BIRDS OF PREY: HUNTRESS

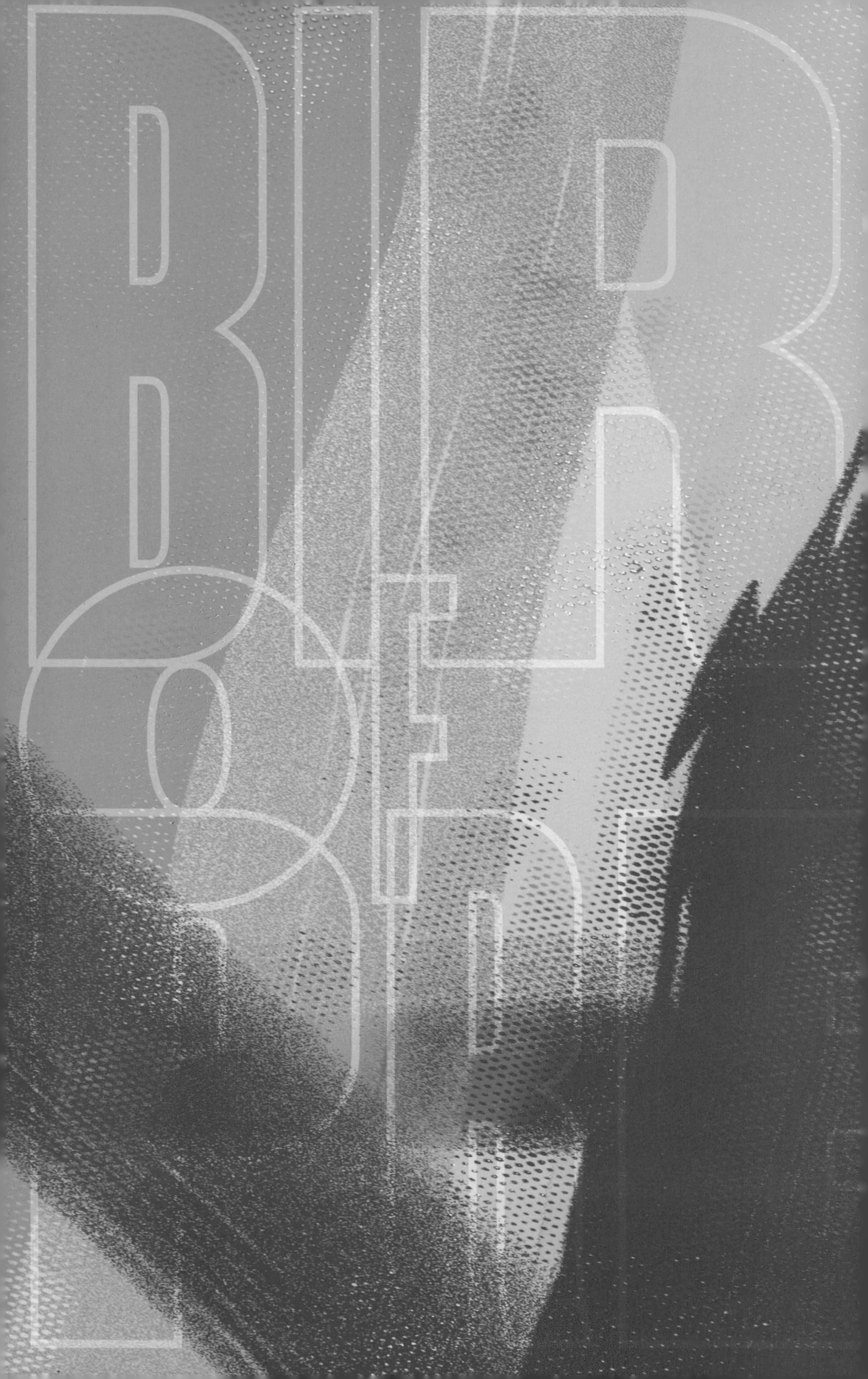

GREG RUCKA
WRITER

RICK BURCHETT
TERRY BEATTY
ARTISTS

TATJANA WOOD
COLORIST

CLEM ROBINS
LETTERER

HUNTRESS

RICK BURCHETT
SERIES COVER ARTIST

TULA LOTAY
COLLECTION COVER ARTIST

BATMAN CREATED BY **BOB KANE** WITH **BILL FINGER**

DENNIS O'NEIL editor – original series
JOSEPH ILLIDGE associate editor – original series
JEB WOODARD group editor – collected editions
ALEX GALER editor – collected edition
STEVE COOK design director – books
MONIQUE NARBONETA publication design
DANIELLE DIGRADO publication production

BOB HARRAS senior vp – editor-in-chief, dc comics
PAT McCALLUM executive editor, dc comics

DAN DiDIO publisher
JIM LEE publisher & chief creative officer
BOBBIE CHASE vp – new publishing initiatives & talent development
DON FALLETTI vp – manufacturing operations & workflow management
LAWRENCE GANEM vp – talent services
ALISON GILL senior vp – manufacturing & operations
HANK KANALZ senior vp – publishing strategy & support services
DAN MIRON vp – publishing operations
NICK J. NAPOLITANO vp – manufacturing administration & design
NANCY SPEARS vp – sales
MICHELE R. WELLS vp & executive editor, young reader

BIRDS OF PREY: HUNTRESS

DC Comics, 2900 West Alameda Ave., Burbank, CA 91505
Printed by LSC Communications, Owensville, MO, USA. 11/29/19. First Printing.
ISBN: 978-1-4012-9890-6

Library of Congress Cataloging-in-Publication Data is available.

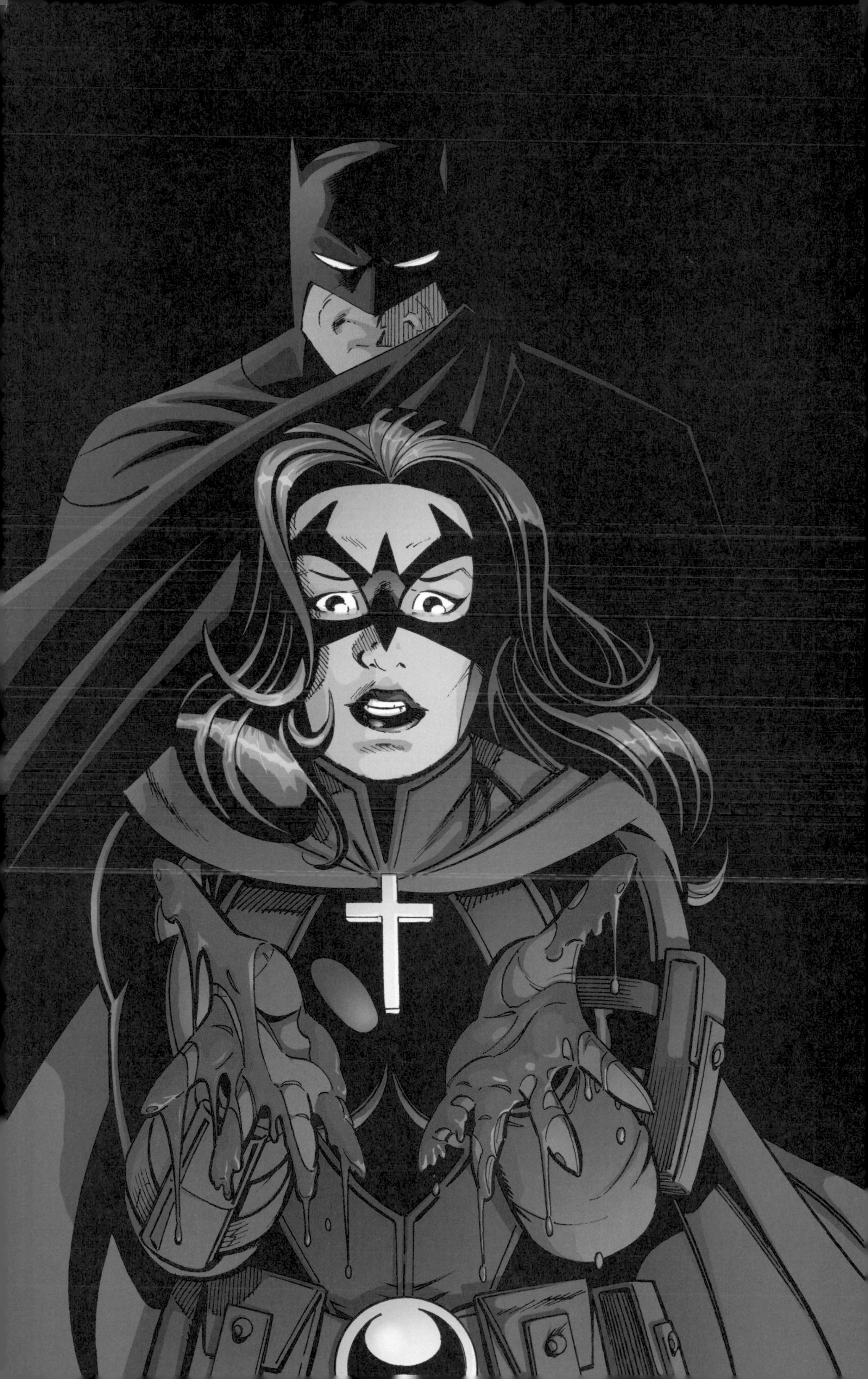

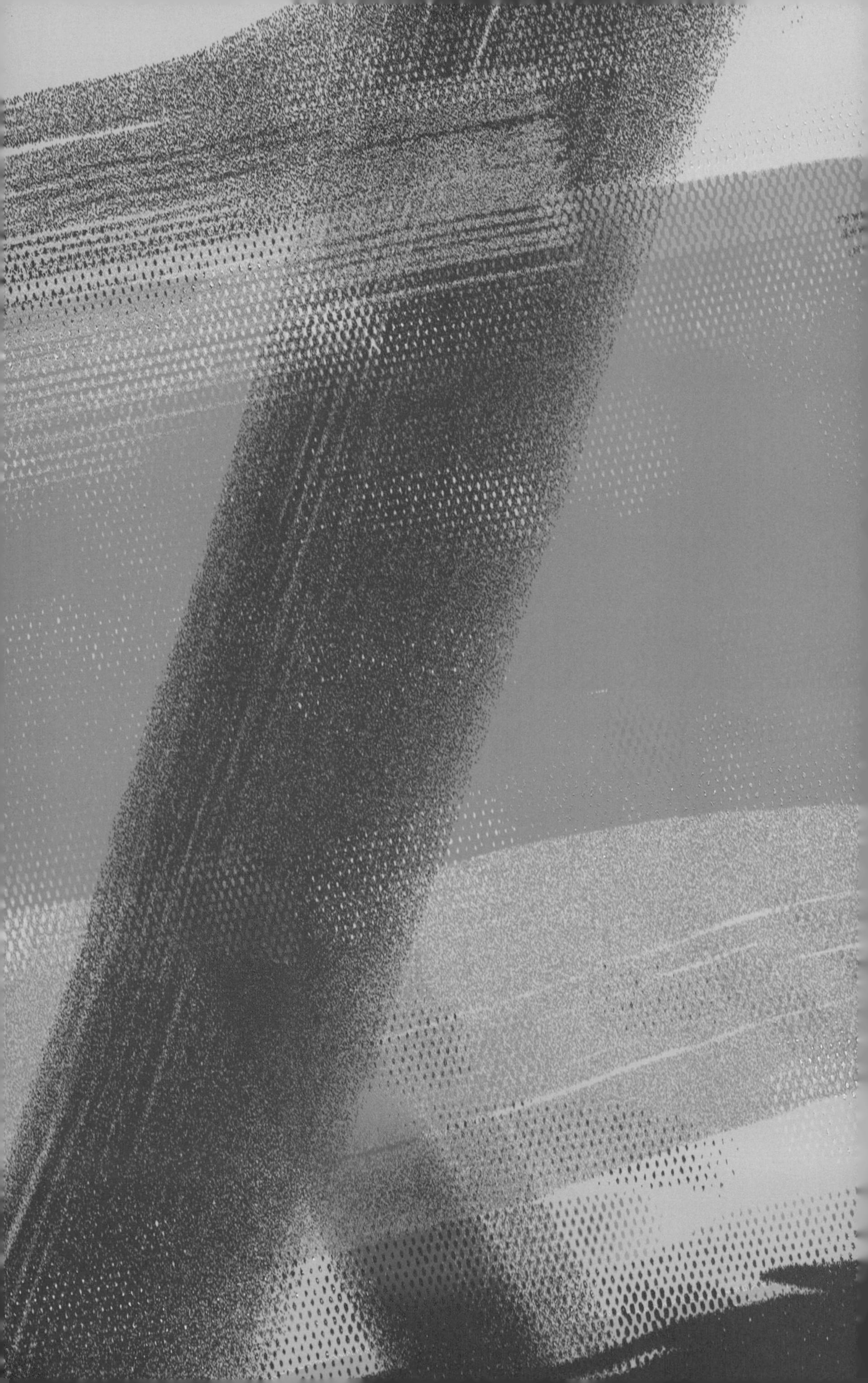

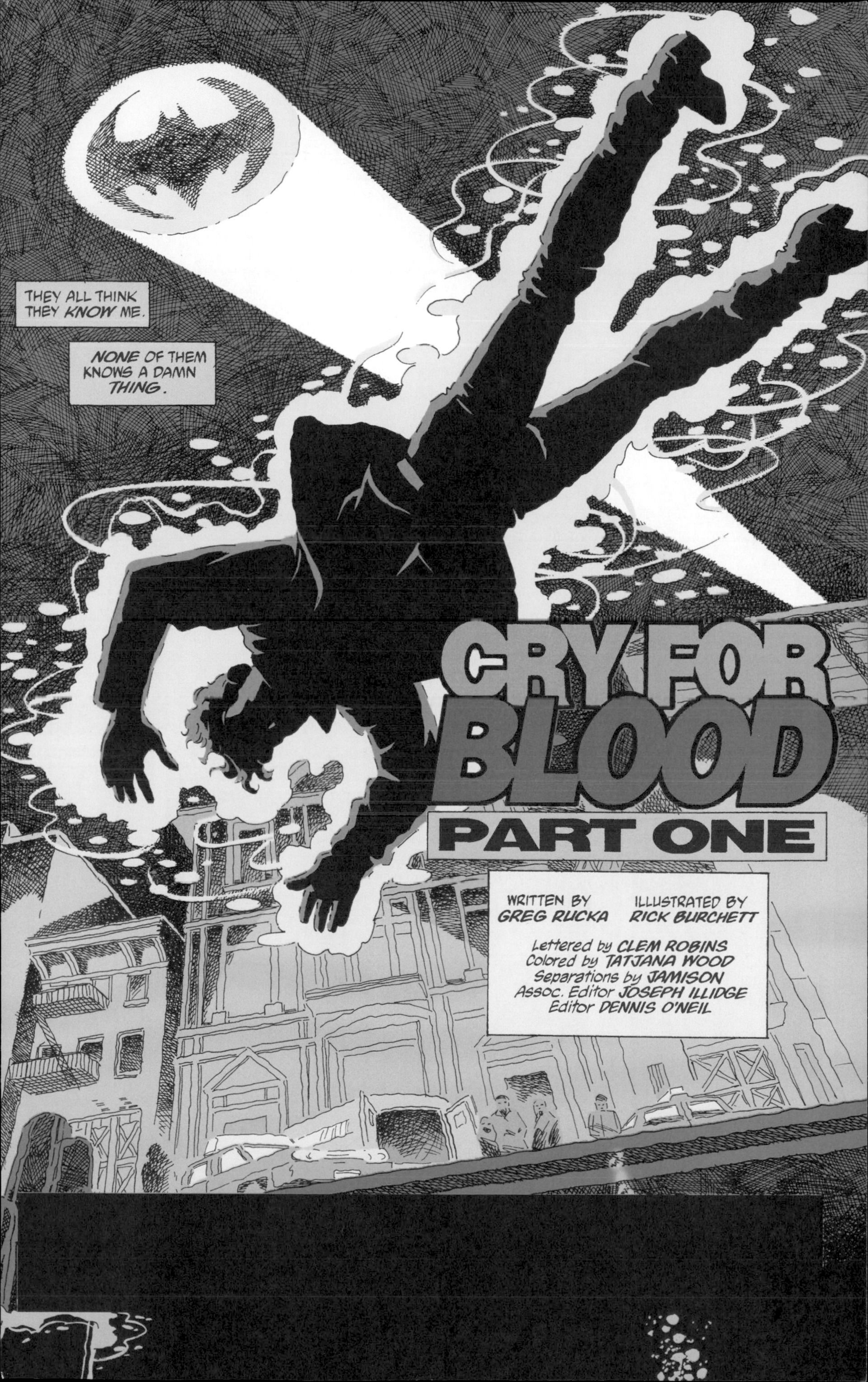
THEY ALL THINK THEY KNOW ME.
NONE OF THEM KNOWS A DAMN THING.
CRY FOR BLOOD
PART ONE
WRITTEN BY GREG RUCKA
ILLUSTRATED BY RICK BURCHETT
Lettered by CLEM ROBINS
Colored by TATJANA WOOD
Separations by JAMISON
Assoc. Editor JOSEPH ILLIDGE
Editor DENNIS O'NEIL

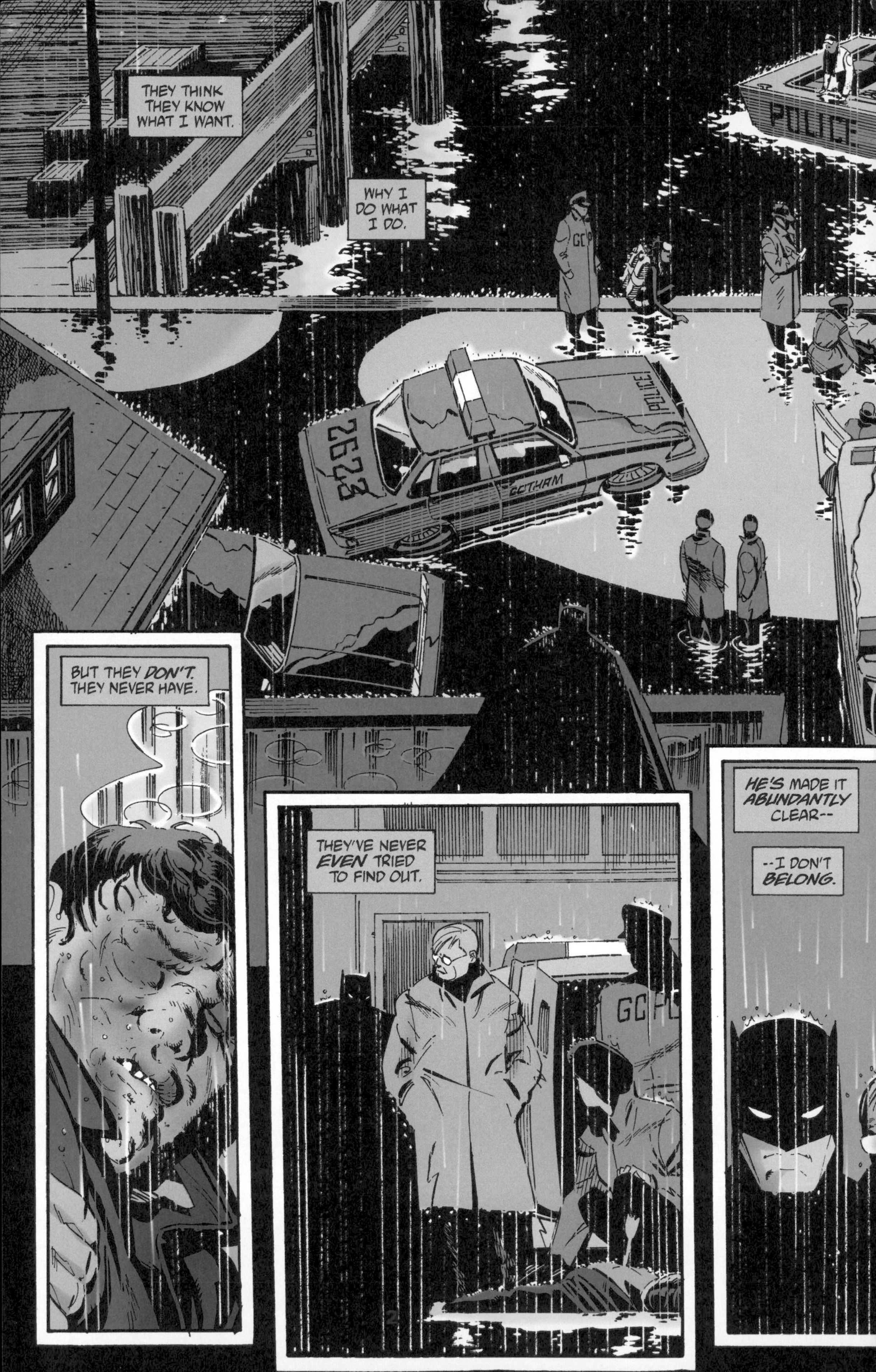
THEY THINK THEY KNOW WHAT I WANT.
WHY I DO WHAT I DO.
POLICE
2623
POLICE
GOTHAM
BUT THEY DON'T. THEY NEVER HAVE.
THEY'VE NEVER EVEN TRIED TO FIND OUT.
GCPD
HE'S MADE IT ABUNDANTLY CLEAR--
--I DON'T BELONG.

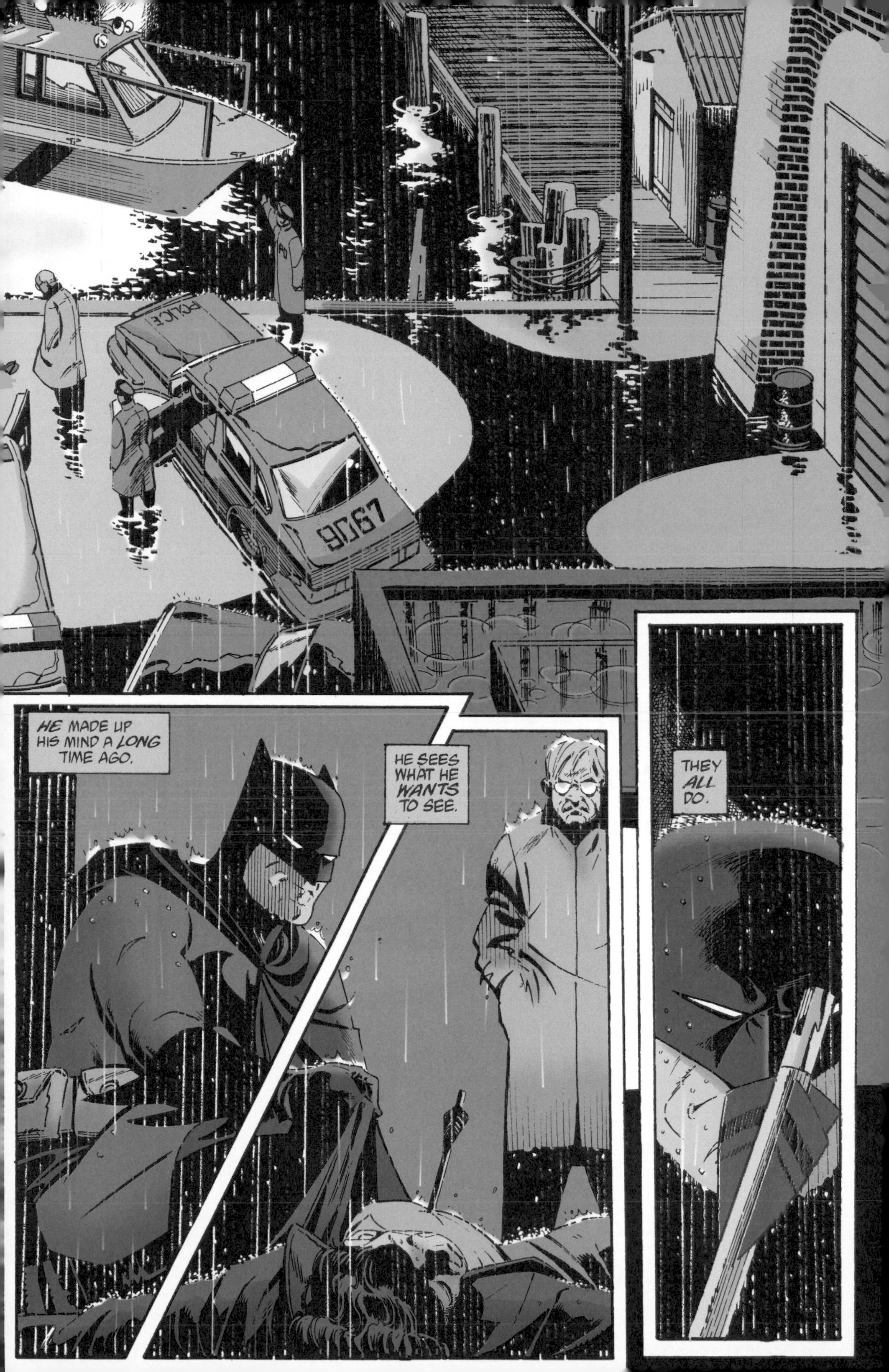

HE MADE UP HIS MIND A LONG TIME AGO.
HE SEES WHAT HE WANTS TO SEE.
THEY ALL DO.

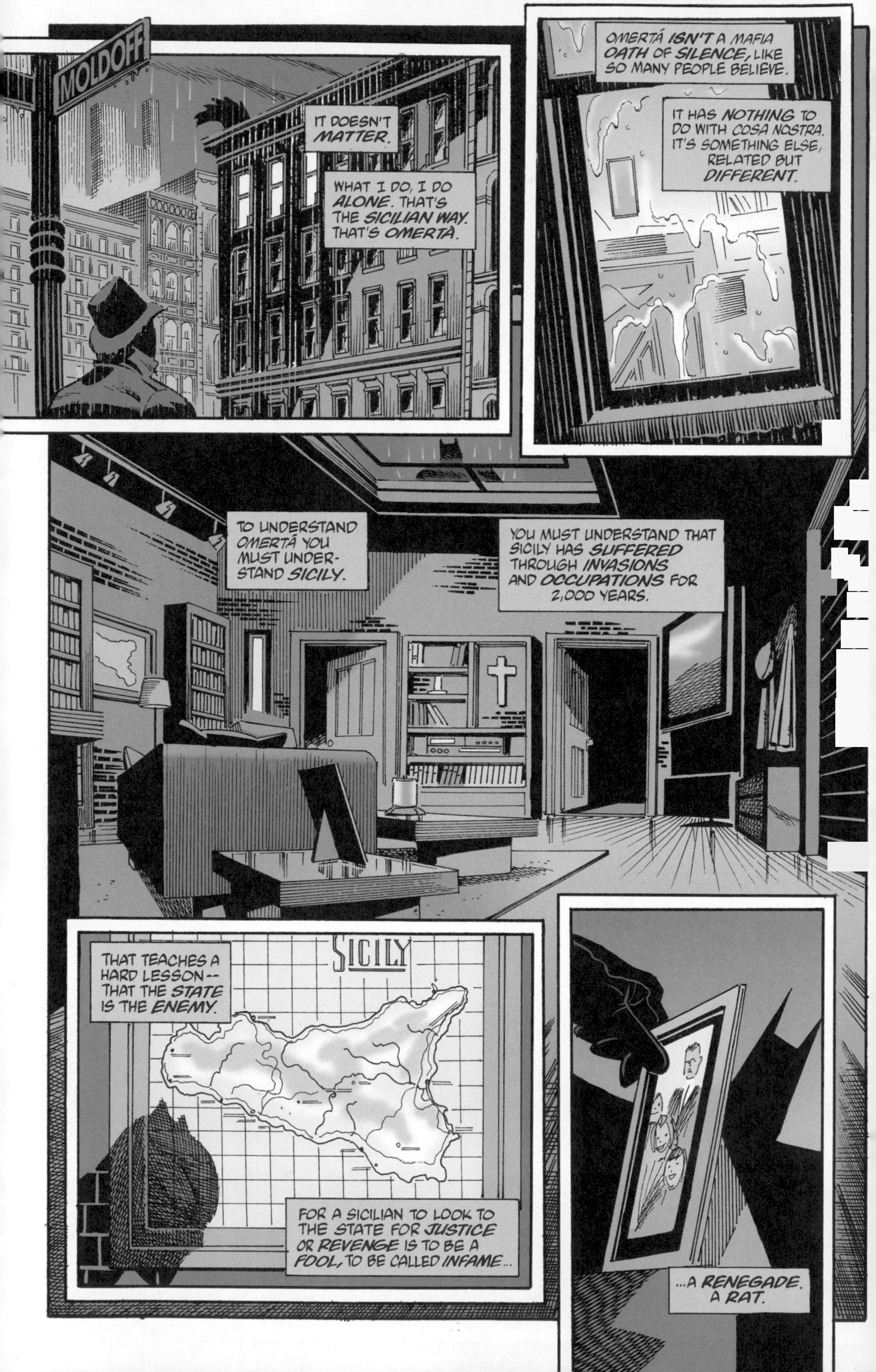
MOLDOFF
IT DOESN'T MATTER.
WHAT I DO, I DO ALONE. THAT'S THE SICILIAN WAY. THAT'S OMERTÀ.
OMERTÀ ISN'T A MAFIA OATH OF SILENCE, LIKE SO MANY PEOPLE BELIEVE.
IT HAS NOTHING TO DO WITH COSA NOSTRA. IT'S SOMETHING ELSE, RELATED BUT DIFFERENT.
TO UNDERSTAND OMERTÀ YOU MUST UNDERSTAND SICILY.
YOU MUST UNDERSTAND THAT SICILY HAS SUFFERED THROUGH INVASIONS AND OCCUPATIONS FOR 2,000 YEARS.
SICILY
THAT TEACHES A HARD LESSON-- THAT THE STATE IS THE ENEMY.
FOR A SICILIAN TO LOOK TO THE STATE FOR JUSTICE OR REVENGE IS TO BE A FOOL, TO BE CALLED INFAME...
...A RENEGADE. A RAT.

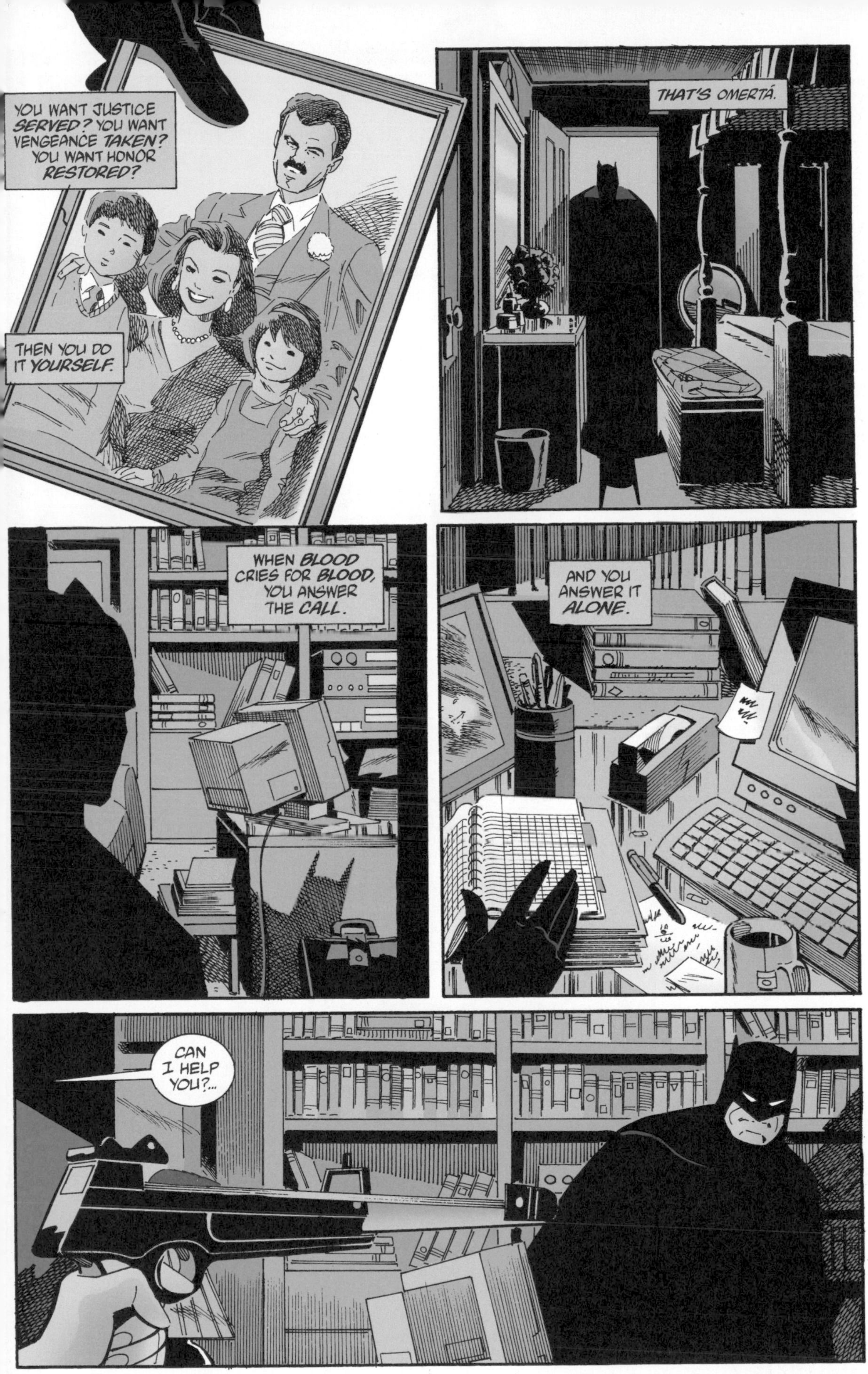

YOU WANT JUSTICE SERVED? YOU WANT VENGEANCE TAKEN? YOU WANT HONOR RESTORED?
THEN YOU DO IT YOURSELF.
THAT'S OMERTÁ.
WHEN BLOOD CRIES FOR BLOOD, YOU ANSWER THE CALL.
AND YOU ANSWER IT ALONE.
CAN I HELP YOU?...

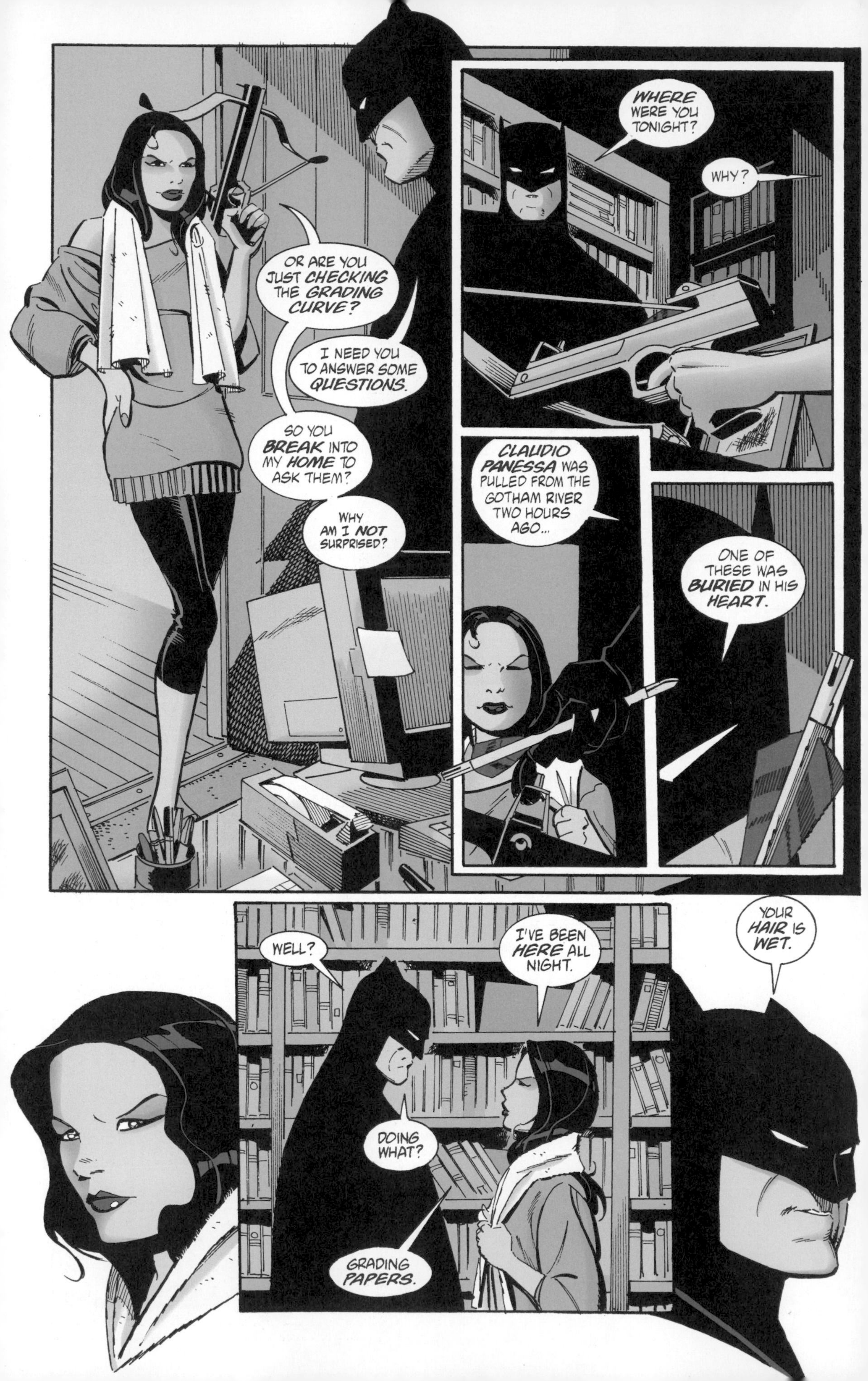
OR ARE YOU JUST CHECKING THE GRADING CURVE?
I NEED YOU TO ANSWER SOME QUESTIONS.
SO YOU BREAK INTO MY HOME TO ASK THEM?
WHY AM I NOT SURPRISED?
WHERE WERE YOU TONIGHT?
WHY?
CLAUDIO PANESSA WAS PULLED FROM THE GOTHAM RIVER TWO HOURS AGO...
ONE OF THESE WAS BURIED IN HIS HEART.
WELL?
I'VE BEEN HERE ALL NIGHT.
DOING WHAT?
GRADING PAPERS.
YOUR HAIR IS WET.

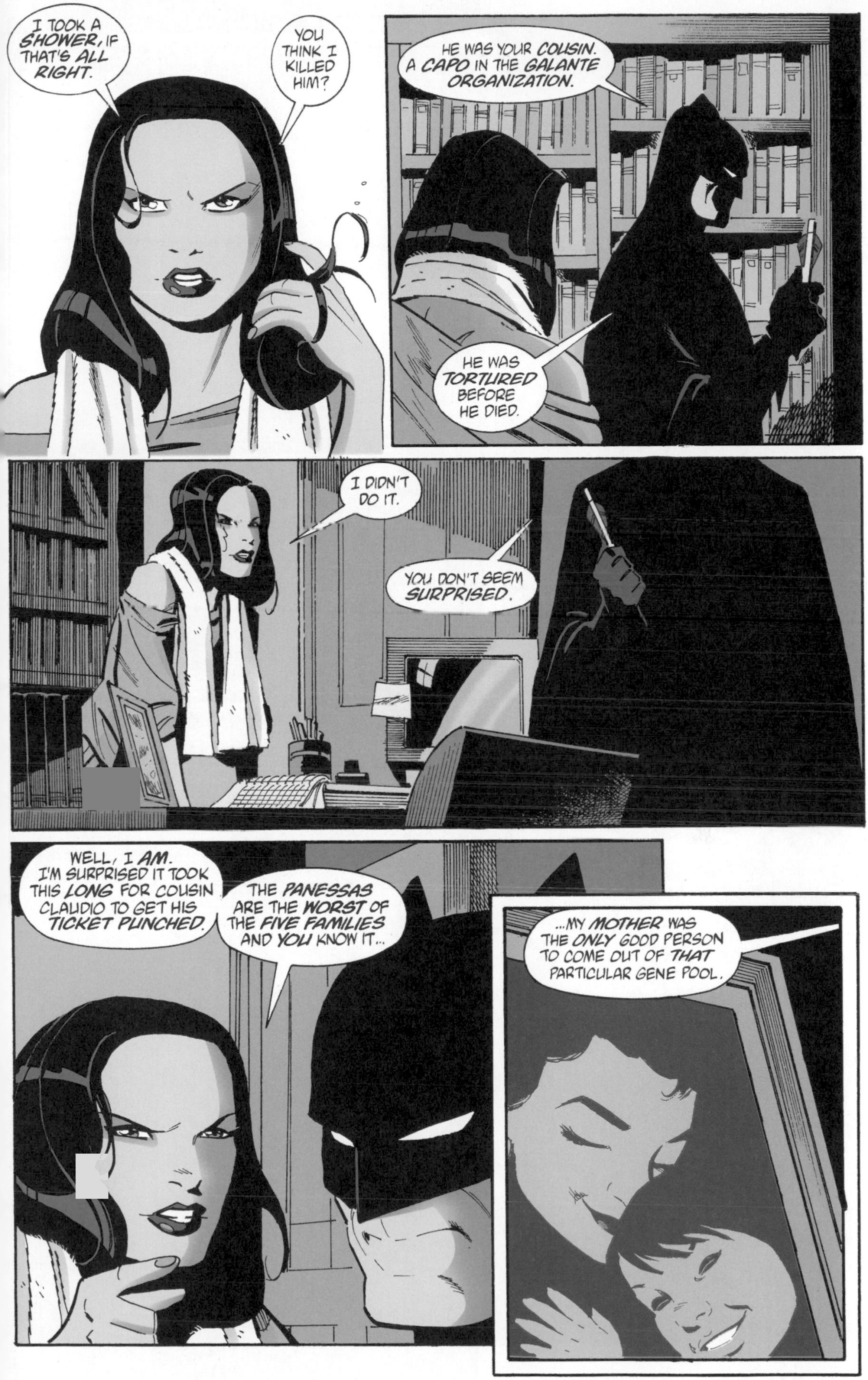
I TOOK A SHOWER, IF THAT'S ALL RIGHT.
YOU THINK I KILLED HIM?
HE WAS YOUR COUSIN. A CAPO IN THE GALANTE ORGANIZATION.
HE WAS TORTURED BEFORE HE DIED.
I DIDN'T DO IT.
YOU DON'T SEEM SURPRISED.
WELL, I AM. I'M SURPRISED IT TOOK THIS LONG FOR COUSIN CLAUDIO TO GET HIS TICKET PUNCHED.
THE PANESSAS ARE THE WORST OF THE FIVE FAMILIES AND YOU KNOW IT...
...MY MOTHER WAS THE ONLY GOOD PERSON TO COME OUT OF THAT PARTICULAR GENE POOL.

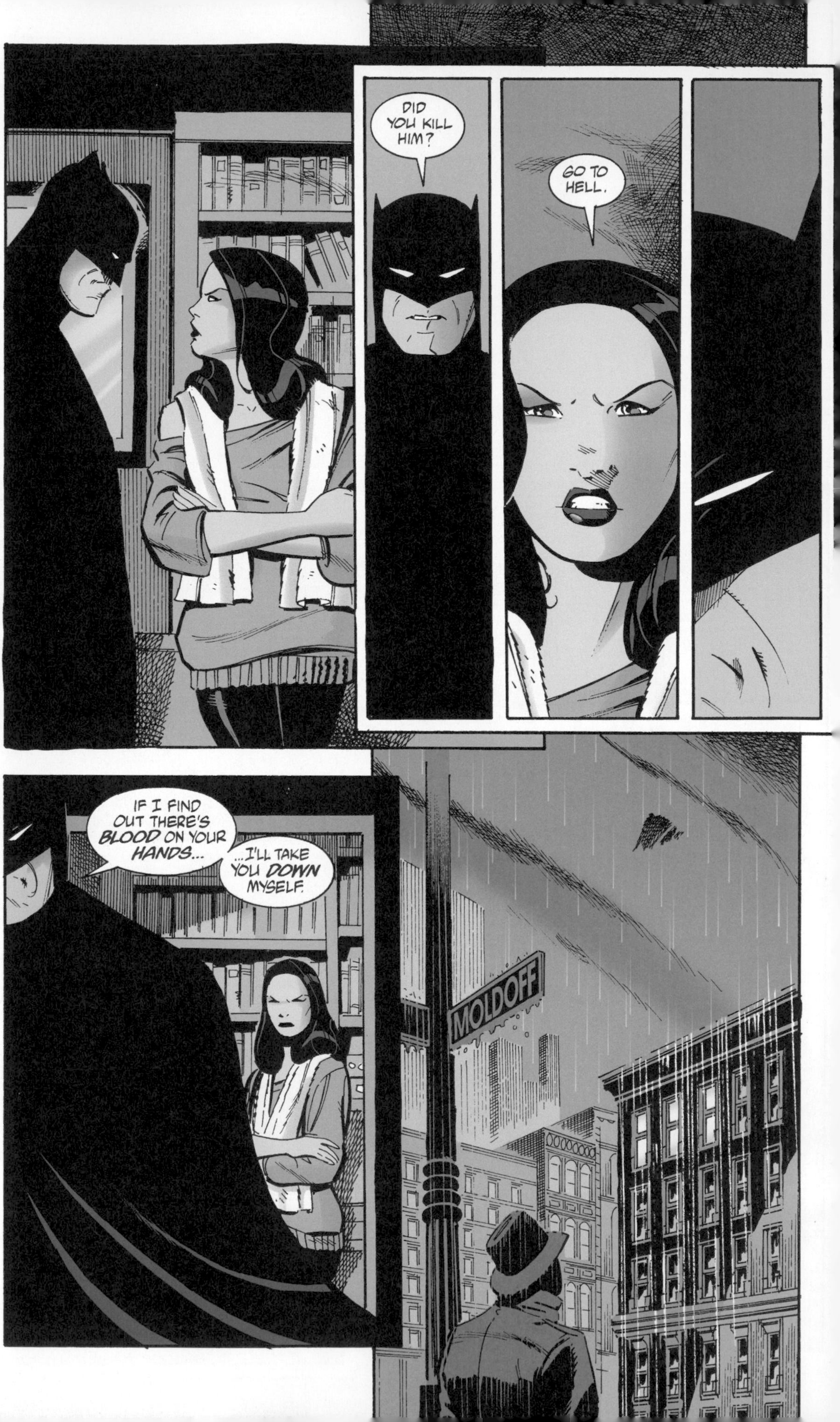
DID YOU KILL HIM?
GO TO HELL.
IF I FIND OUT THERE'S BLOOD ON YOUR HANDS...
...I'LL TAKE YOU DOWN MYSELF.
MOLDOFF

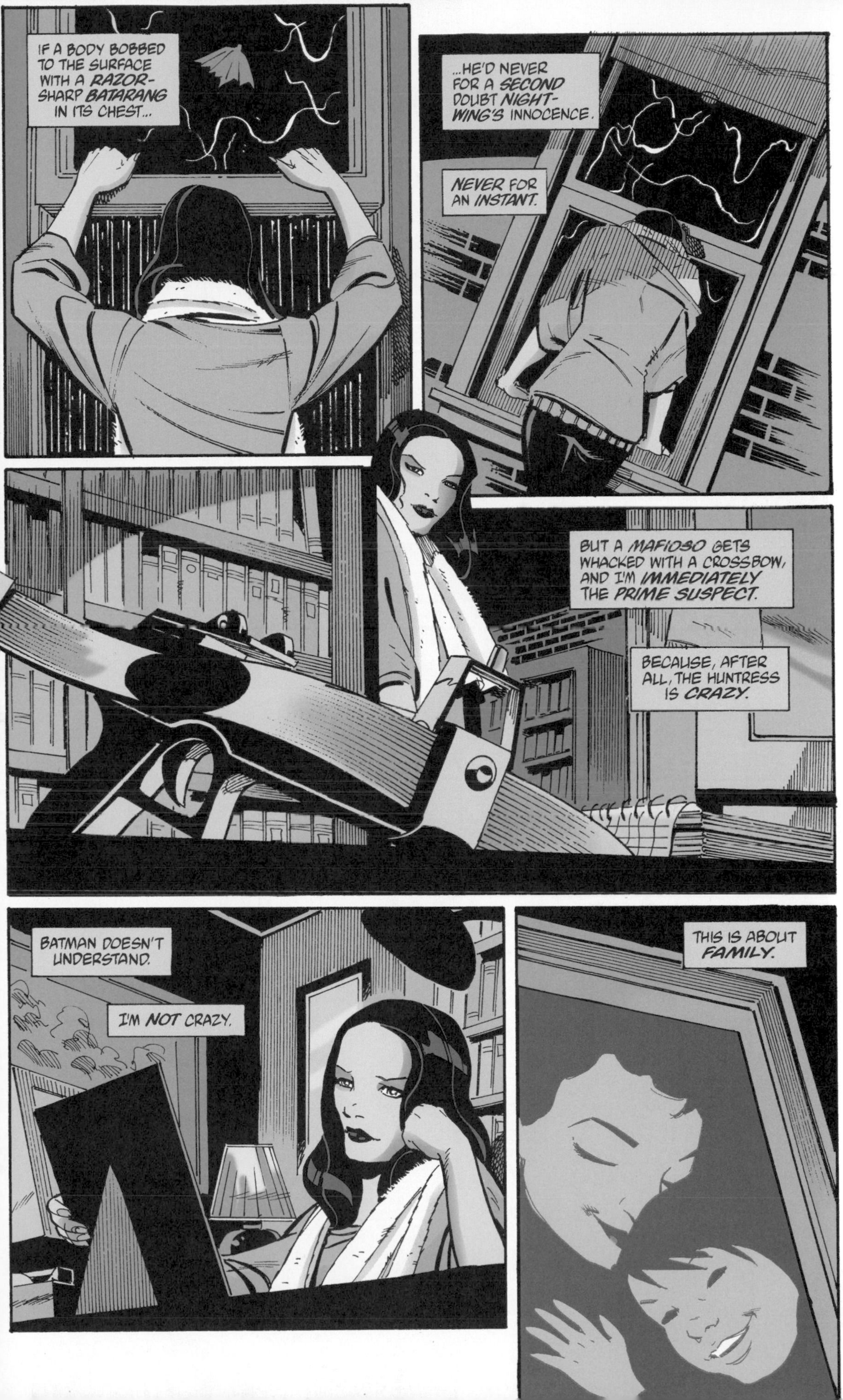
IF A BODY BOBBED TO THE SURFACE WITH A RAZOR-SHARP BATARANG IN ITS CHEST...
...HE'D NEVER FOR A SECOND DOUBT NIGHT-WING'S INNOCENCE.
NEVER FOR AN INSTANT.
BUT A MAFIOSO GETS WHACKED WITH A CROSSBOW, AND I'M IMMEDIATELY THE PRIME SUSPECT.
BECAUSE, AFTER ALL, THE HUNTRESS IS CRAZY.
BATMAN DOESN'T UNDERSTAND.
I'M NOT CRAZY.
THIS IS ABOUT FAMILY.

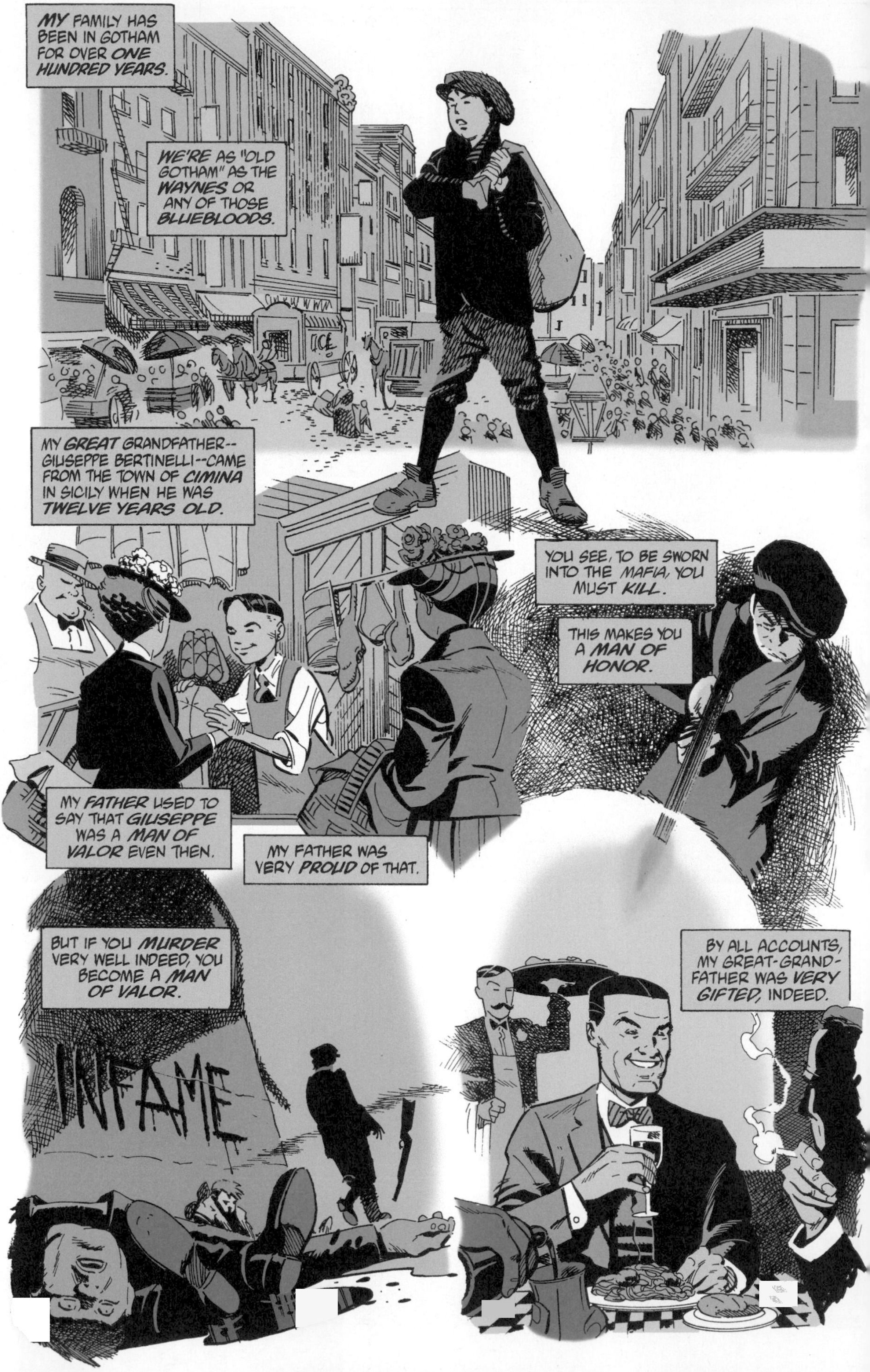
MY FAMILY HAS BEEN IN GOTHAM FOR OVER ONE HUNDRED YEARS.
WE'RE AS "OLD GOTHAM" AS THE WAYNES OR ANY OF THOSE BLUEBLOODS.
MY GREAT GRANDFATHER--GIUSEPPE BERTINELLI--CAME FROM THE TOWN OF CIMINA IN SICILY WHEN HE WAS TWELVE YEARS OLD.
MY FATHER USED TO SAY THAT GIUSEPPE WAS A MAN OF VALOR EVEN THEN.
MY FATHER WAS VERY PROUD OF THAT.
YOU SEE, TO BE SWORN INTO THE MAFIA, YOU MUST KILL.
THIS MAKES YOU A MAN OF HONOR.
BUT IF YOU MURDER VERY WELL INDEED, YOU BECOME A MAN OF VALOR.
INFAME
BY ALL ACCOUNTS, MY GREAT-GRAND-FATHER WAS VERY GIFTED, INDEED.

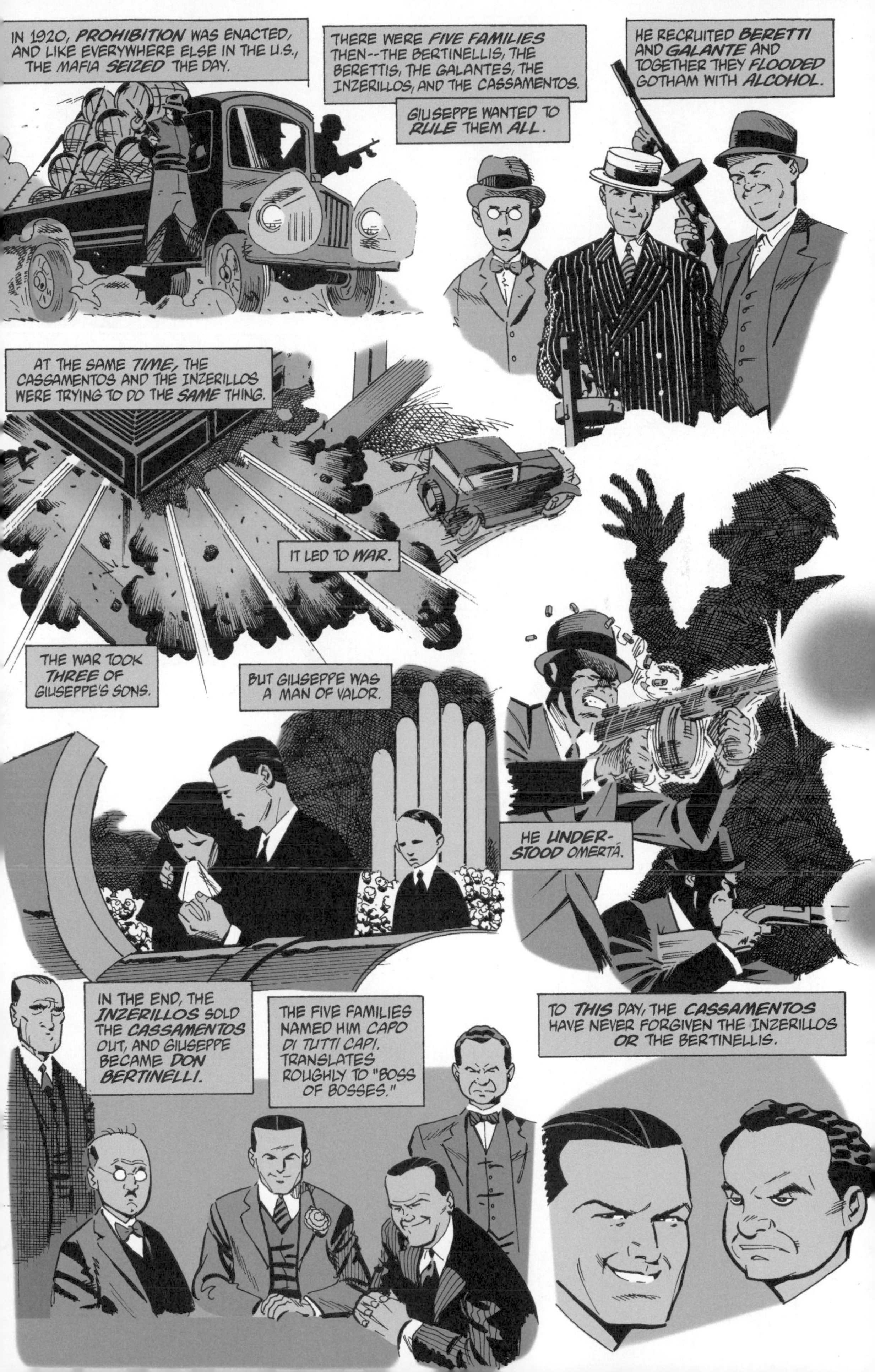
IN 1920, PROHIBITION WAS ENACTED, AND LIKE EVERYWHERE ELSE IN THE U.S., THE MAFIA SEIZED THE DAY.
THERE WERE FIVE FAMILIES THEN--THE BERTINELLIS, THE BERETTIS, THE GALANTES, THE INZERILLOS, AND THE CASSAMENTOS.
GIUSEPPE WANTED TO RULE THEM ALL.
HE RECRUITED BERETTI AND GALANTE AND TOGETHER THEY FLOODED GOTHAM WITH ALCOHOL.
AT THE SAME TIME, THE CASSAMENTOS AND THE INZERILLOS WERE TRYING TO DO THE SAME THING.
IT LED TO WAR.
THE WAR TOOK THREE OF GIUSEPPE'S SONS.
BUT GIUSEPPE WAS A MAN OF VALOR.
HE UNDER-STOOD OMERTÁ.
IN THE END, THE INZERILLOS SOLD THE CASSAMENTOS OUT, AND GIUSEPPE BECAME DON BERTINELLI.
THE FIVE FAMILIES NAMED HIM CAPO DI TUTTI CAPI. TRANSLATES ROUGHLY TO "BOSS OF BOSSES."
TO THIS DAY, THE CASSAMENTOS HAVE NEVER FORGIVEN THE INZERILLOS OR THE BERTINELLIS.

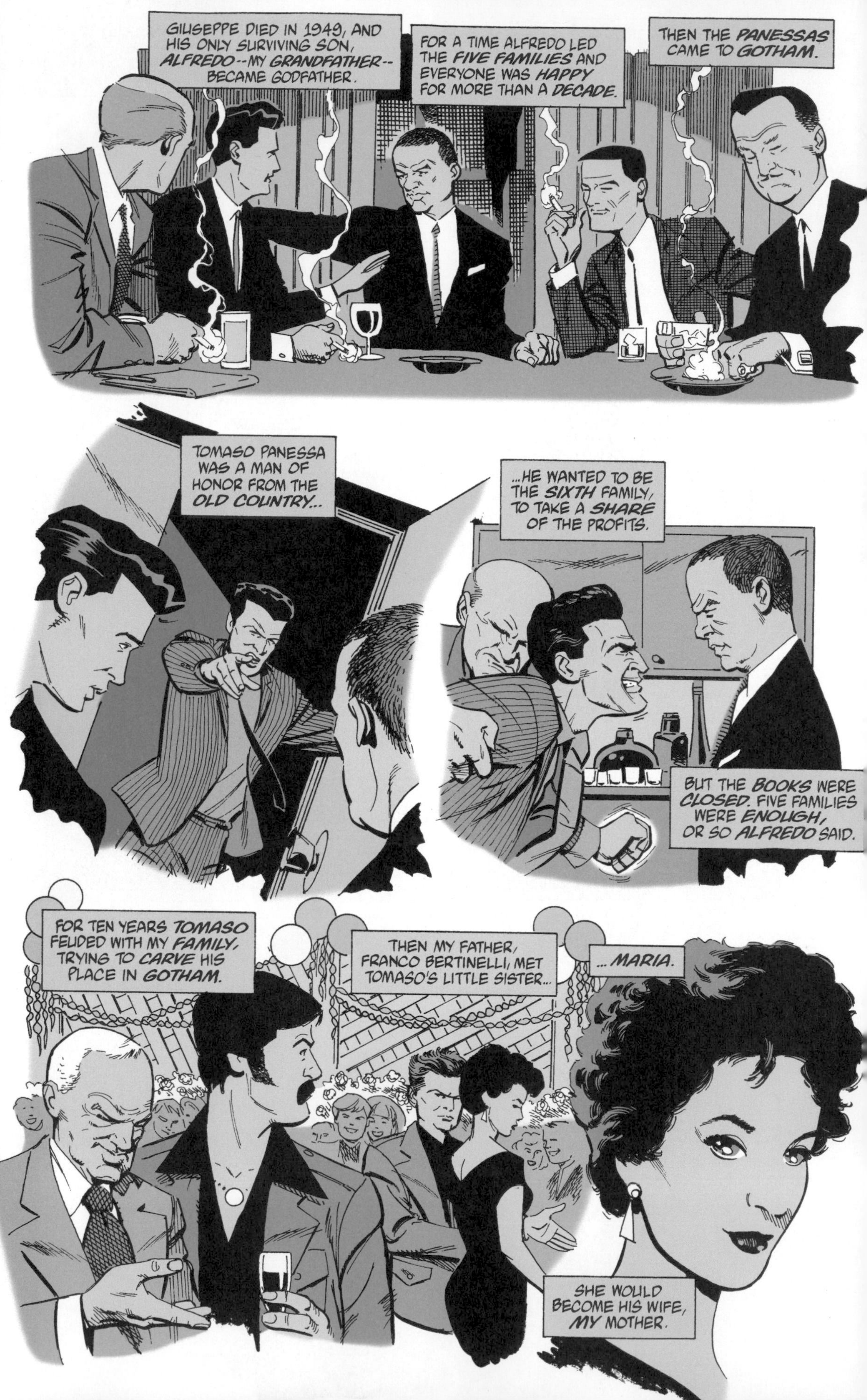
GIUSEPPE DIED IN 1949, AND HIS ONLY SURVIVING SON, ALFREDO--MY GRANDFATHER--BECAME GODFATHER.
FOR A TIME ALFREDO LED THE FIVE FAMILIES AND EVERYONE WAS HAPPY FOR MORE THAN A DECADE.
THEN THE PANESSAS CAME TO GOTHAM.
TOMASO PANESSA WAS A MAN OF HONOR FROM THE OLD COUNTRY...
...HE WANTED TO BE THE SIXTH FAMILY, TO TAKE A SHARE OF THE PROFITS.
BUT THE BOOKS WERE CLOSED. FIVE FAMILIES WERE ENOUGH, OR SO ALFREDO SAID.
FOR TEN YEARS TOMASO FEUDED WITH MY FAMILY, TRYING TO CARVE HIS PLACE IN GOTHAM.
THEN MY FATHER, FRANCO BERTINELLI, MET TOMASO'S LITTLE SISTER...
...MARIA.
SHE WOULD BECOME HIS WIFE, MY MOTHER.

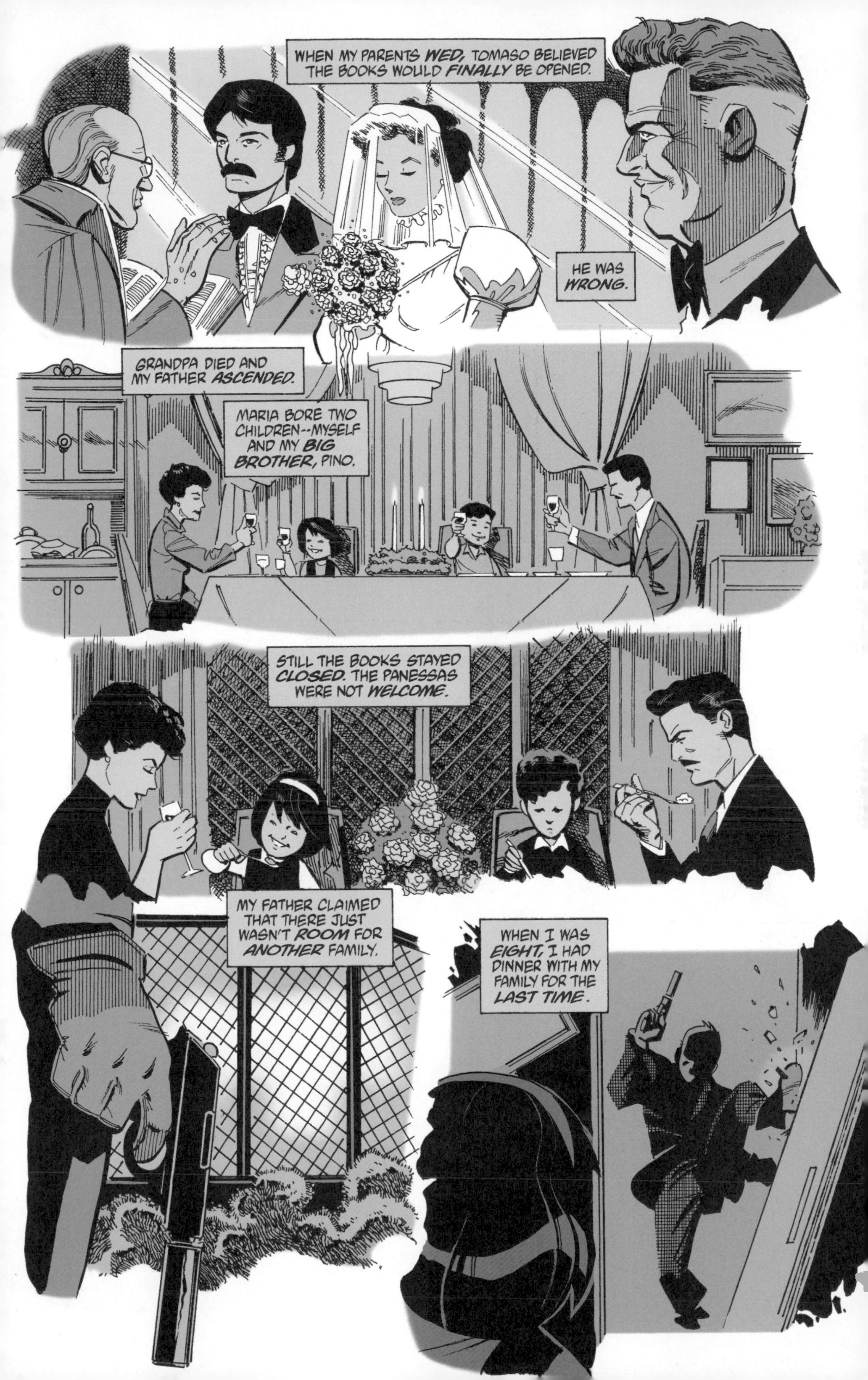
WHEN MY PARENTS WED, TOMASO BELIEVED THE BOOKS WOULD FINALLY BE OPENED.
HE WAS WRONG.
GRANDPA DIED AND MY FATHER ASCENDED.
MARIA BORE TWO CHILDREN--MYSELF AND MY BIG BROTHER, PINO.
STILL THE BOOKS STAYED CLOSED. THE PANESSAS WERE NOT WELCOME.
MY FATHER CLAIMED THAT THERE JUST WASN'T ROOM FOR ANOTHER FAMILY.
WHEN I WAS EIGHT, I HAD DINNER WITH MY FAMILY FOR THE LAST TIME.

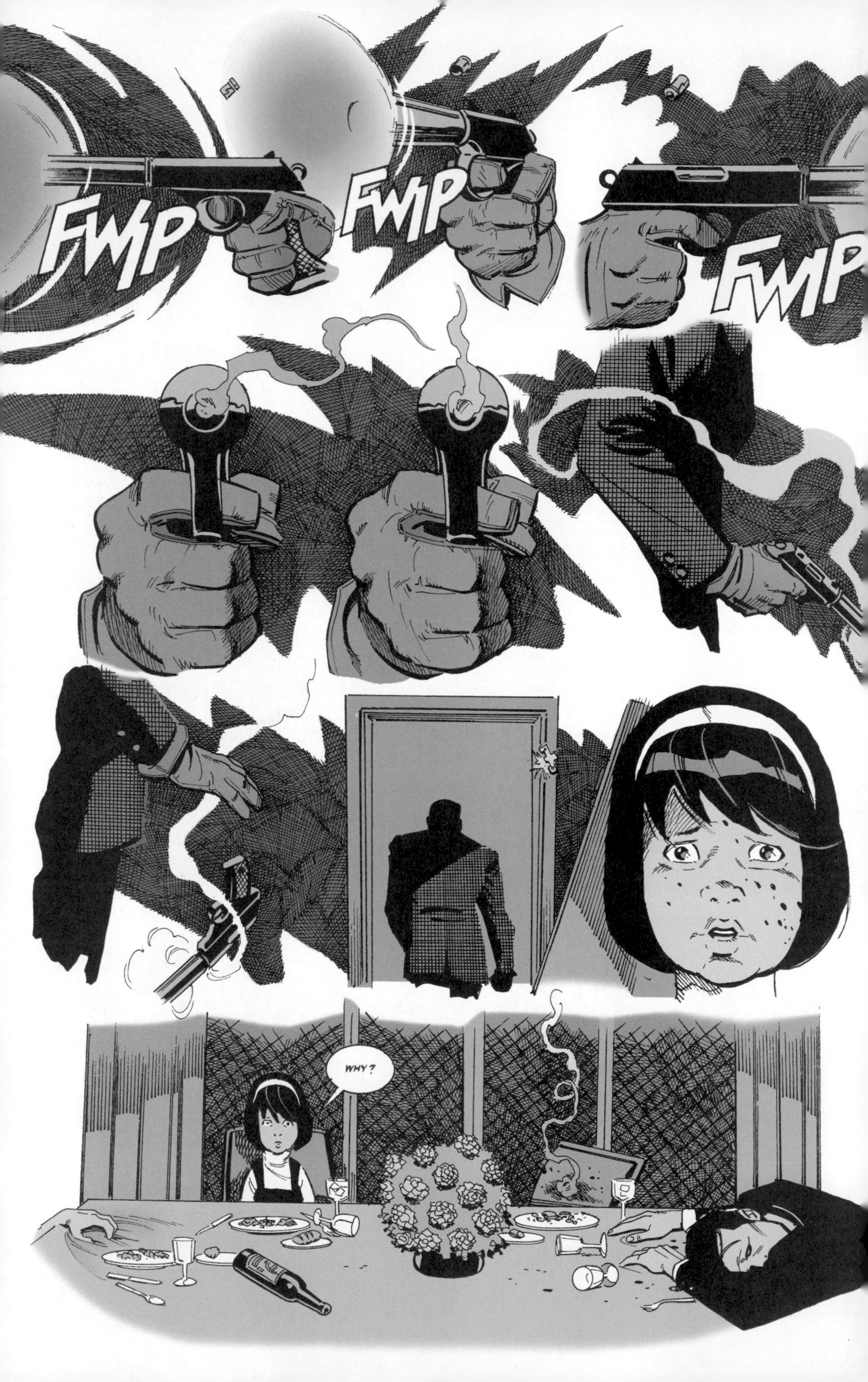
FWP
FWP
FWP
WHY?

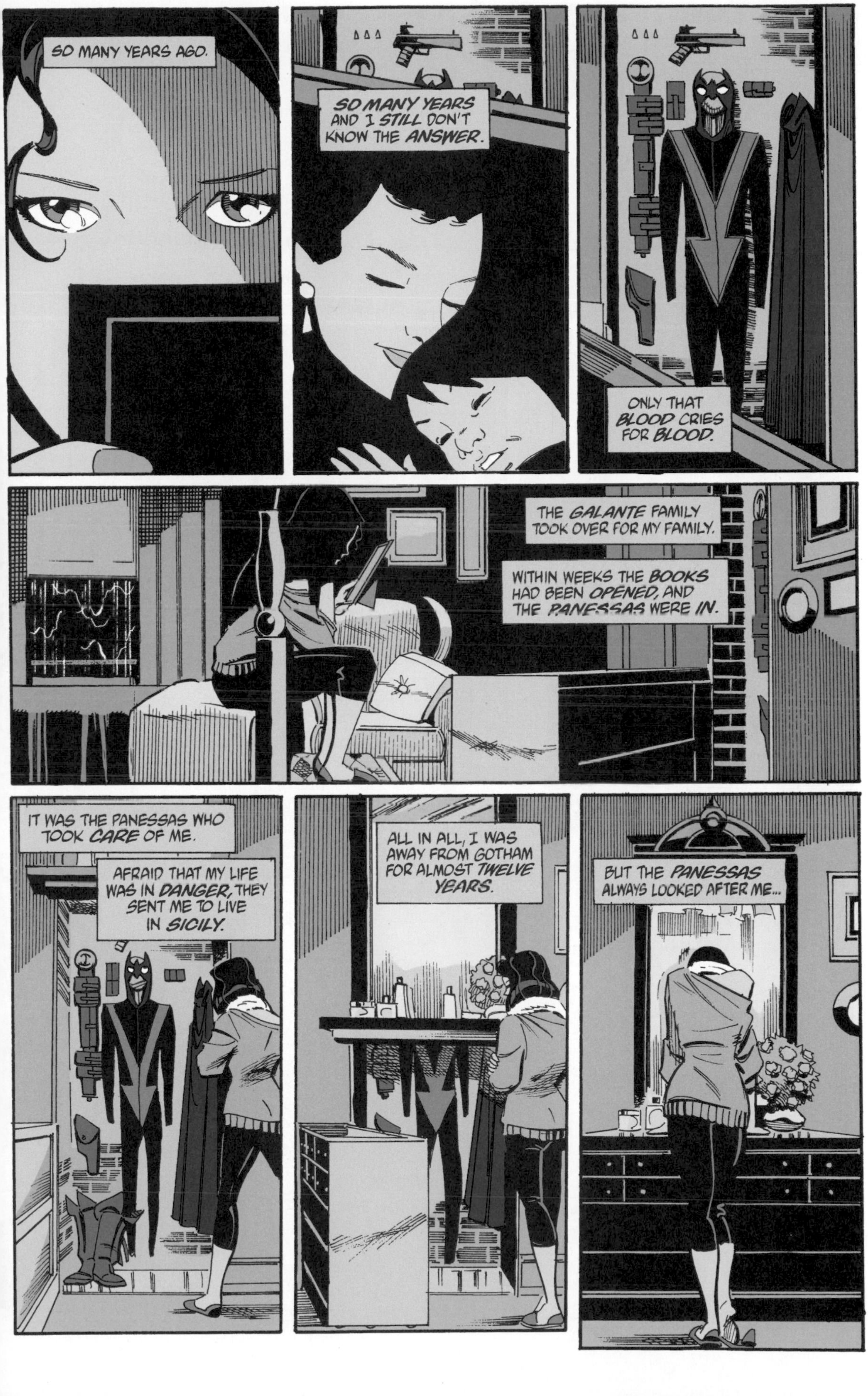
SO MANY YEARS AGO.
SO MANY YEARS AND I STILL DON'T KNOW THE ANSWER.
ONLY THAT BLOOD CRIES FOR BLOOD.
THE GALANTE FAMILY TOOK OVER FOR MY FAMILY.
WITHIN WEEKS THE BOOKS HAD BEEN OPENED, AND THE PANESSAS WERE IN.
IT WAS THE PANESSAS WHO TOOK CARE OF ME.
AFRAID THAT MY LIFE WAS IN DANGER, THEY SENT ME TO LIVE IN SICILY.
ALL IN ALL, I WAS AWAY FROM GOTHAM FOR ALMOST TWELVE YEARS.
BUT THE PANESSAS ALWAYS LOOKED AFTER ME...

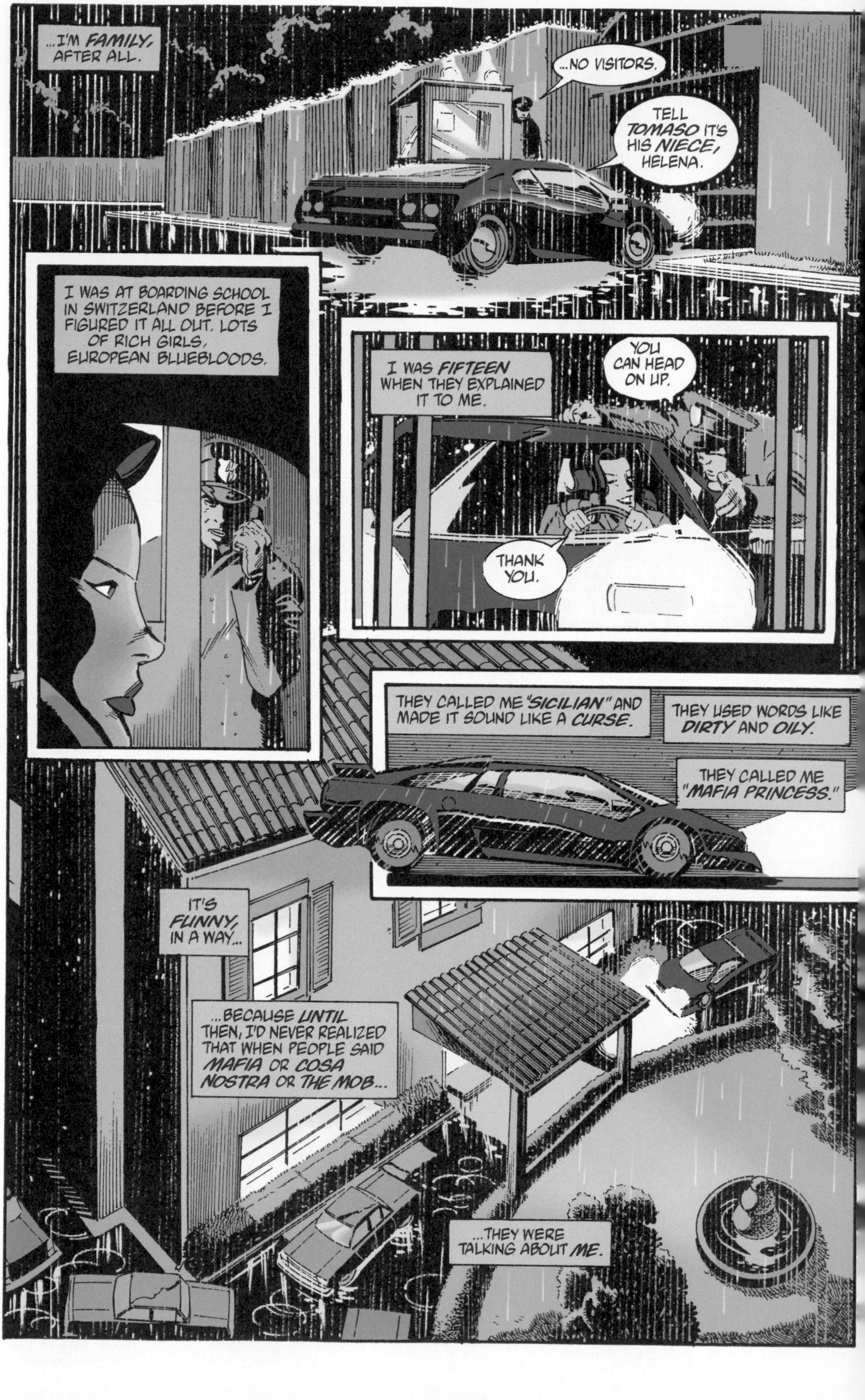
...I'M FAMILY, AFTER ALL.
...NO VISITORS.
TELL TOMASO IT'S HIS NIECE, HELENA.
I WAS AT BOARDING SCHOOL IN SWITZERLAND BEFORE I FIGURED IT ALL OUT. LOTS OF RICH GIRLS, EUROPEAN BLUEBLOODS.
I WAS FIFTEEN WHEN THEY EXPLAINED IT TO ME.
YOU CAN HEAD ON UP.
THANK YOU.
THEY CALLED ME "SICILIAN" AND MADE IT SOUND LIKE A CURSE.
THEY USED WORDS LIKE DIRTY AND OILY.
THEY CALLED ME "MAFIA PRINCESS."
IT'S FUNNY, IN A WAY...
...BECAUSE UNTIL THEN, I'D NEVER REALIZED THAT WHEN PEOPLE SAID MAFIA OR COSA NOSTRA OR THE MOB...
...THEY WERE TALKING ABOUT ME.

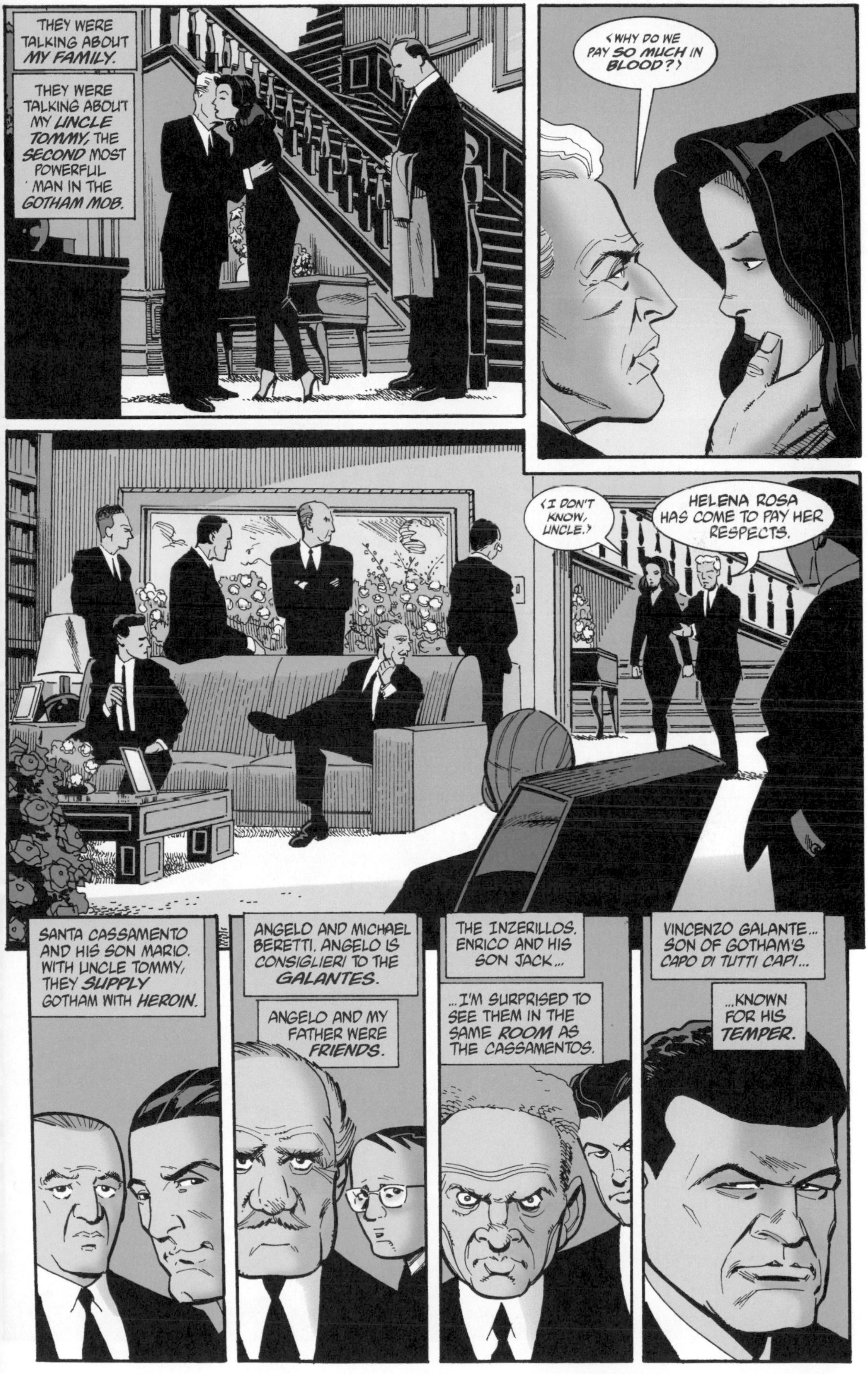
THEY WERE TALKING ABOUT MY FAMILY.
THEY WERE TALKING ABOUT MY UNCLE TOMMY, THE SECOND MOST POWERFUL MAN IN THE GOTHAM MOB.
<WHY DO WE PAY SO MUCH IN BLOOD?>
<I DON'T KNOW, UNCLE.>
HELENA ROSA HAS COME TO PAY HER RESPECTS.
SANTA CASSAMENTO AND HIS SON MARIO. WITH UNCLE TOMMY, THEY SUPPLY GOTHAM WITH HEROIN.
ANGELO AND MICHAEL BERETTI. ANGELO IS CONSIGLIERI TO THE GALANTES.
ANGELO AND MY FATHER WERE FRIENDS.
THE INZERILLOS. ENRICO AND HIS SON JACK...
...I'M SURPRISED TO SEE THEM IN THE SAME ROOM AS THE CASSAMENTOS.
VINCENZO GALANTE... SON OF GOTHAM'S CAPO DI TUTTI CAPI...
...KNOWN FOR HIS TEMPER.

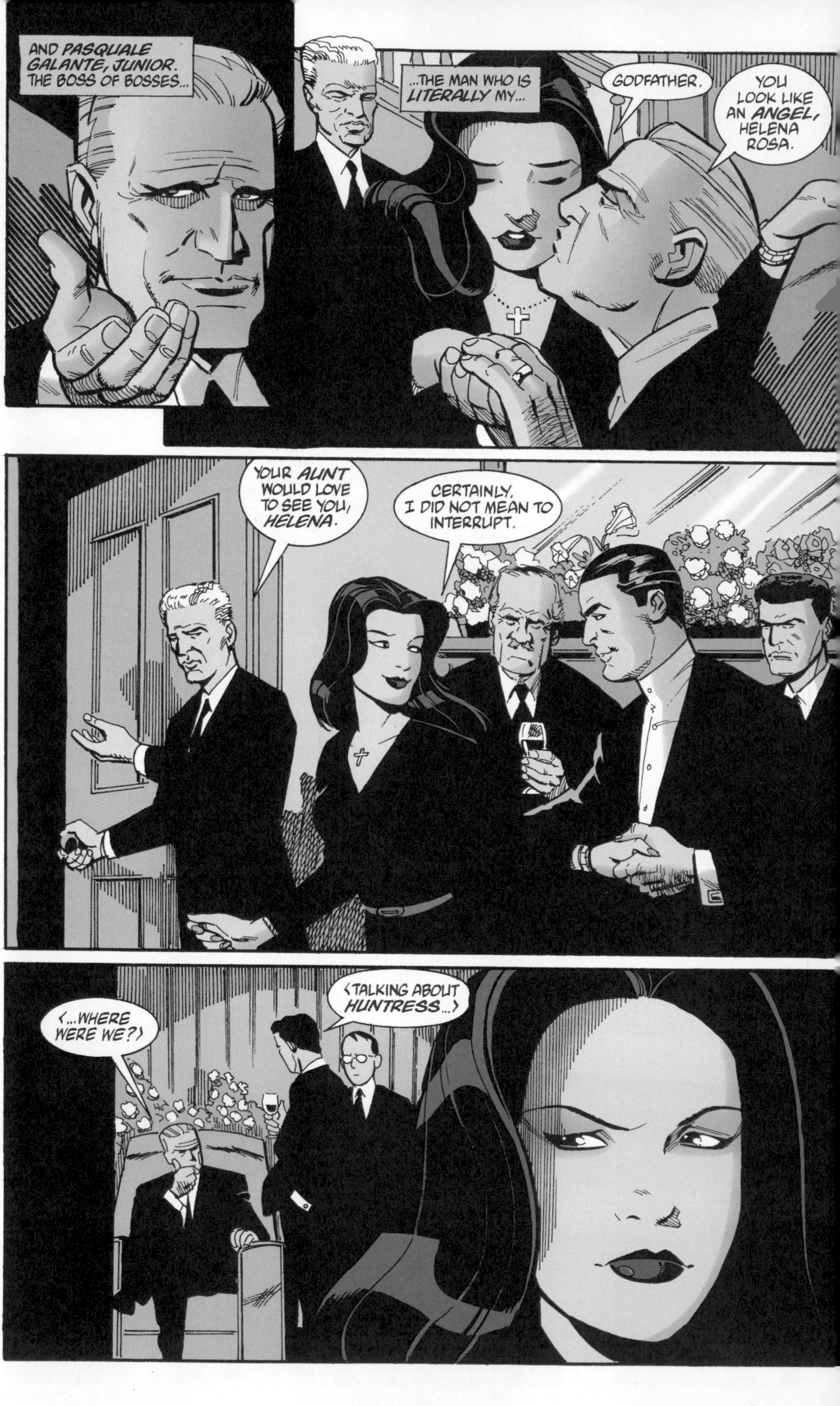
AND PASQUALE GALANTE, JUNIOR. THE BOSS OF BOSSES...
...THE MAN WHO IS LITERALLY MY...
GODFATHER.
YOU LOOK LIKE AN ANGEL, HELENA ROSA.
YOUR AUNT WOULD LOVE TO SEE YOU, HELENA.
CERTAINLY. I DID NOT MEAN TO INTERRUPT.
<...WHERE WERE WE?>
<TALKING ABOUT HUNTRESS...>

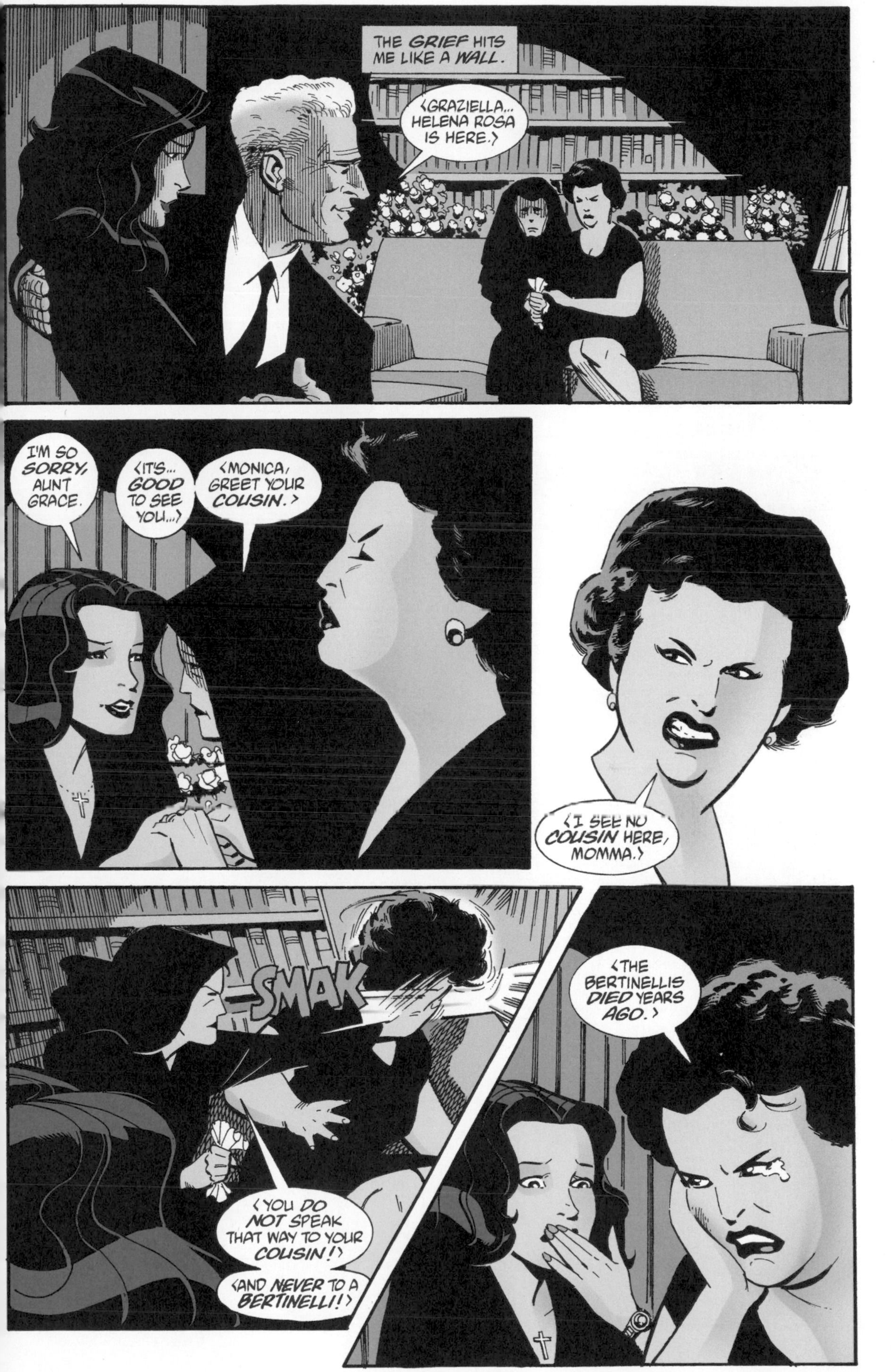
THE GRIEF HITS ME LIKE A WALL.
‹GRAZIELLA... HELENA ROSA IS HERE.›
I'M SO SORRY, AUNT GRACE.
‹IT'S... GOOD TO SEE YOU...›
‹MONICA, GREET YOUR COUSIN.›
‹I SEE NO COUSIN HERE, MOMMA.›
SMAK
‹YOU DO NOT SPEAK THAT WAY TO YOUR COUSIN!›
‹AND NEVER TO A BERTINELLI!›
‹THE BERTINELLIS DIED YEARS AGO.›

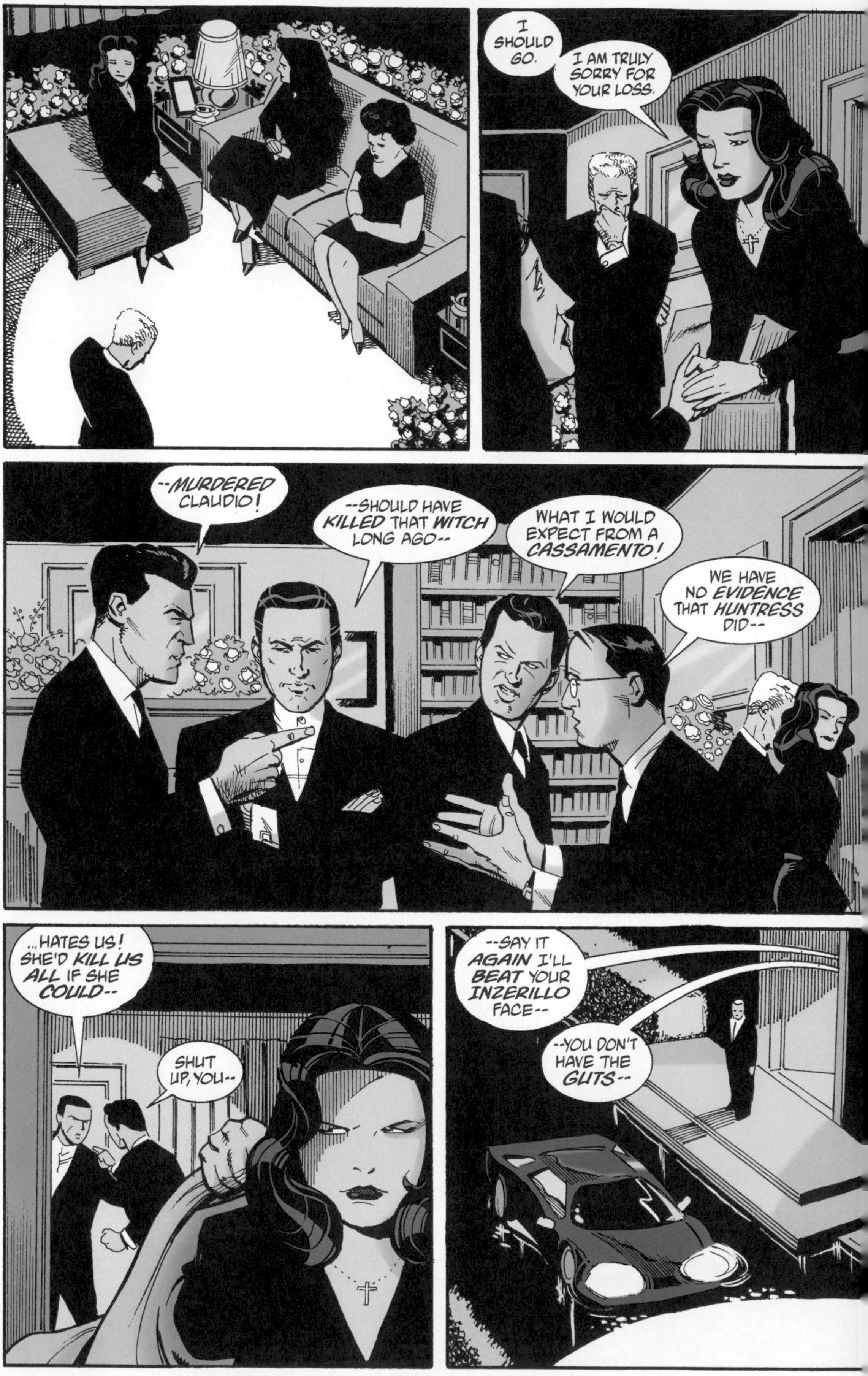
I SHOULD GO.
I AM TRULY SORRY FOR YOUR LOSS.
--MURDERED CLAUDIO!
--SHOULD HAVE KILLED THAT WITCH LONG AGO--
WHAT I WOULD EXPECT FROM A CASSAMENTO!
WE HAVE NO EVIDENCE THAT HUNTRESS DID--
...HATES US! SHE'D KILL US ALL IF SHE COULD--
SHUT UP, YOU--
--SAY IT AGAIN I'LL BEAT YOUR INZERILLO FACE--
--YOU DON'T HAVE THE GUTS--

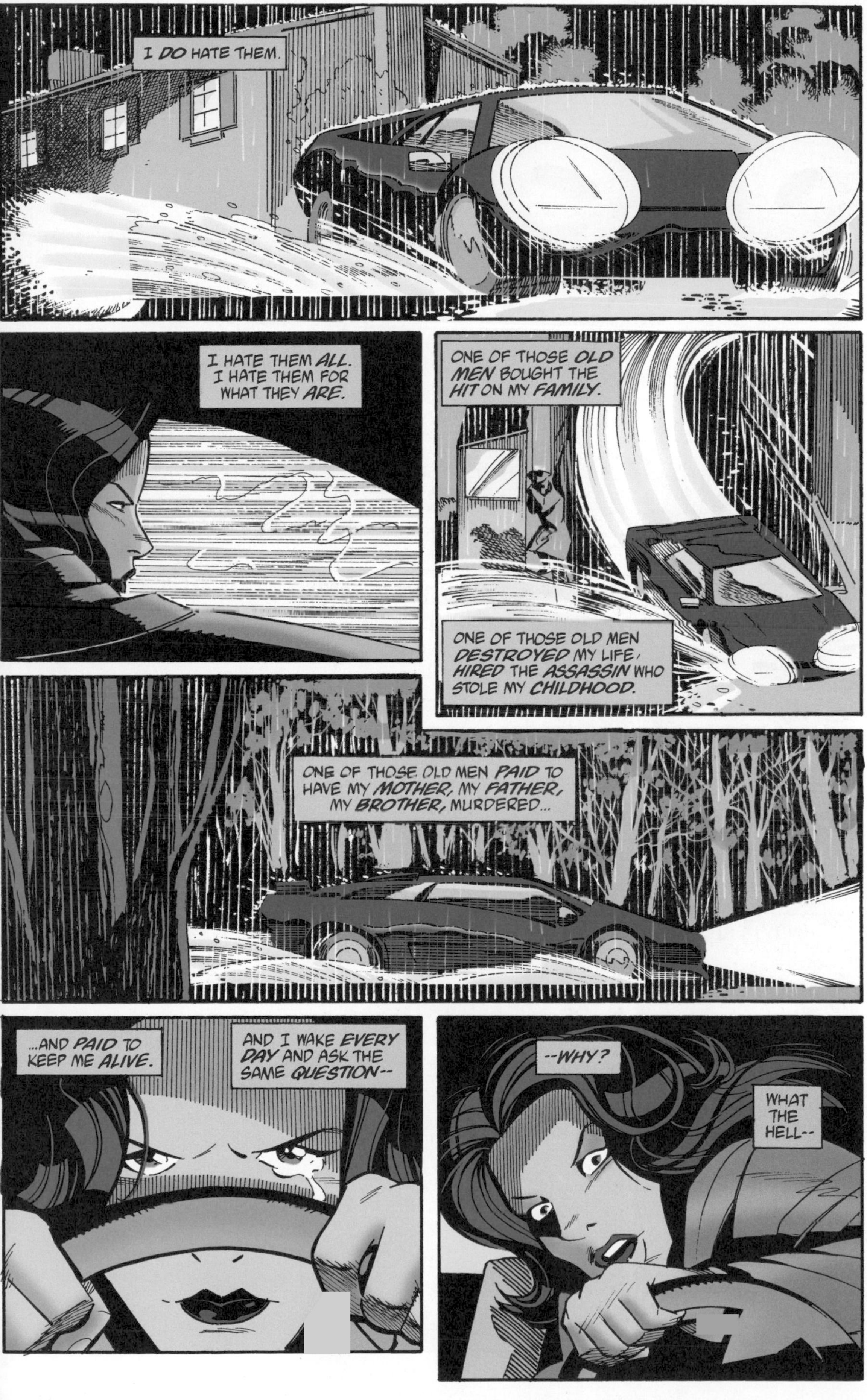
I DO HATE THEM.
I HATE THEM ALL. I HATE THEM FOR WHAT THEY ARE.
ONE OF THOSE OLD MEN BOUGHT THE HIT ON MY FAMILY.
ONE OF THOSE OLD MEN DESTROYED MY LIFE, HIRED THE ASSASSIN WHO STOLE MY CHILDHOOD.
ONE OF THOSE OLD MEN PAID TO HAVE MY MOTHER, MY FATHER, MY BROTHER, MURDERED...
...AND PAID TO KEEP ME ALIVE.
AND I WAKE EVERY DAY AND ASK THE SAME QUESTION--
--WHY?
WHAT THE HELL--

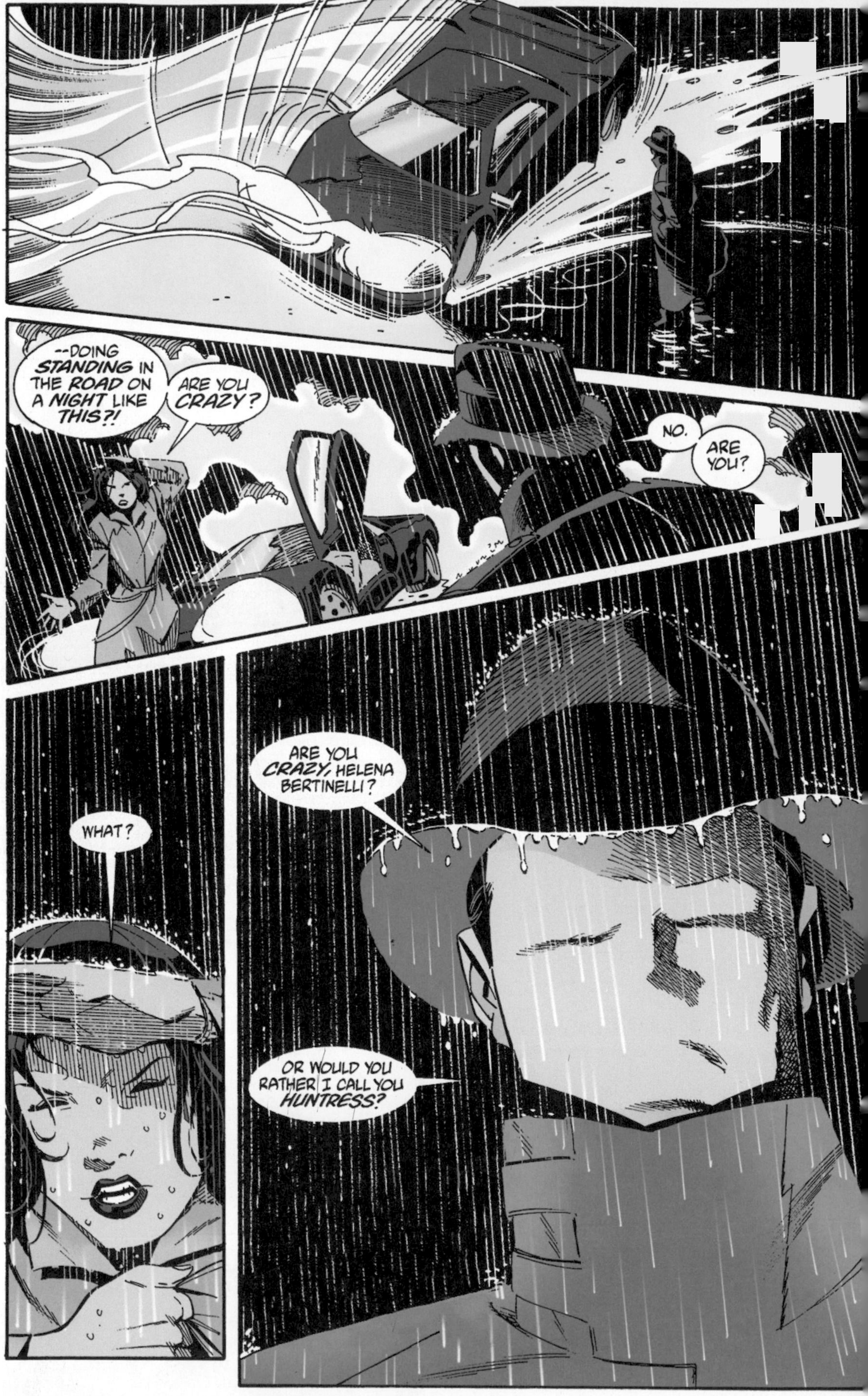
--DOING STANDING IN THE ROAD ON A NIGHT LIKE THIS?!
ARE YOU CRAZY?
NO.
ARE YOU?
WHAT?
ARE YOU CRAZY, HELENA BERTINELLI?
OR WOULD YOU RATHER I CALL YOU HUNTRESS?

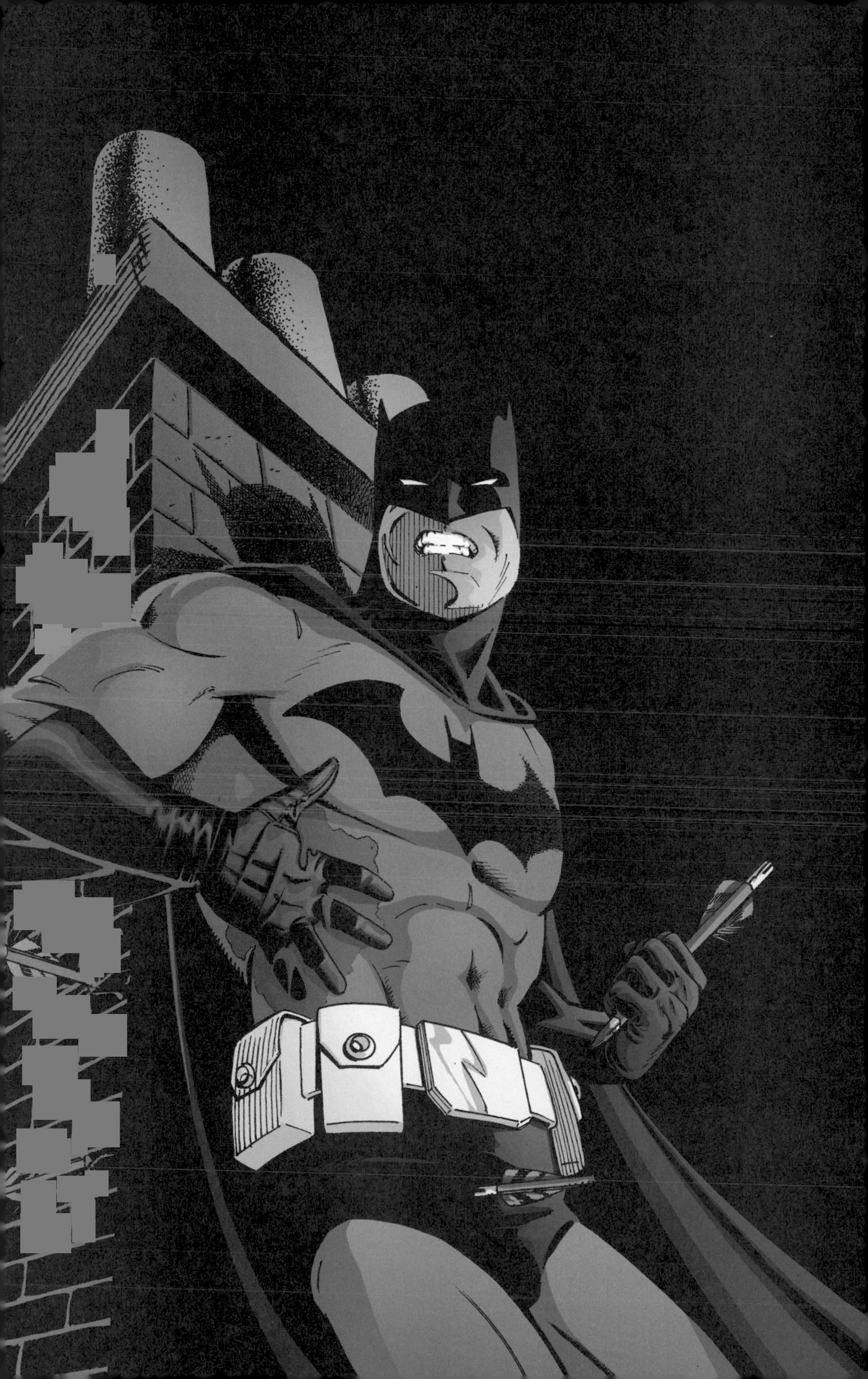

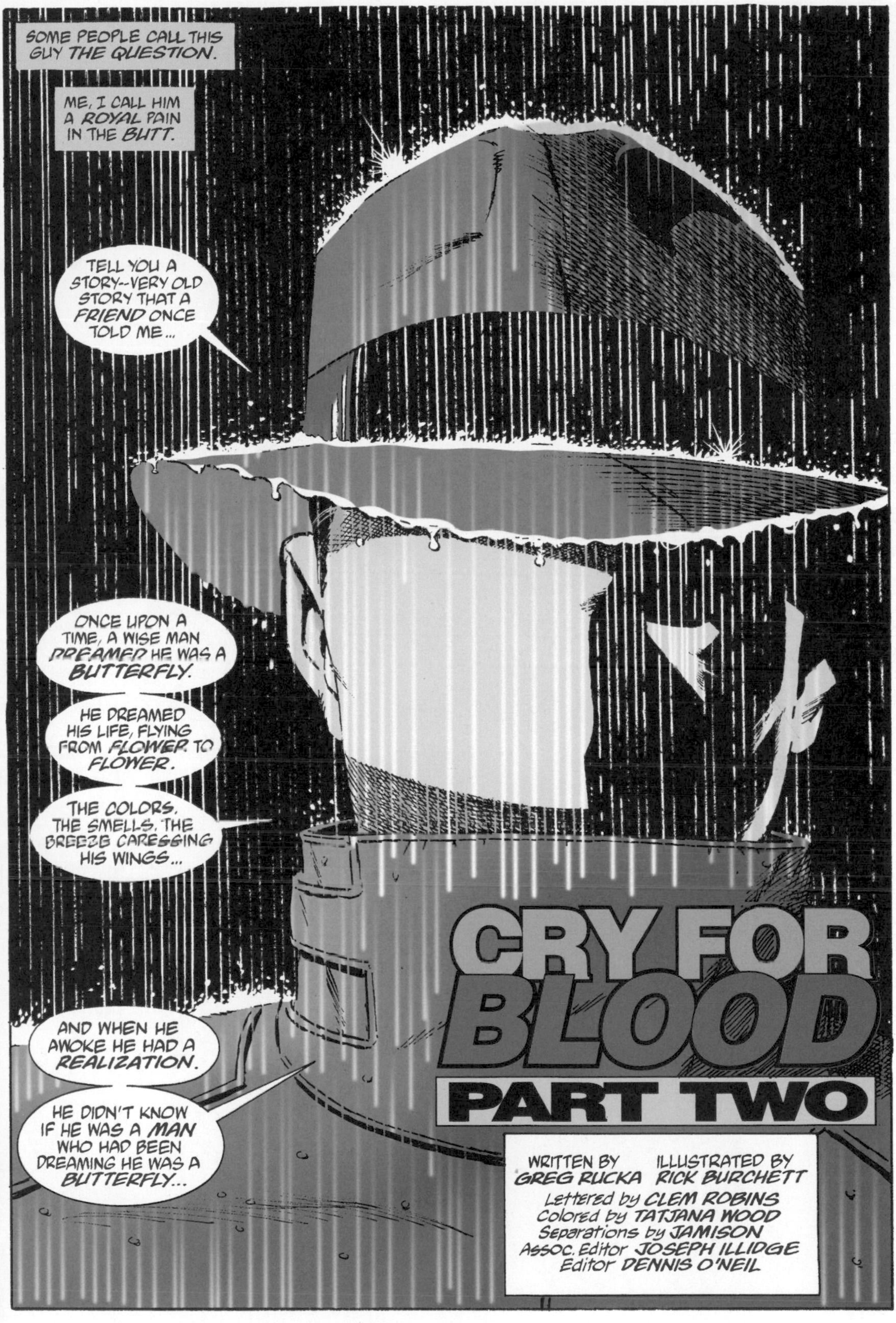
SOME PEOPLE CALL THIS GUY THE QUESTION.
ME, I CALL HIM A ROYAL PAIN IN THE BUTT.
TELL YOU A STORY--VERY OLD STORY THAT A FRIEND ONCE TOLD ME...
ONCE UPON A TIME, A WISE MAN DREAMED HE WAS A BUTTERFLY.
HE DREAMED HIS LIFE, FLYING FROM FLOWER TO FLOWER.
THE COLORS. THE SMELLS. THE BREEZE CARESSING HIS WINGS...
CRY FOR BLOOD
PART TWO
AND WHEN HE AWOKE HE HAD A REALIZATION.
HE DIDN'T KNOW IF HE WAS A MAN WHO HAD BEEN DREAMING HE WAS A BUTTERFLY...
WRITTEN BY GREG RUCKA
ILLUSTRATED BY RICK BURCHETT
Lettered by CLEM ROBINS
Colored by TATJANA WOOD
Separations by JAMISON
Assoc. Editor JOSEPH ILLIDGE
Editor DENNIS O'NEIL

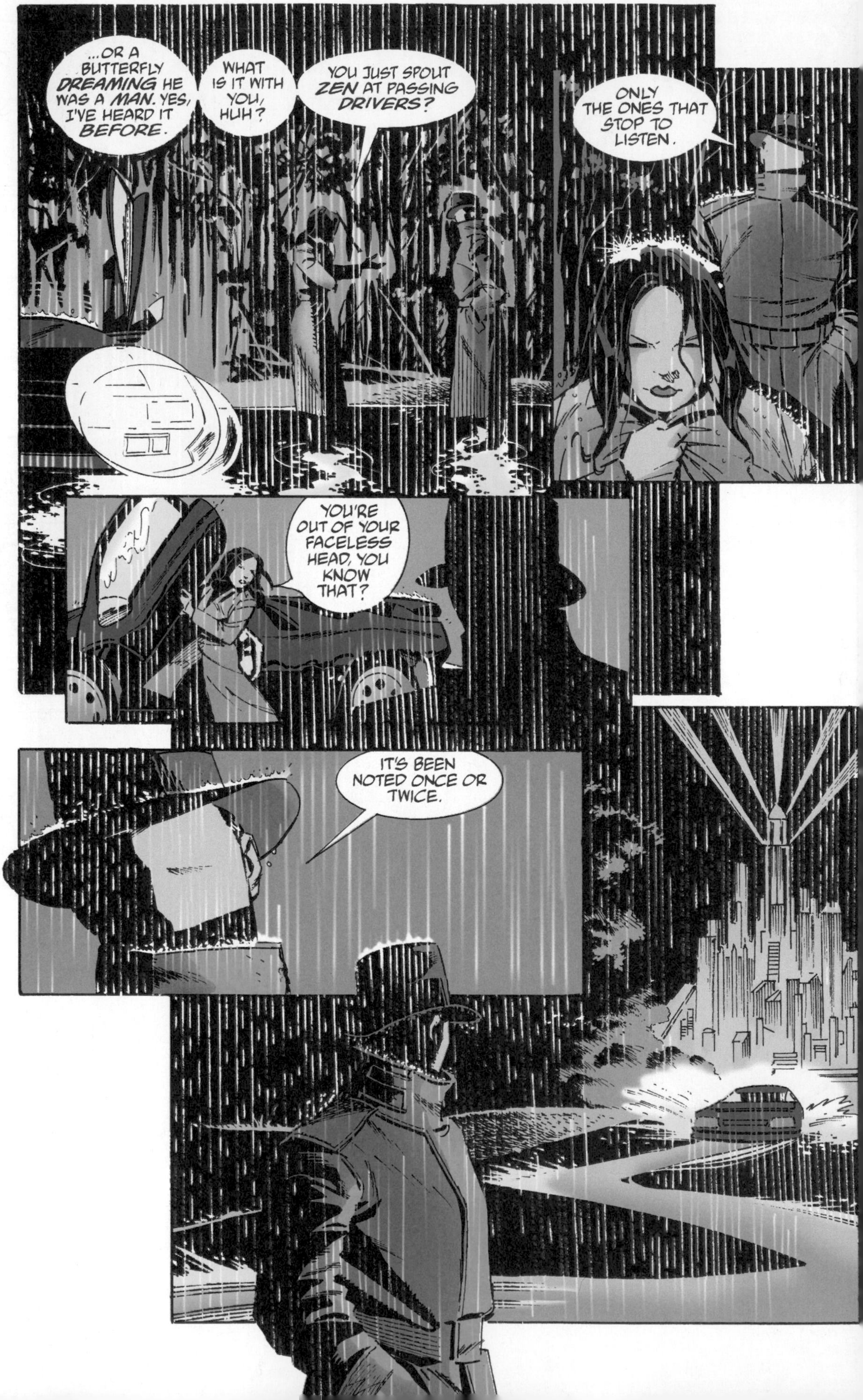
...OR A BUTTERFLY DREAMING HE WAS A MAN. YES, I'VE HEARD IT BEFORE.
WHAT IS IT WITH YOU, HUH?
YOU JUST SPOUT ZEN AT PASSING DRIVERS?
ONLY THE ONES THAT STOP TO LISTEN.
YOU'RE OUT OF YOUR FACELESS HEAD, YOU KNOW THAT?
IT'S BEEN NOTED ONCE OR TWICE.

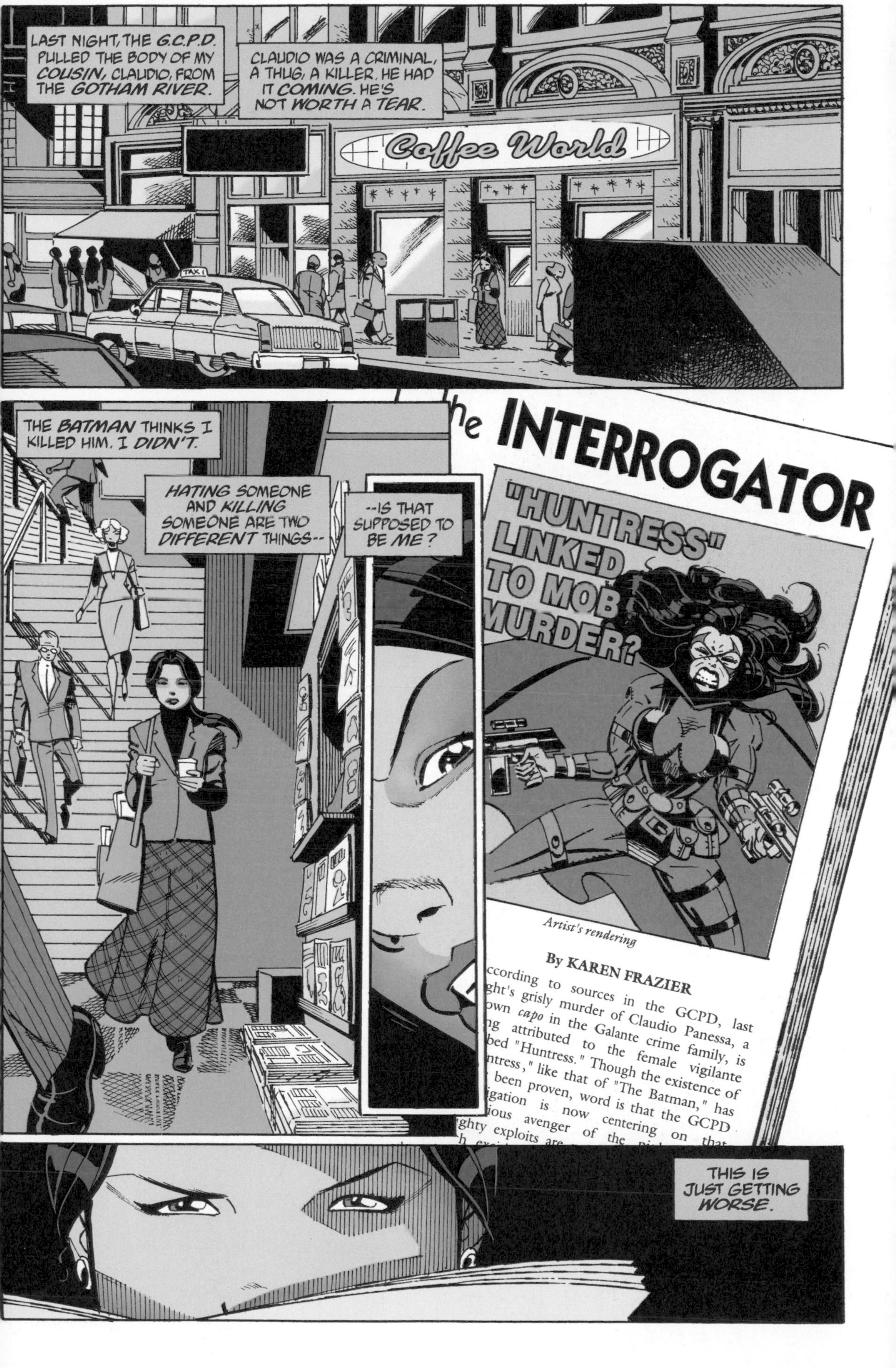

LAST NIGHT, THE G.C.P.D. PULLED THE BODY OF MY COUSIN, CLAUDIO, FROM THE GOTHAM RIVER.
CLAUDIO WAS A CRIMINAL, A THUG, A KILLER. HE HAD IT COMING. HE'S NOT WORTH A TEAR.
Coffee World
TAXI
THE BATMAN THINKS I KILLED HIM. I DIDN'T.
HATING SOMEONE AND KILLING SOMEONE ARE TWO DIFFERENT THINGS--
--IS THAT SUPPOSED TO BE ME?
he INTERROGATOR
"HUNTRESS" LINKED TO MOB MURDER?
Artist's rendering
By KAREN FRAZIER
ccording to sources in the GCPD, last
ght's grisly murder of Claudio Panessa, a
own capo in the Galante crime family, is
ng attributed to the female vigilante
bed "Huntress." Though the existence of
ntress," like that of "The Batman," has
been proven, word is that the GCPD
igation is now centering on that
ious avenger of the
ghty exploits are
THIS IS JUST GETTING WORSE.

SOMEONE IS SETTING ME UP. SETTING *HUNTRESS* UP.

SOMEONE *PAID* FOR THIS STORY.

...PAID FRAZIER. SHE'S *MOBBED-UP*, I'M *SURE* OF IT.

By KAREN FRAZIER

...ording to sources in the GCPD
...ht's grisly murder of Claudio Pan
...own *capo* in the Galante crime fa
...ing attributed to the female v
...abbed "Huntress,"...ugh the exis
...untress," like...The Batm
...ever been prov...ering
...vestigation is...nigh
...ysterious ave...hro
...mighty exploits...mi
...each exciting

BUT IF THE COPS REALLY *ARE* AFTER ME, MY LIFE IS ABOUT TO BECOME A *LOT* MORE COMPLICATED.

BATMAN *KNOWS* WHO I *AM*, HE KNOWS ALMOST *EVERYTHING* ABOUT ME.

IF HE THINKS I'M *GUILTY*, THERE'S *NOTHING* TO KEEP HIM FROM SHARING THAT INFORMATION WITH *GORDON*.

AND THEN *GORDON* ARRESTS THE ONLY SURVIVING *BERTINELLI*... AND *HUNTRESS* IS UNMASKED FOR ALL TO SEE.

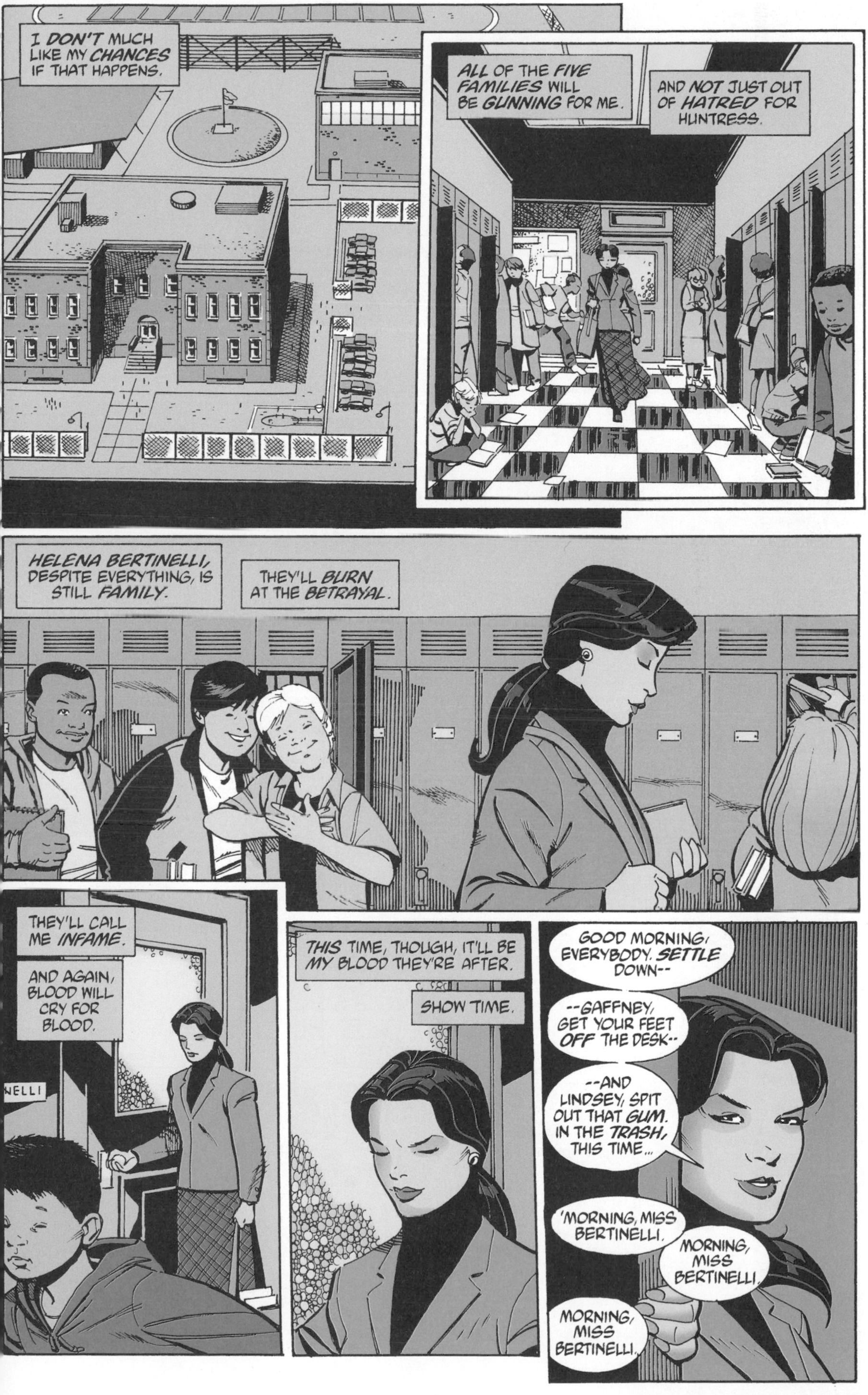
I DON'T MUCH LIKE MY CHANCES IF THAT HAPPENS.
ALL OF THE FIVE FAMILIES WILL BE GUNNING FOR ME.
AND NOT JUST OUT OF HATRED FOR HUNTRESS.
HELENA BERTINELLI, DESPITE EVERYTHING, IS STILL FAMILY.
THEY'LL BURN AT THE BETRAYAL.
THEY'LL CALL ME INFAME.
AND AGAIN, BLOOD WILL CRY FOR BLOOD.
NELLI
THIS TIME, THOUGH, IT'LL BE MY BLOOD THEY'RE AFTER.
SHOW TIME.
GOOD MORNING, EVERYBODY. SETTLE DOWN--
--GAFFNEY, GET YOUR FEET OFF THE DESK--
--AND LINDSEY, SPIT OUT THAT GUM. IN THE TRASH, THIS TIME...
'MORNING, MISS BERTINELLI.
MORNING, MISS BERTINELLI.
MORNING, MISS BERTINELLI.

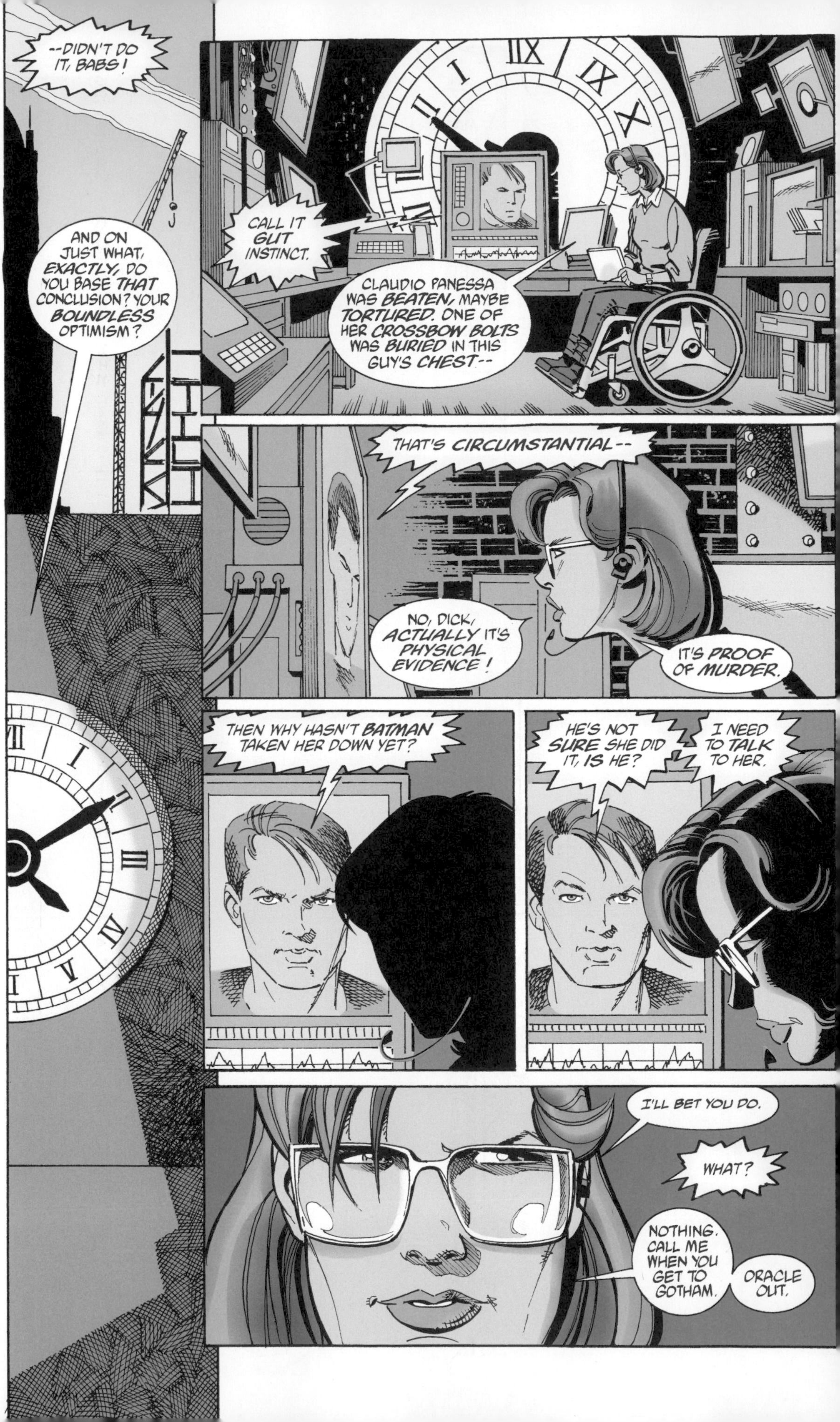
--DIDN'T DO IT, BABS!
AND ON JUST WHAT, EXACTLY, DO YOU BASE THAT CONCLUSION? YOUR BOUNDLESS OPTIMISM?
CALL IT GUT INSTINCT.
CLAUDIO PANESSA WAS BEATEN, MAYBE TORTURED. ONE OF HER CROSSBOW BOLTS WAS BURIED IN THIS GUY'S CHEST--
THAT'S CIRCUMSTANTIAL--
NO, DICK, ACTUALLY IT'S PHYSICAL EVIDENCE!
IT'S PROOF OF MURDER.
THEN WHY HASN'T BATMAN TAKEN HER DOWN YET?
HE'S NOT SURE SHE DID IT, IS HE?
I NEED TO TALK TO HER.
I'LL BET YOU DO.
WHAT?
NOTHING. CALL ME WHEN YOU GET TO GOTHAM.
ORACLE OUT.

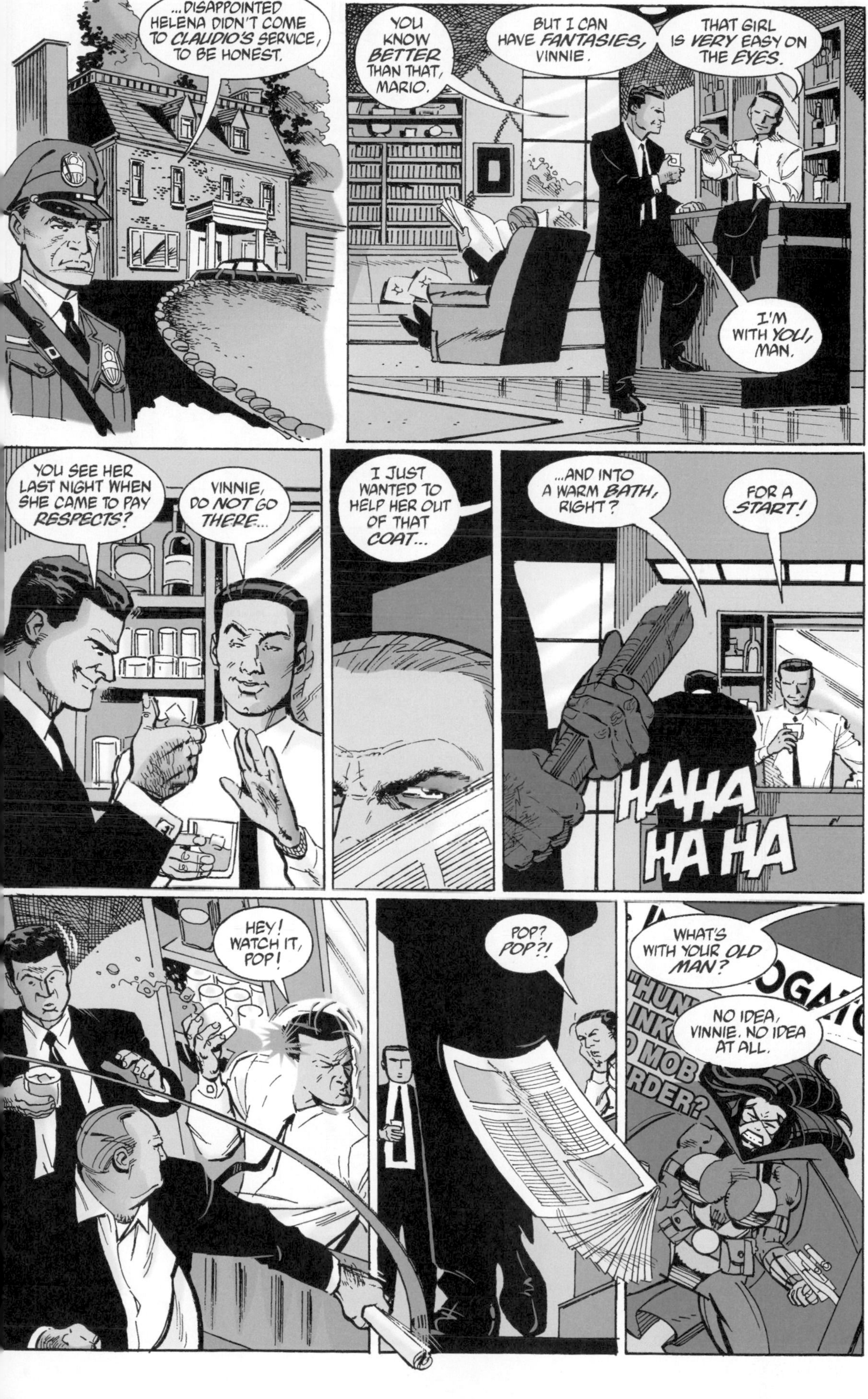
...DISAPPOINTED HELENA DIDN'T COME TO CLAUDIO'S SERVICE, TO BE HONEST.
YOU KNOW BETTER THAN THAT, MARIO.
BUT I CAN HAVE FANTASIES, VINNIE.
THAT GIRL IS VERY EASY ON THE EYES.
I'M WITH YOU, MAN.
YOU SEE HER LAST NIGHT WHEN SHE CAME TO PAY RESPECTS?
VINNIE, DO NOT GO THERE...
I JUST WANTED TO HELP HER OUT OF THAT COAT...
...AND INTO A WARM BATH, RIGHT?
FOR A START!
HAHA HA HA
HEY! WATCH IT, POP!
POP? POP?!
WHAT'S WITH YOUR OLD MAN?
NO IDEA, VINNIE. NO IDEA AT ALL.

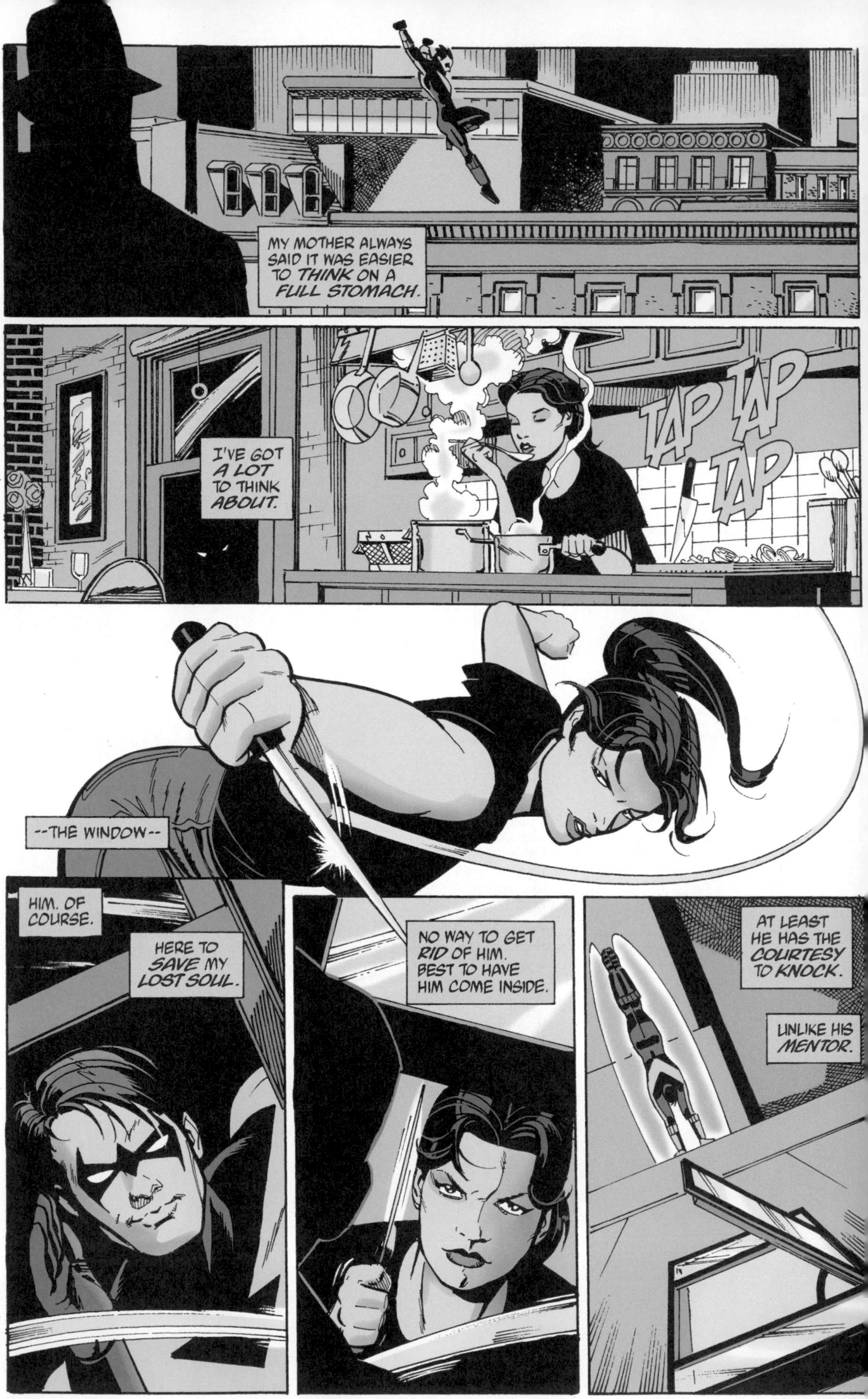
MY MOTHER ALWAYS SAID IT WAS EASIER TO THINK ON A FULL STOMACH.
I'VE GOT A LOT TO THINK ABOUT.
TAP TAP TAP
--THE WINDOW--
HIM. OF COURSE.
HERE TO SAVE MY LOST SOUL.
NO WAY TO GET RID OF HIM. BEST TO HAVE HIM COME INSIDE.
AT LEAST HE HAS THE COURTESY TO KNOCK.
UNLIKE HIS MENTOR.

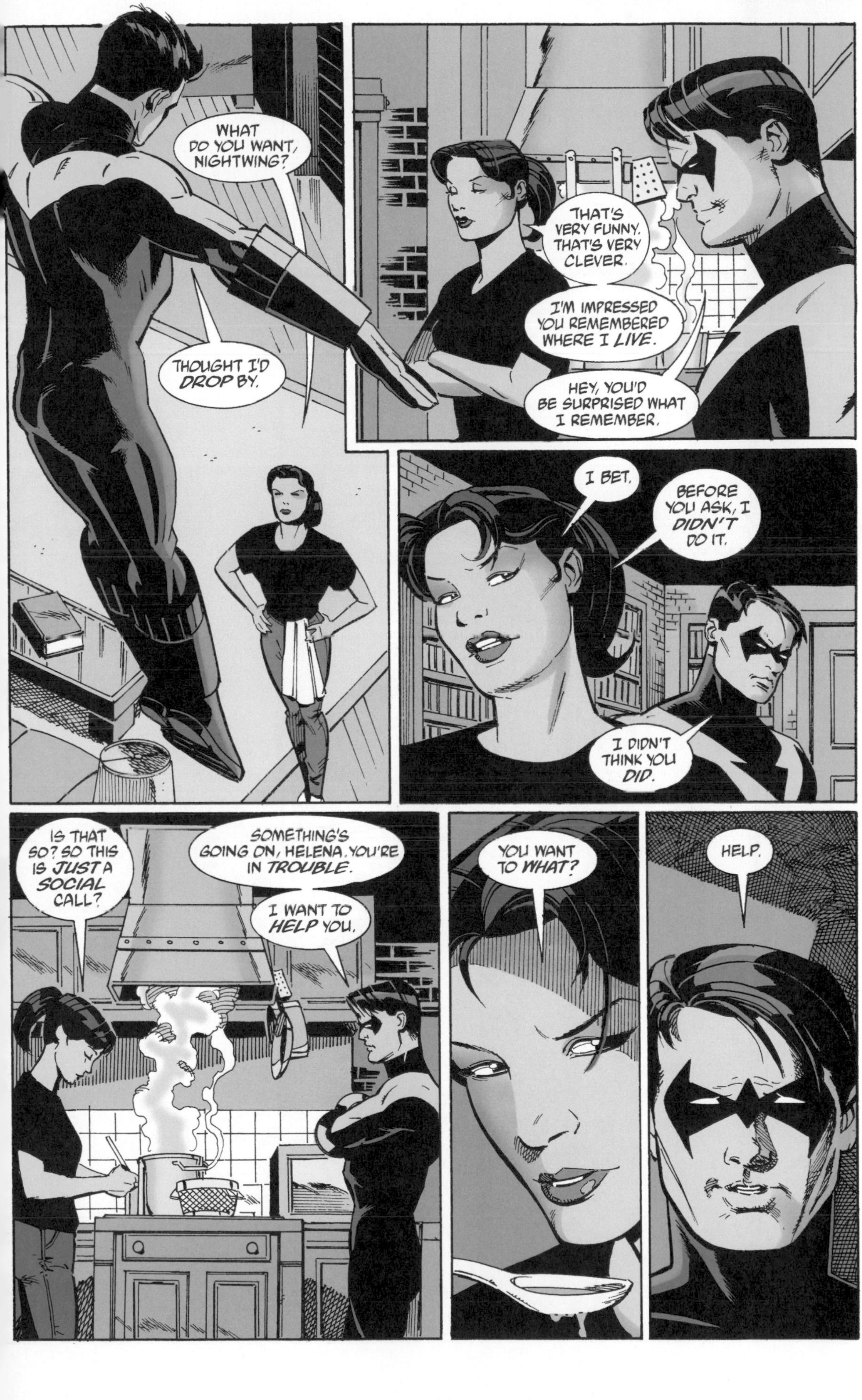
WHAT DO YOU WANT, NIGHTWING?
THOUGHT I'D DROP BY.
THAT'S VERY FUNNY. THAT'S VERY CLEVER.
I'M IMPRESSED YOU REMEMBERED WHERE I LIVE.
HEY, YOU'D BE SURPRISED WHAT I REMEMBER.
I BET.
BEFORE YOU ASK, I DIDN'T DO IT.
I DIDN'T THINK YOU DID.
IS THAT SO? SO THIS IS JUST A SOCIAL CALL?
SOMETHING'S GOING ON, HELENA. YOU'RE IN TROUBLE.
I WANT TO HELP YOU.
YOU WANT TO WHAT?
HELP.

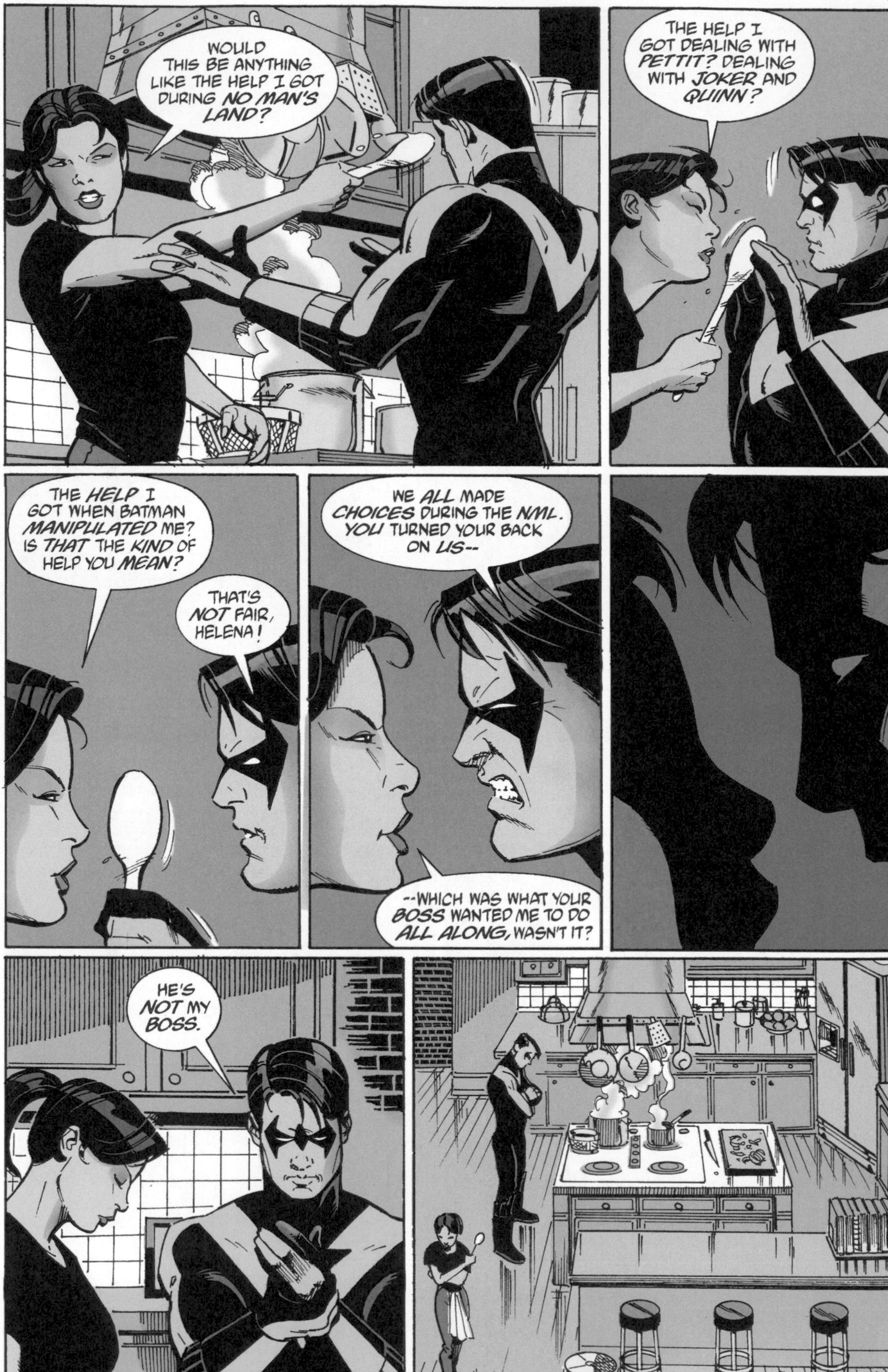
WOULD THIS BE ANYTHING LIKE THE HELP I GOT DURING NO MAN'S LAND?
THE HELP I GOT DEALING WITH PETTIT? DEALING WITH JOKER AND QUINN?
THE HELP I GOT WHEN BATMAN MANIPULATED ME? IS THAT THE KIND OF HELP YOU MEAN?
THAT'S NOT FAIR, HELENA!
WE ALL MADE CHOICES DURING THE NML. YOU TURNED YOUR BACK ON US--
--WHICH WAS WHAT YOUR BOSS WANTED ME TO DO ALL ALONG, WASN'T IT?
HE'S NOT MY BOSS.

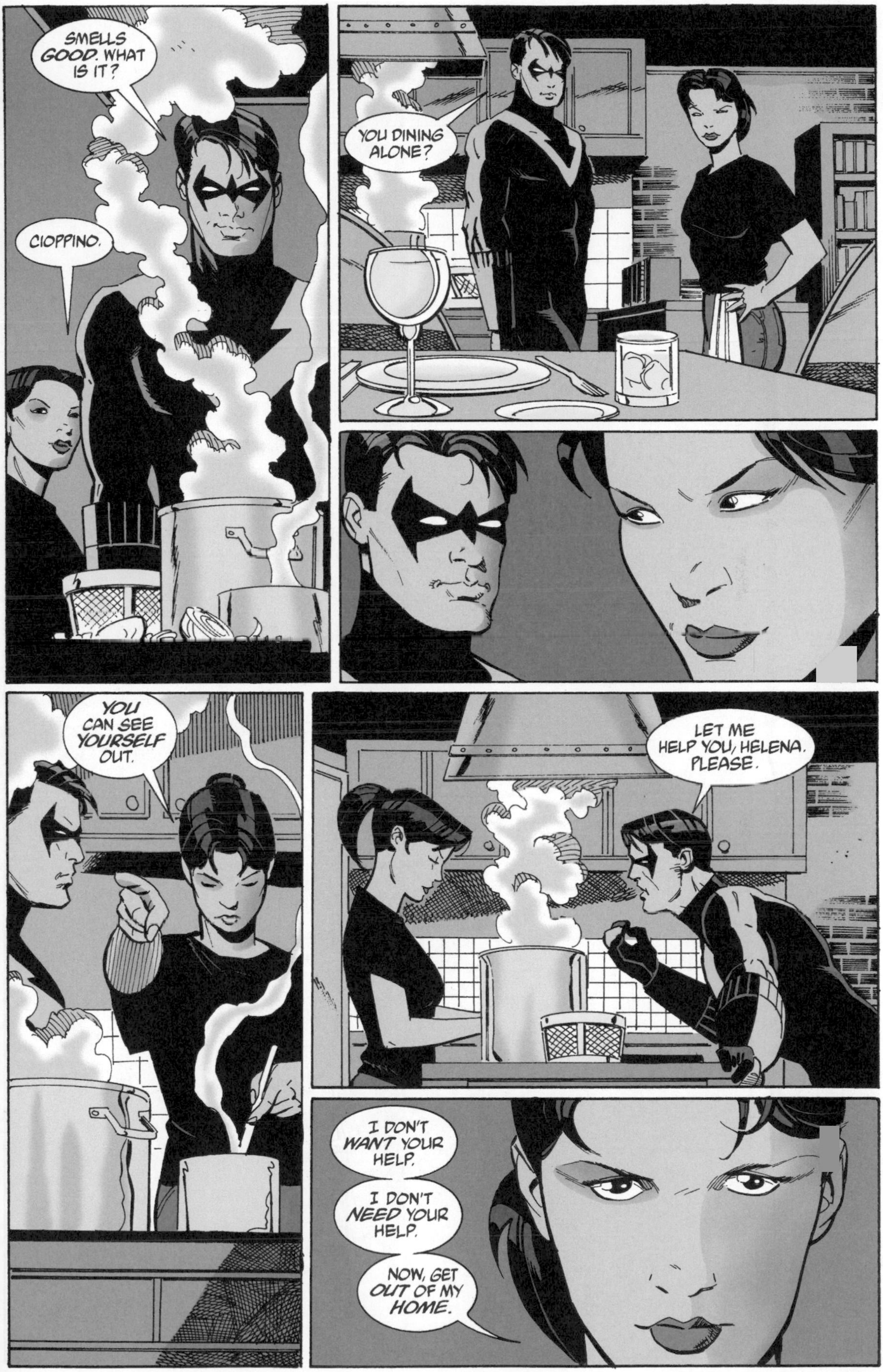
SMELLS GOOD. WHAT IS IT?
CIOPPINO.
YOU DINING ALONE?
YOU CAN SEE YOURSELF OUT.
LET ME HELP YOU, HELENA. PLEASE.
I DON'T WANT YOUR HELP.
I DON'T NEED YOUR HELP.
NOW, GET OUT OF MY HOME.

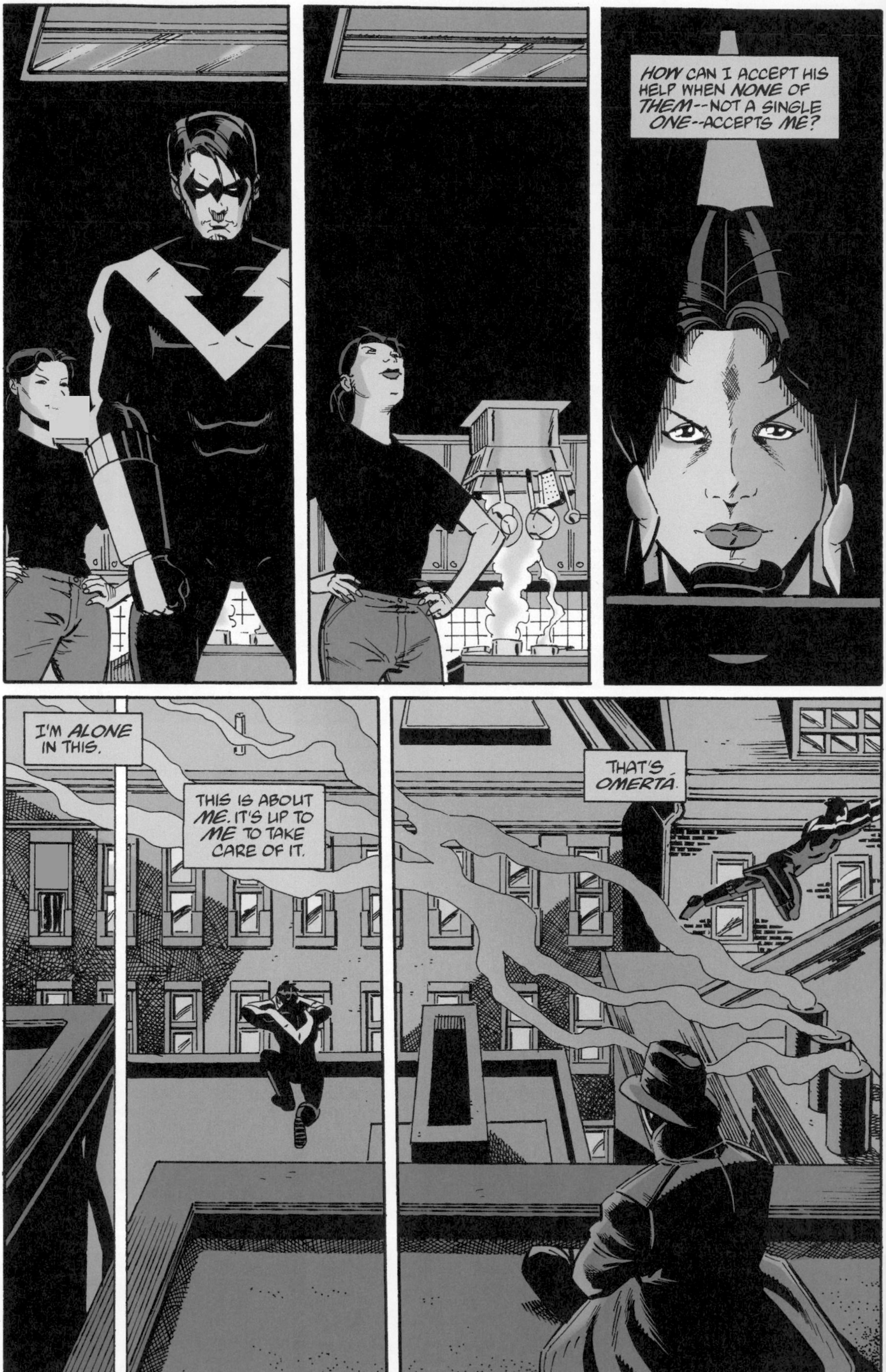
HOW CAN I ACCEPT HIS HELP WHEN NONE OF THEM--NOT A SINGLE ONE--ACCEPTS ME?
I'M ALONE IN THIS.
THIS IS ABOUT ME. IT'S UP TO ME TO TAKE CARE OF IT.
THAT'S OMERTÁ.

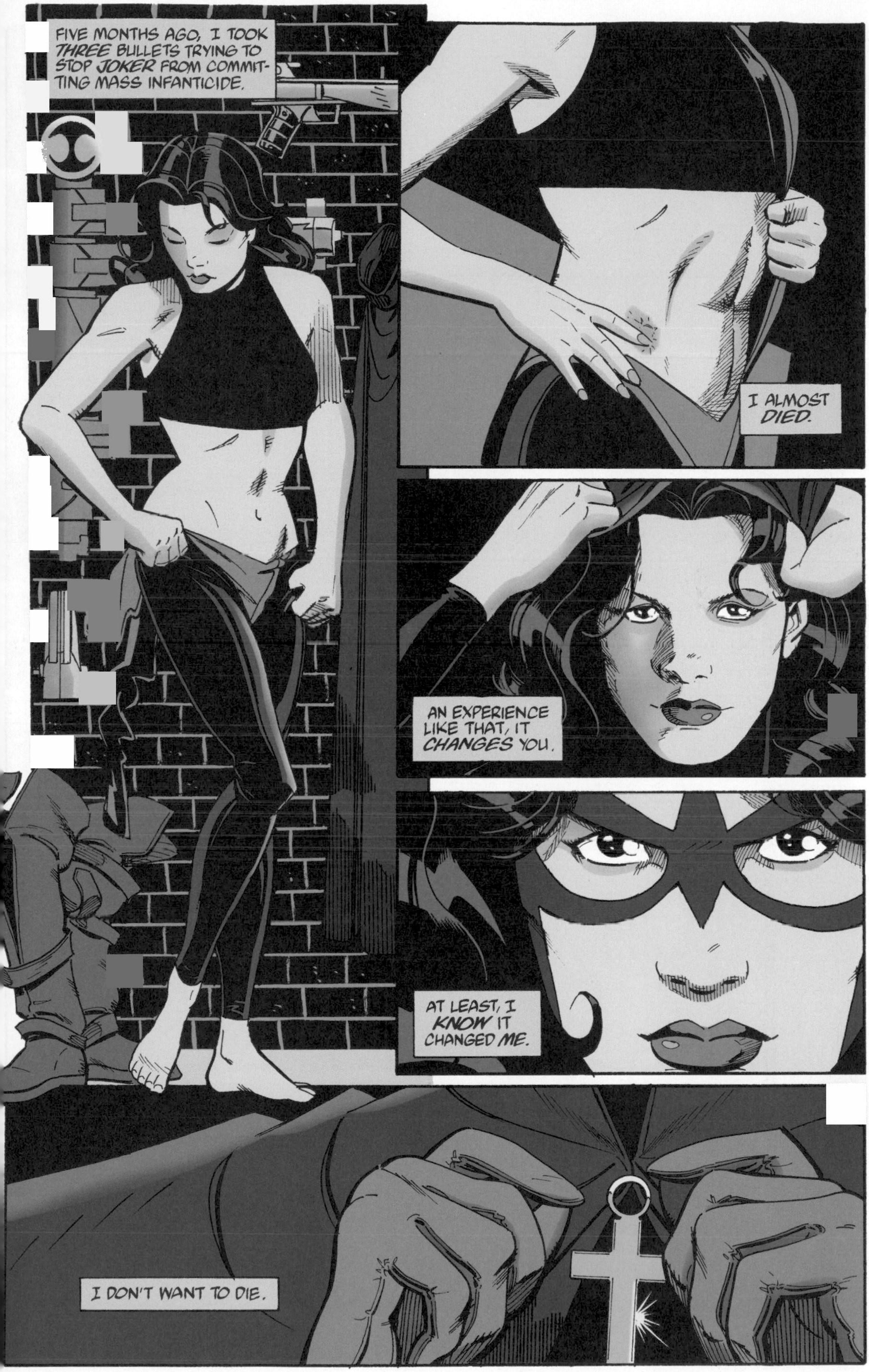
FIVE MONTHS AGO, I TOOK THREE BULLETS TRYING TO STOP JOKER FROM COMMITTING MASS INFANTICIDE.
I ALMOST DIED.
AN EXPERIENCE LIKE THAT, IT CHANGES YOU.
AT LEAST, I KNOW IT CHANGED ME.
I DON'T WANT TO DIE.

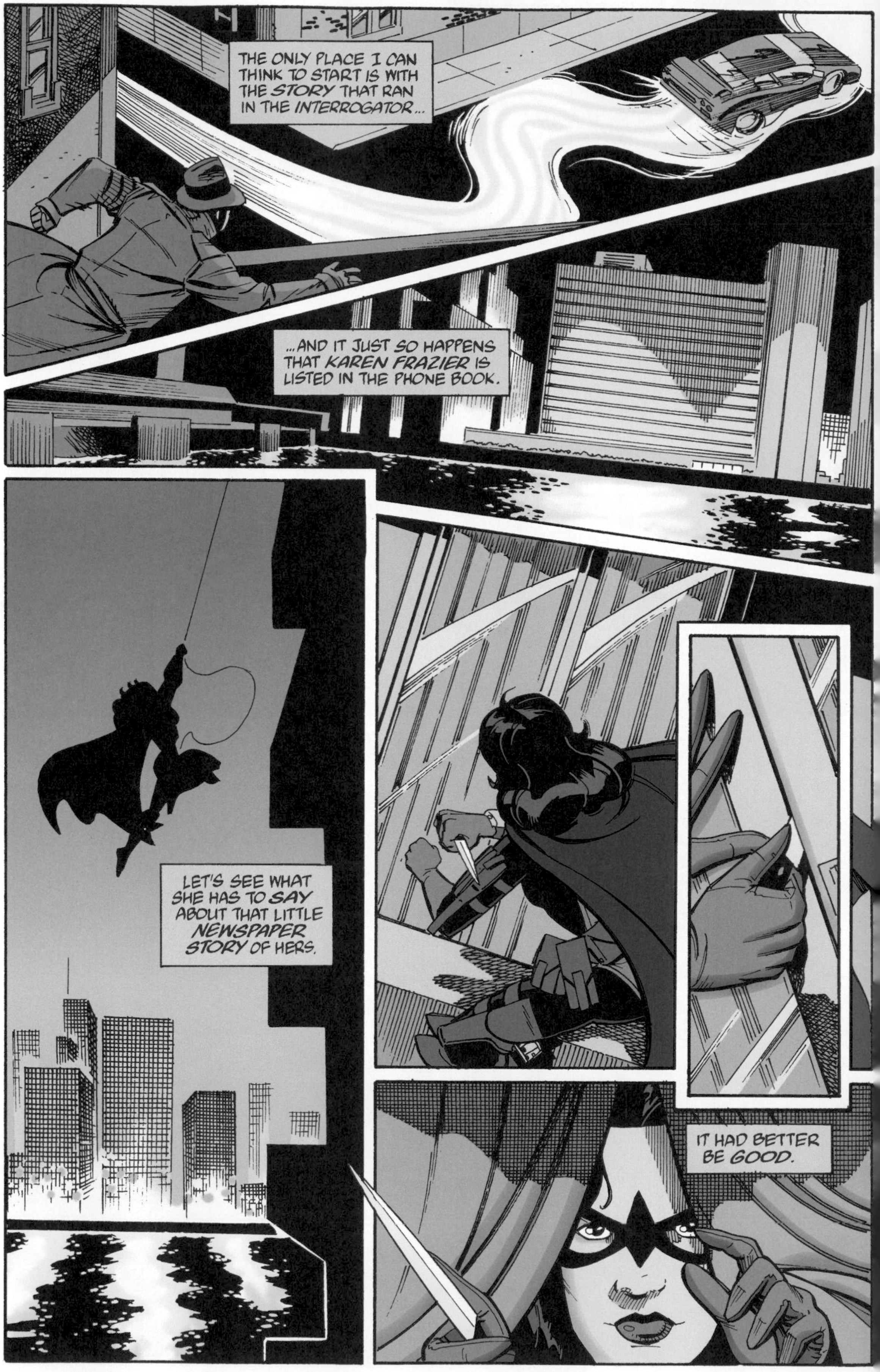
THE ONLY PLACE I CAN THINK TO START IS WITH THE STORY THAT RAN IN THE INTERROGATOR...
...AND IT JUST SO HAPPENS THAT KAREN FRAZIER IS LISTED IN THE PHONE BOOK.
LET'S SEE WHAT SHE HAS TO SAY ABOUT THAT LITTLE NEWSPAPER STORY OF HERS.
IT HAD BETTER BE GOOD.

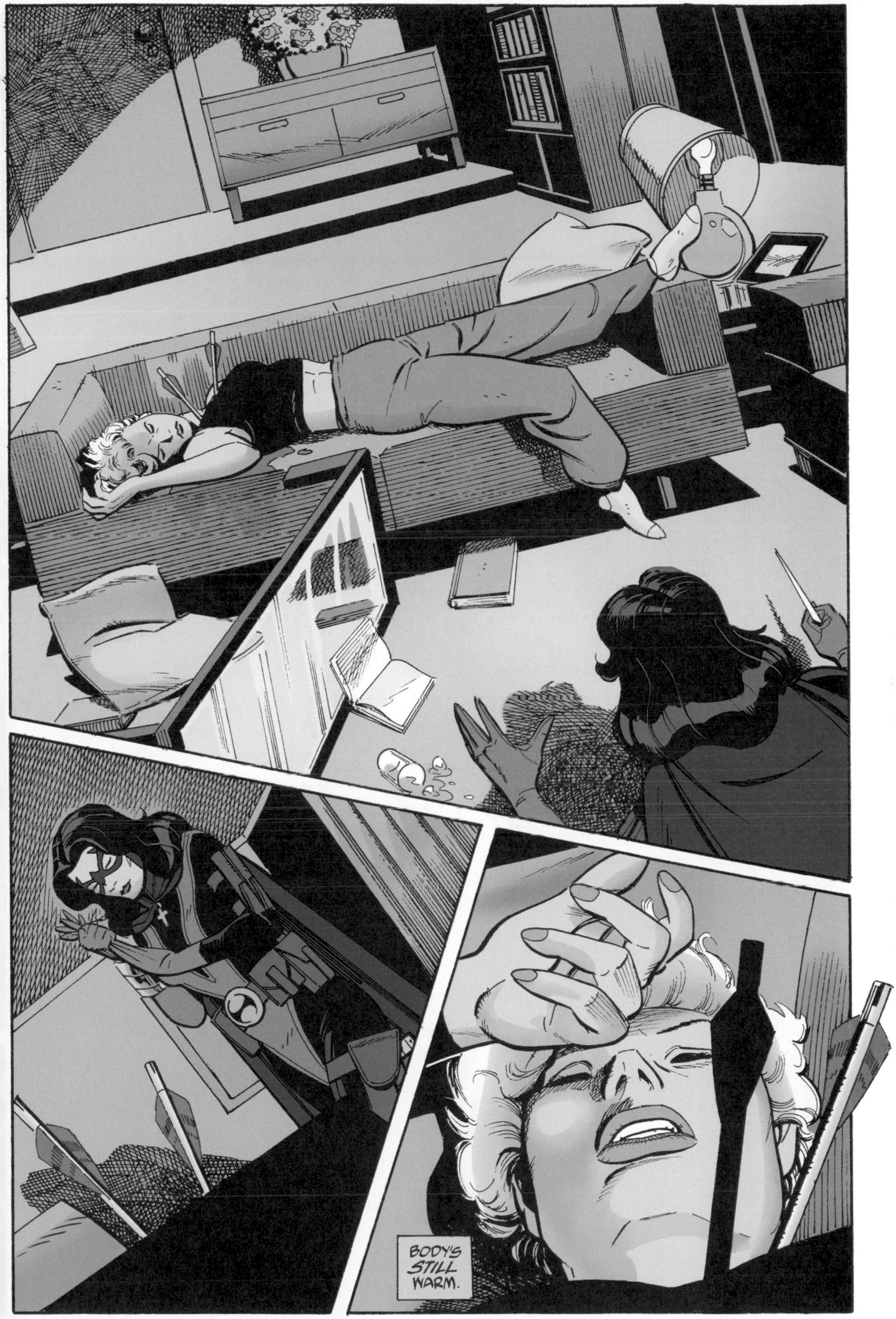
BODY'S STILL WARM.

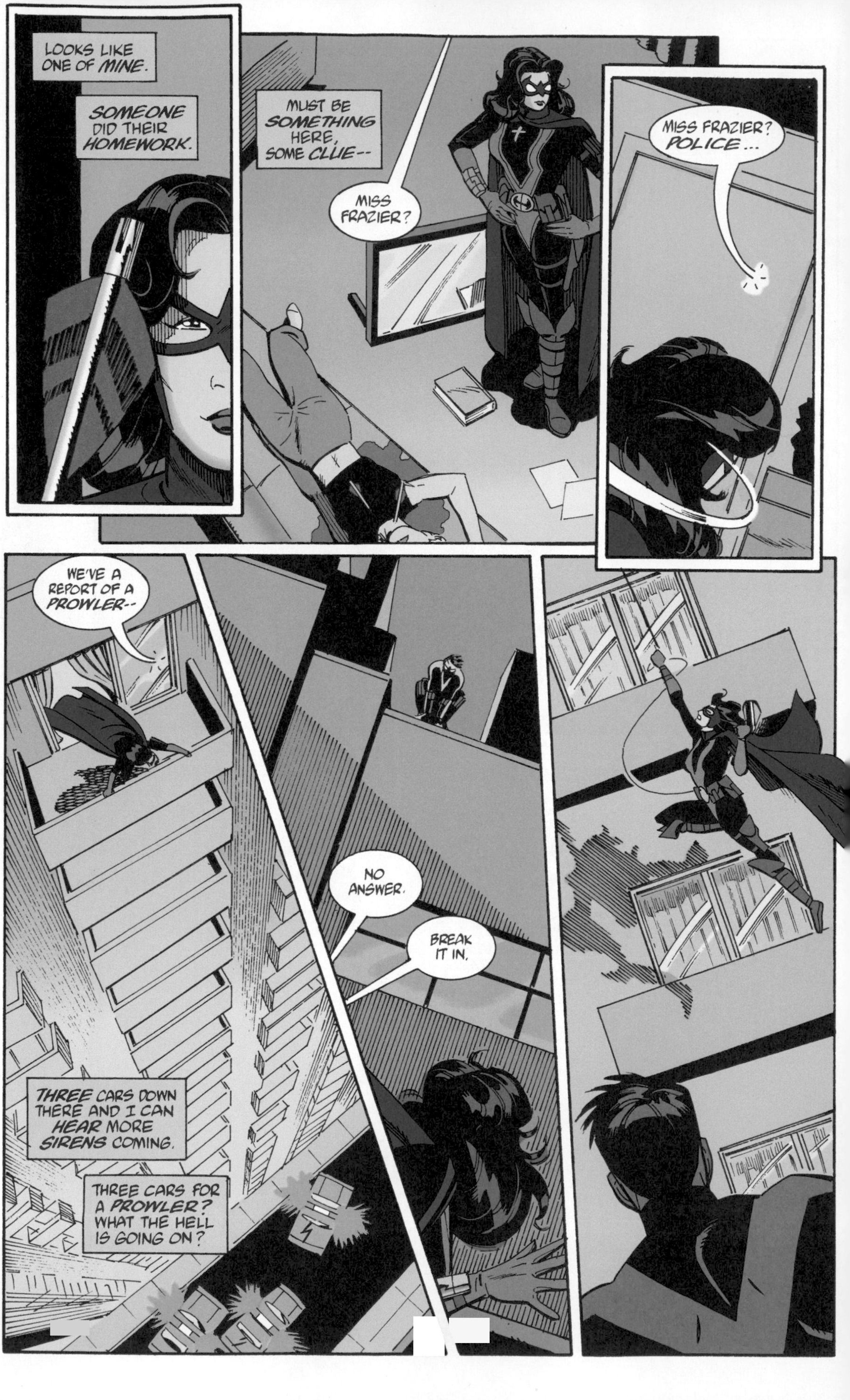
LOOKS LIKE ONE OF MINE.
SOMEONE DID THEIR HOMEWORK.
MUST BE SOMETHING HERE, SOME CLUE--
MISS FRAZIER?
MISS FRAZIER? POLICE...
WE'VE A REPORT OF A PROWLER--
THREE CARS DOWN THERE AND I CAN HEAR MORE SIRENS COMING.
THREE CARS FOR A PROWLER? WHAT THE HELL IS GOING ON?
NO ANSWER.
BREAK IT IN.

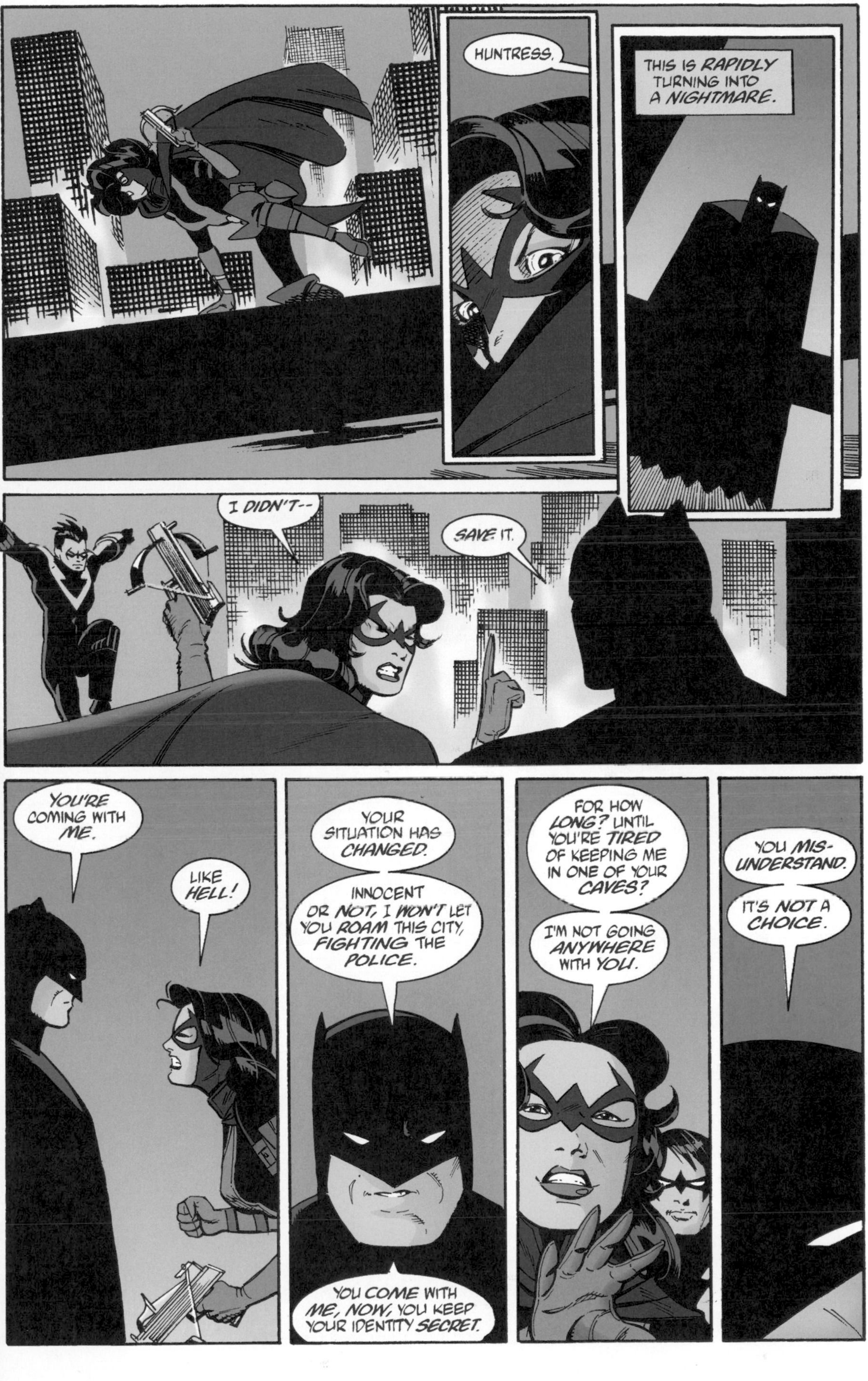
HUNTRESS.
THIS IS RAPIDLY TURNING INTO A NIGHTMARE.
I DIDN'T--
SAVE IT.
YOU'RE COMING WITH ME.
LIKE HELL!
YOUR SITUATION HAS CHANGED.
INNOCENT OR NOT, I WON'T LET YOU ROAM THIS CITY, FIGHTING THE POLICE.
YOU COME WITH ME, NOW, YOU KEEP YOUR IDENTITY SECRET.
FOR HOW LONG? UNTIL YOU'RE TIRED OF KEEPING ME IN ONE OF YOUR CAVES?
I'M NOT GOING ANYWHERE WITH YOU.
YOU MIS-UNDERSTAND.
IT'S NOT A CHOICE.

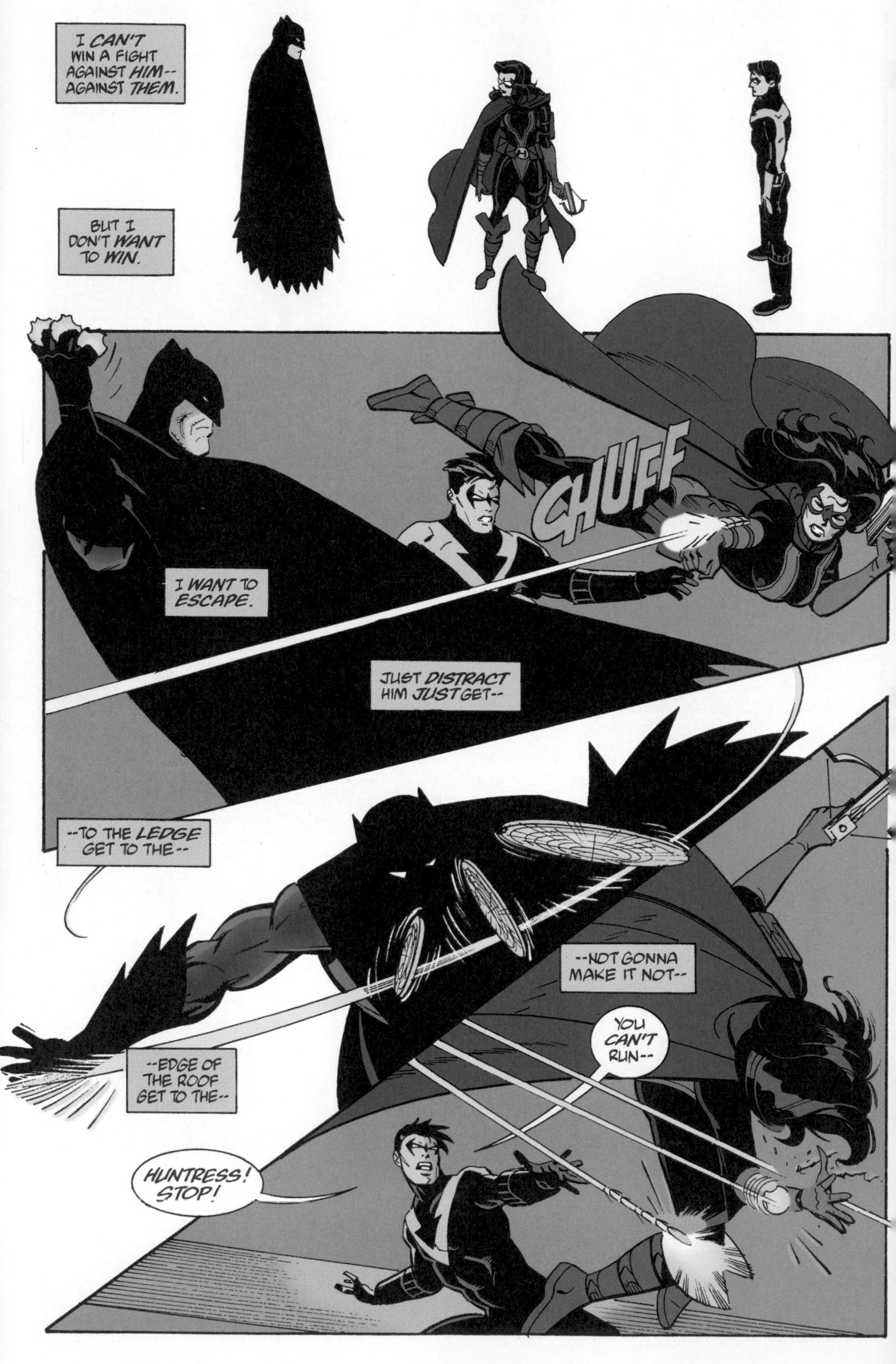

I CAN'T WIN A FIGHT AGAINST HIM-- AGAINST THEM.
BUT I DON'T WANT TO WIN.
I WANT TO ESCAPE.
CHUFF
JUST DISTRACT HIM JUST GET--
--TO THE LEDGE GET TO THE--
--NOT GONNA MAKE IT NOT--
YOU CAN'T RUN--
--EDGE OF THE ROOF GET TO THE--
HUNTRESS! STOP!

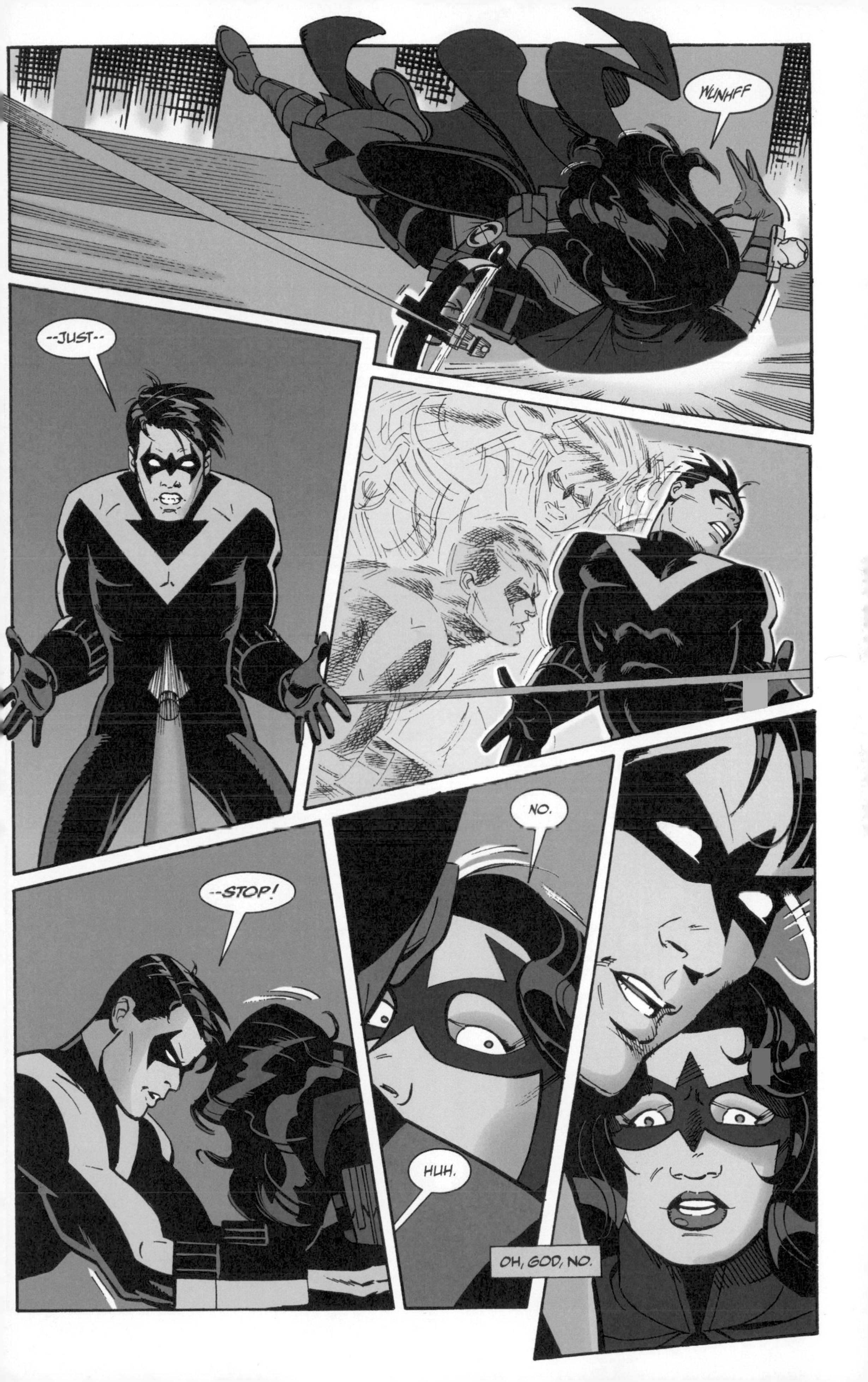
WUNHFF
--JUST--
--STOP!
NO.
HUH.
OH, GOD, NO.

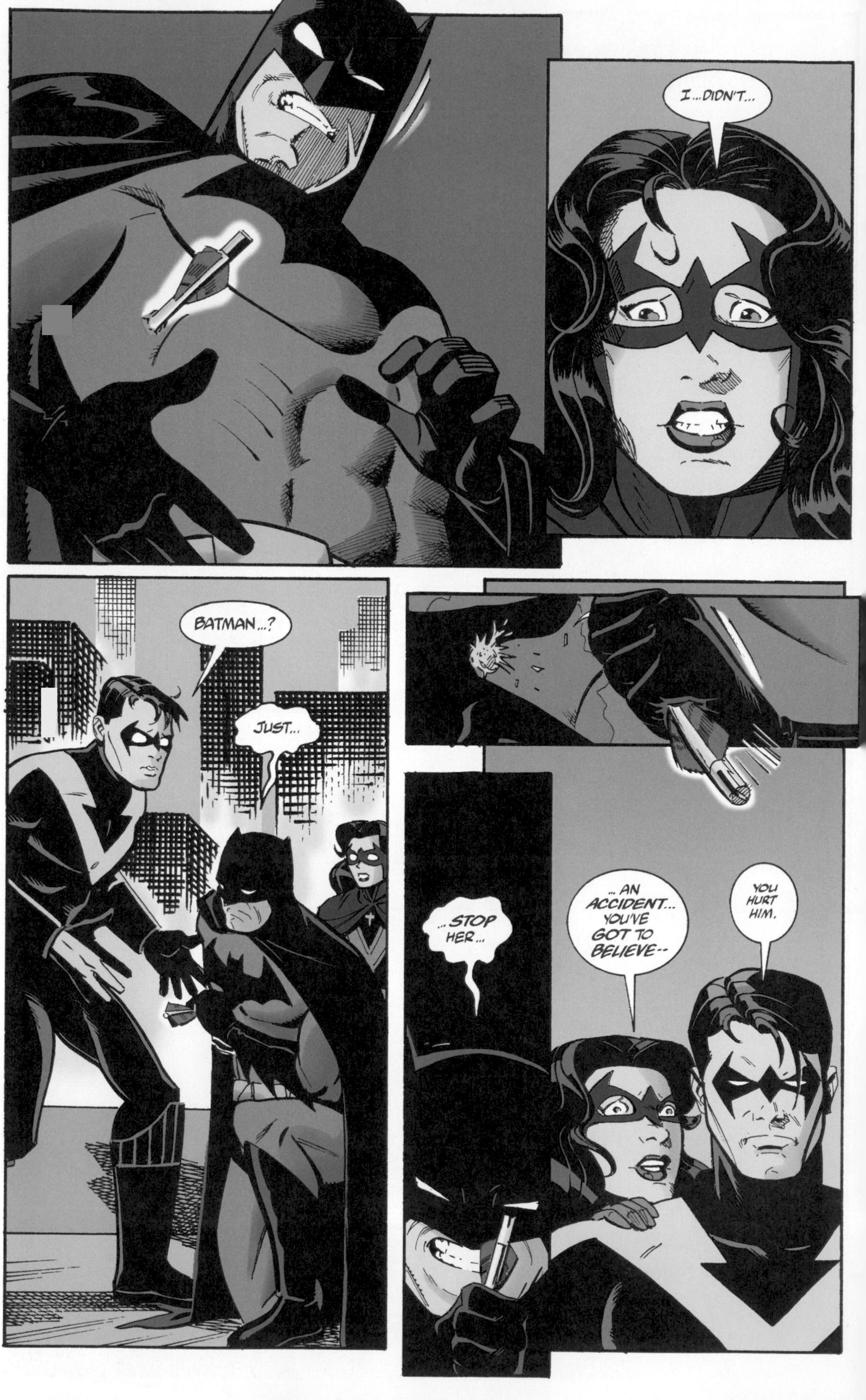
I...DIDN'T...
BATMAN...?
JUST...
...STOP HER...
... AN ACCIDENT... YOU'VE GOT TO BELIEVE--
YOU HURT HIM.

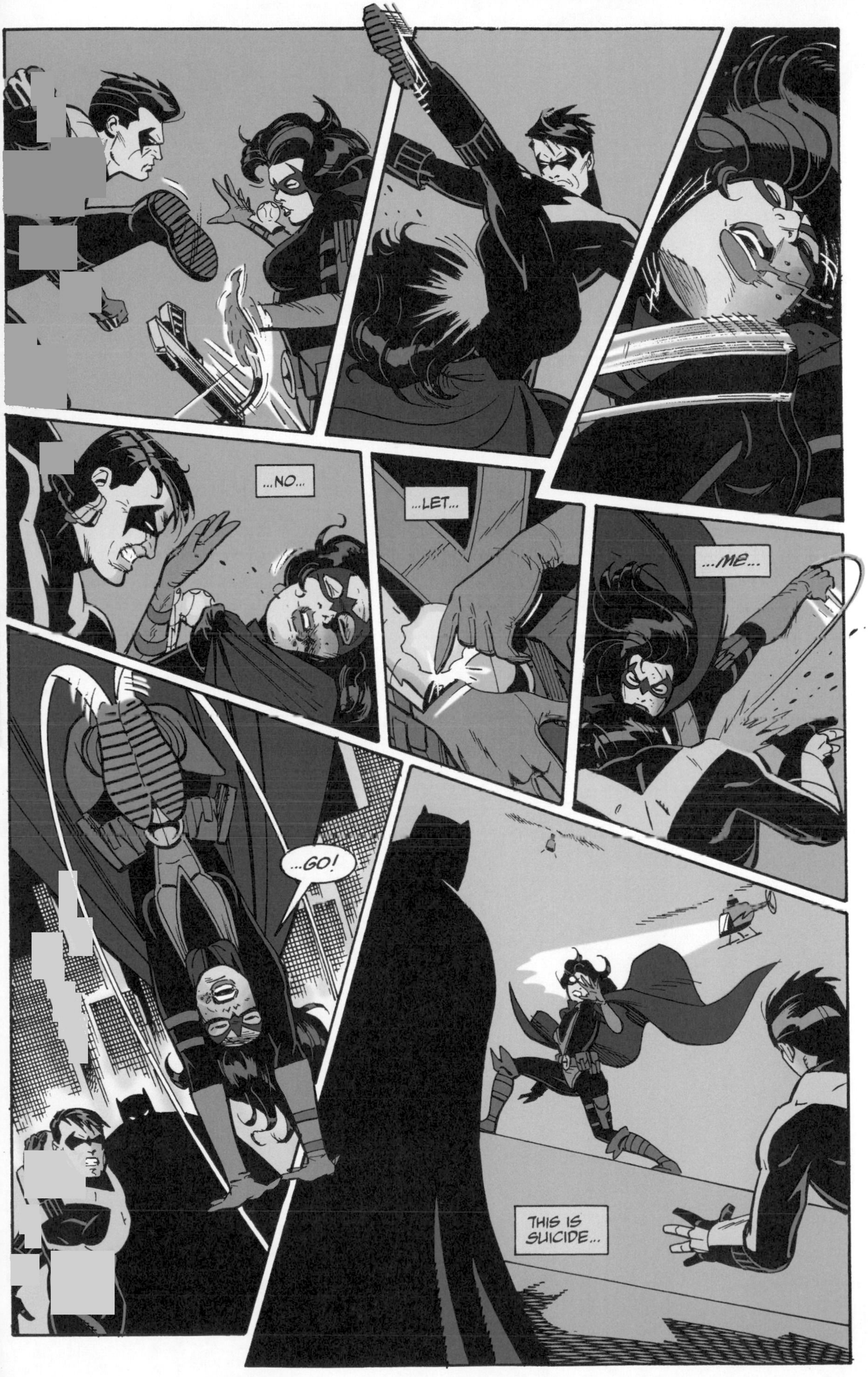
...NO...
...LET...
...ME...
...GO!
THIS IS SUICIDE...

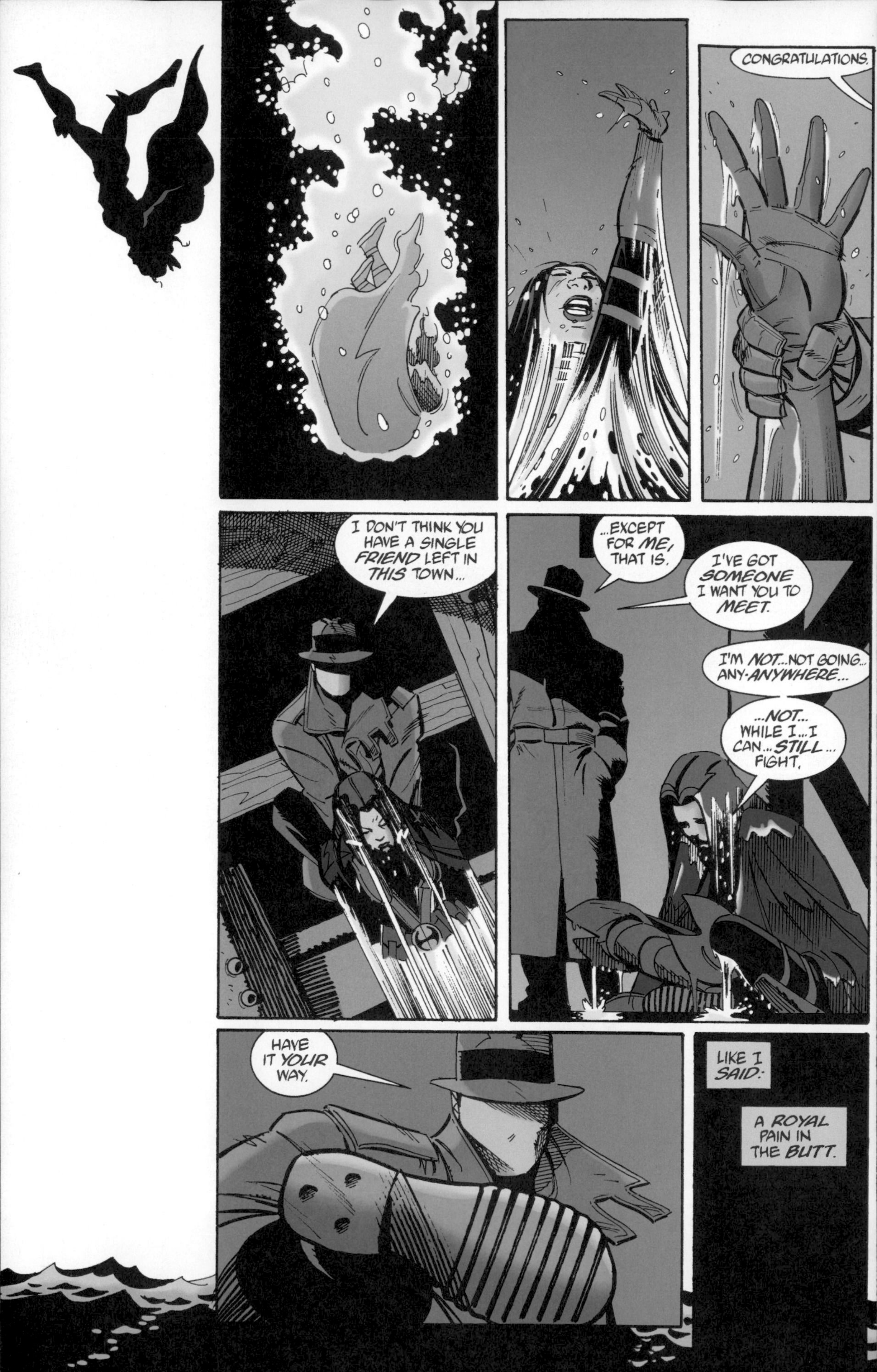
CONGRATULATIONS.
I DON'T THINK YOU HAVE A SINGLE FRIEND LEFT IN THIS TOWN...
...EXCEPT FOR ME, THAT IS.
I'VE GOT SOMEONE I WANT YOU TO MEET.
I'M NOT...NOT GOING... ANY-ANYWHERE...
...NOT... WHILE I...I CAN...STILL... FIGHT.
HAVE IT YOUR WAY.
LIKE I SAID:
A ROYAL PAIN IN THE BUTT.

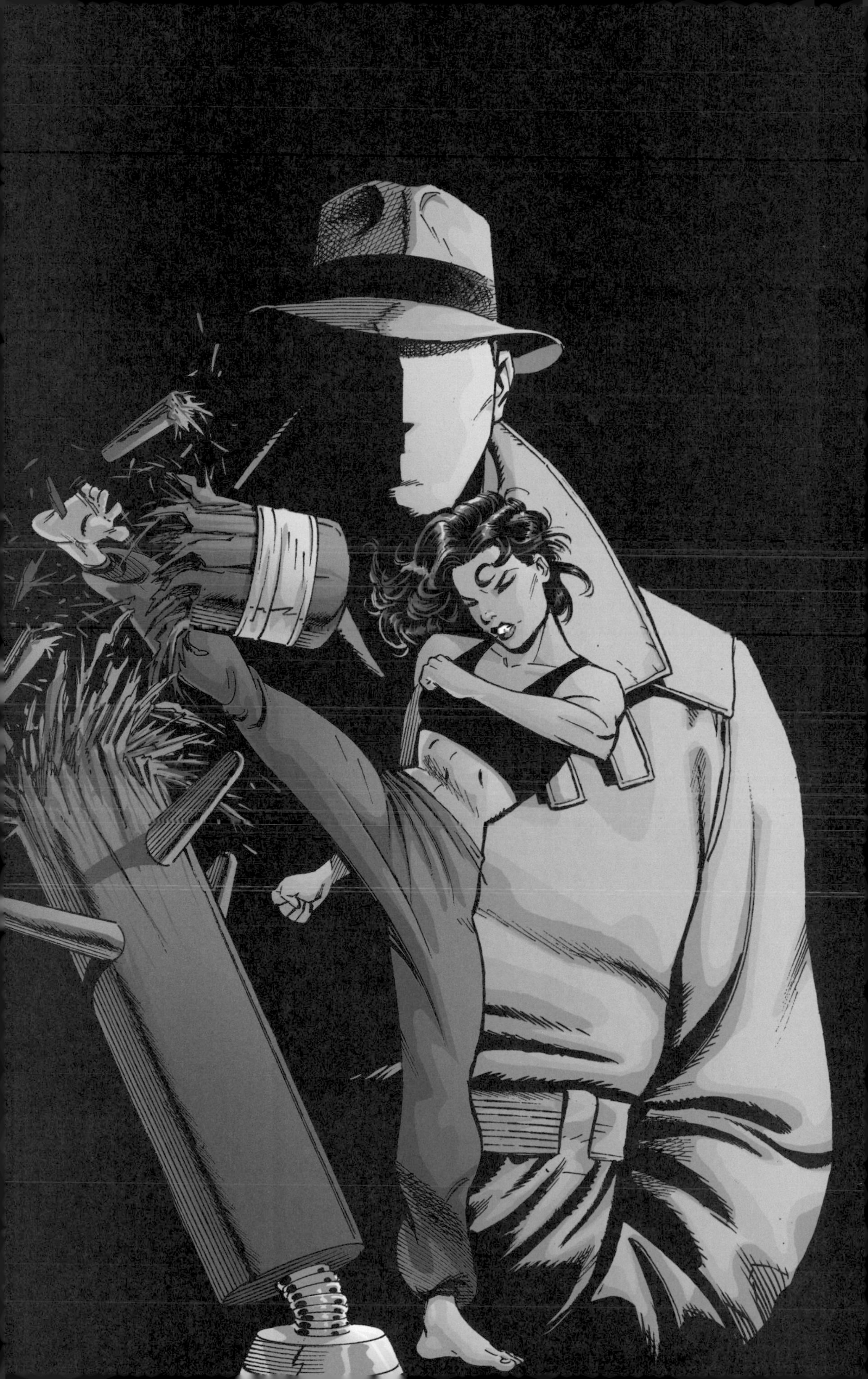

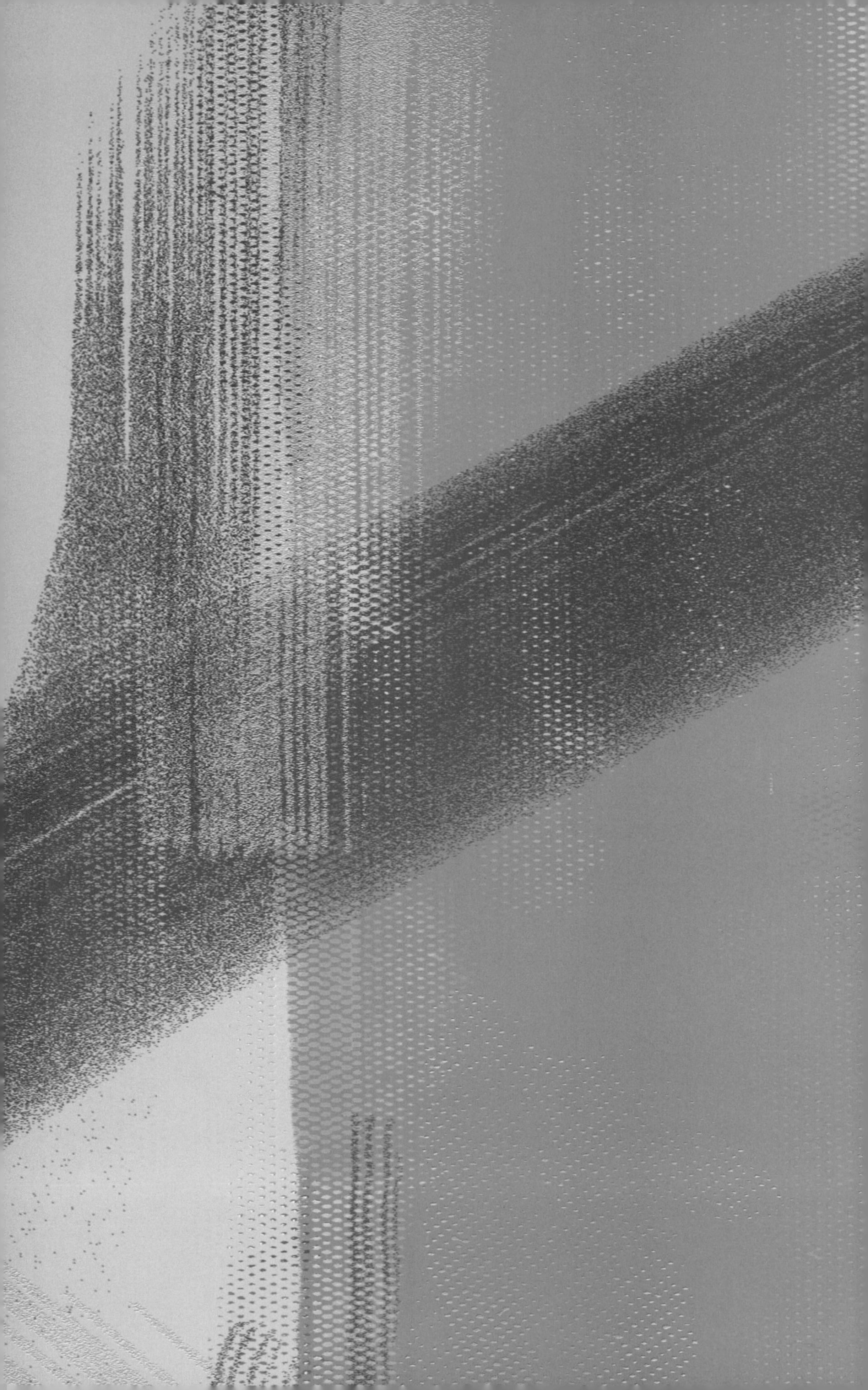

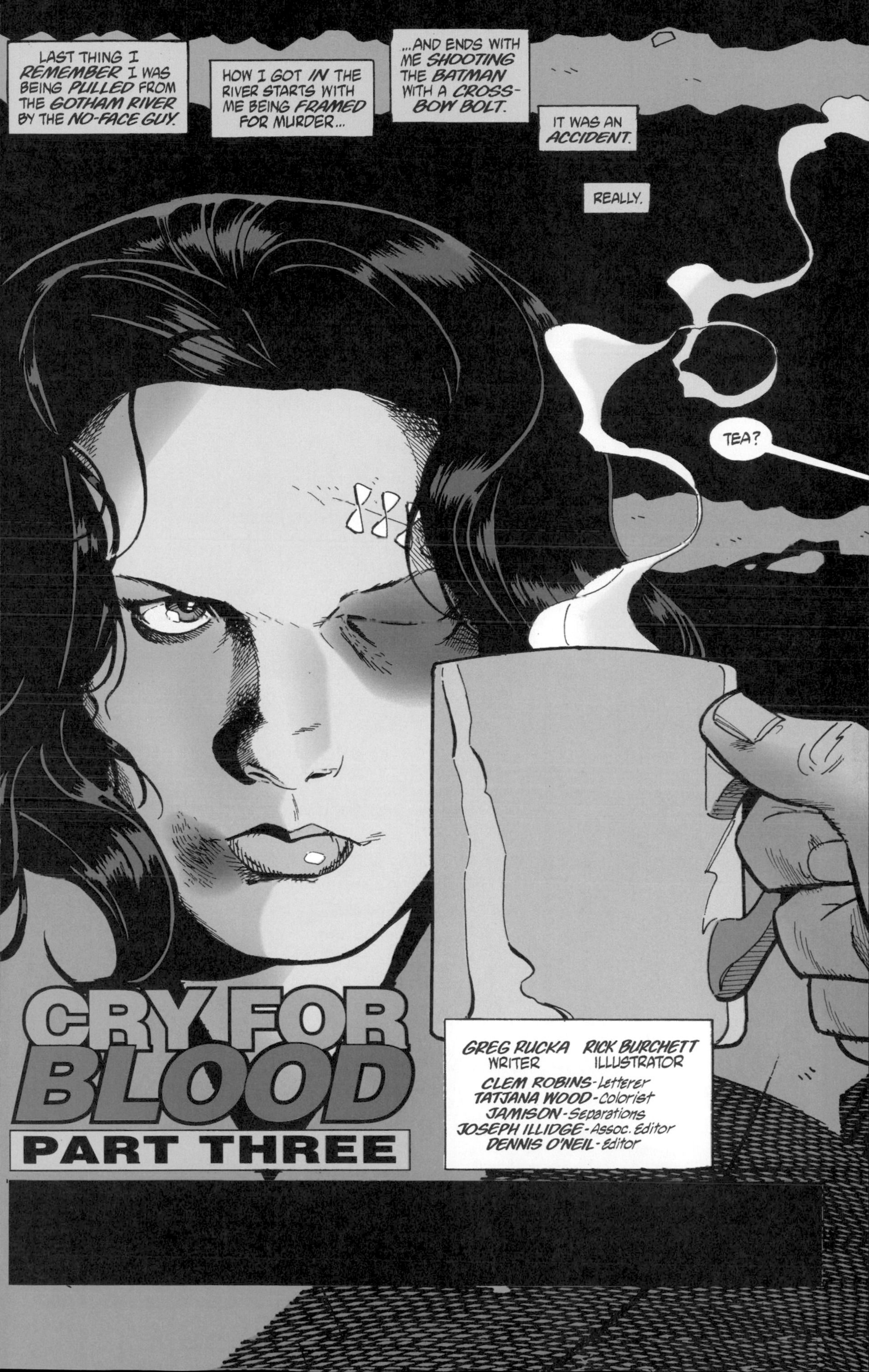
LAST THING I REMEMBER I WAS BEING PULLED FROM THE GOTHAM RIVER BY THE NO-FACE GUY.
HOW I GOT IN THE RIVER STARTS WITH ME BEING FRAMED FOR MURDER...
...AND ENDS WITH ME SHOOTING THE BATMAN WITH A CROSS-BOW BOLT.
IT WAS AN ACCIDENT.
REALLY.
TEA?
CRY FOR BLOOD
PART THREE
GREG RUCKA WRITER
RICK BURCHETT ILLUSTRATOR
CLEM ROBINS-Letterer
TATJANA WOOD-Colorist
JAMISON-Separations
JOSEPH ILLIDGE-Assoc. Editor
DENNIS O'NEIL-Editor

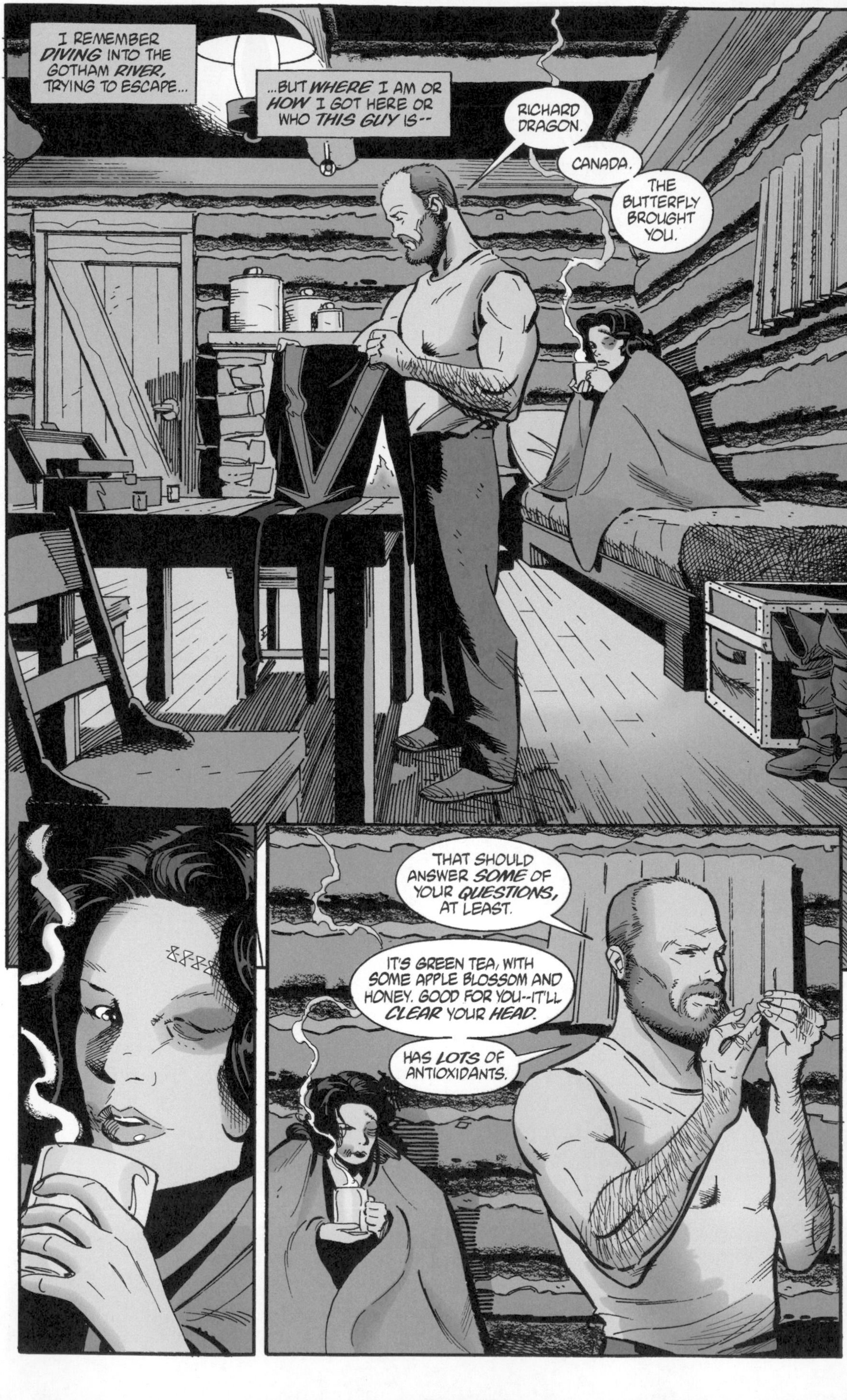
I REMEMBER DIVING INTO THE GOTHAM RIVER, TRYING TO ESCAPE...
...BUT WHERE I AM OR HOW I GOT HERE OR WHO THIS GUY IS--
RICHARD DRAGON.
CANADA.
THE BUTTERFLY BROUGHT YOU.
THAT SHOULD ANSWER SOME OF YOUR QUESTIONS, AT LEAST.
IT'S GREEN TEA, WITH SOME APPLE BLOSSOM AND HONEY. GOOD FOR YOU--IT'LL CLEAR YOUR HEAD.
HAS LOTS OF ANTIOXIDANTS.

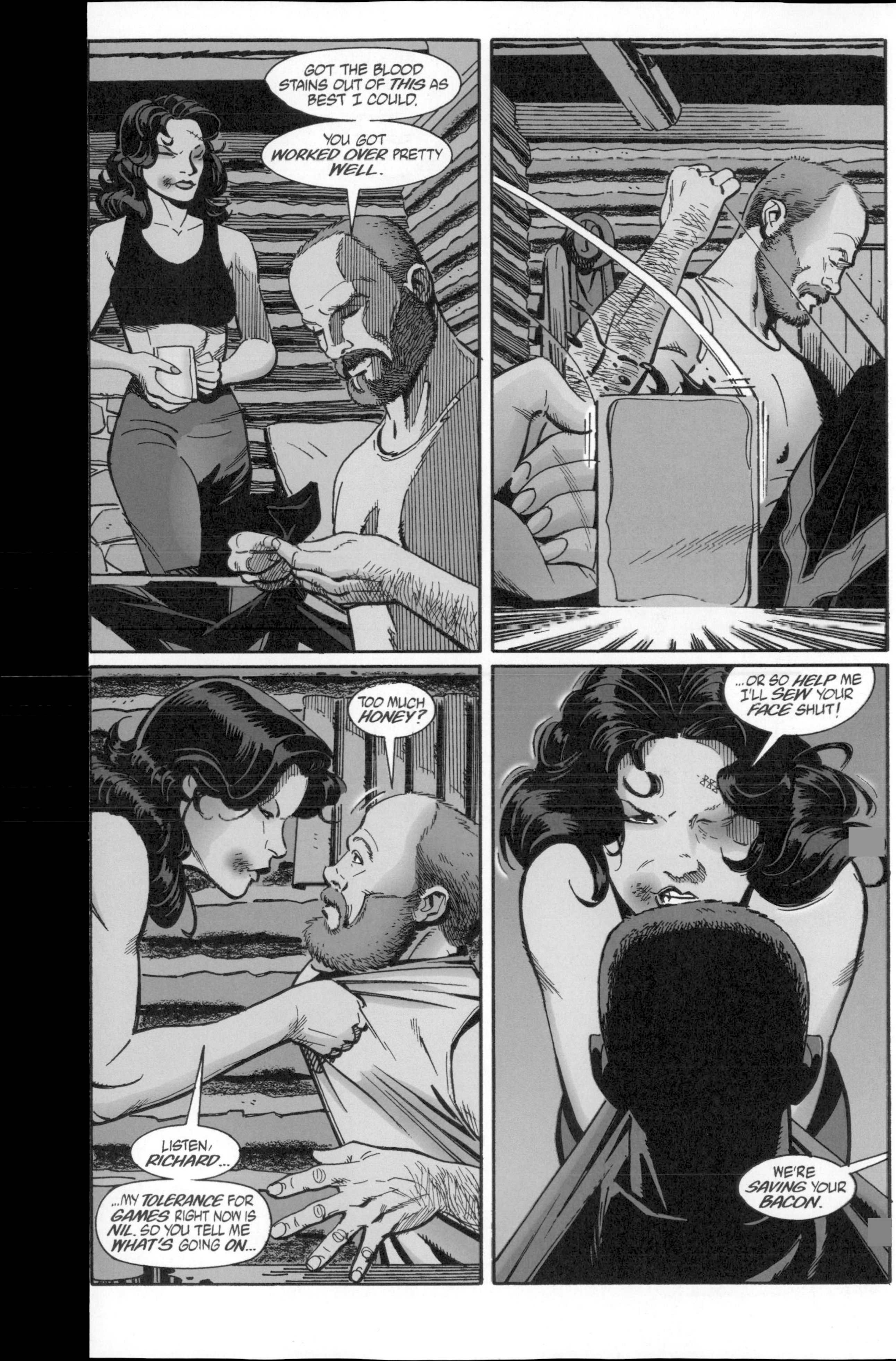
GOT THE BLOOD STAINS OUT OF THIS AS BEST I COULD.
YOU GOT WORKED OVER PRETTY WELL.
TOO MUCH HONEY?
LISTEN, RICHARD...
...MY TOLERANCE FOR GAMES RIGHT NOW IS NIL. SO YOU TELL ME WHAT'S GOING ON...
...OR SO HELP ME I'LL SEW YOUR FACE SHUT!
WE'RE SAVING YOUR BACON.

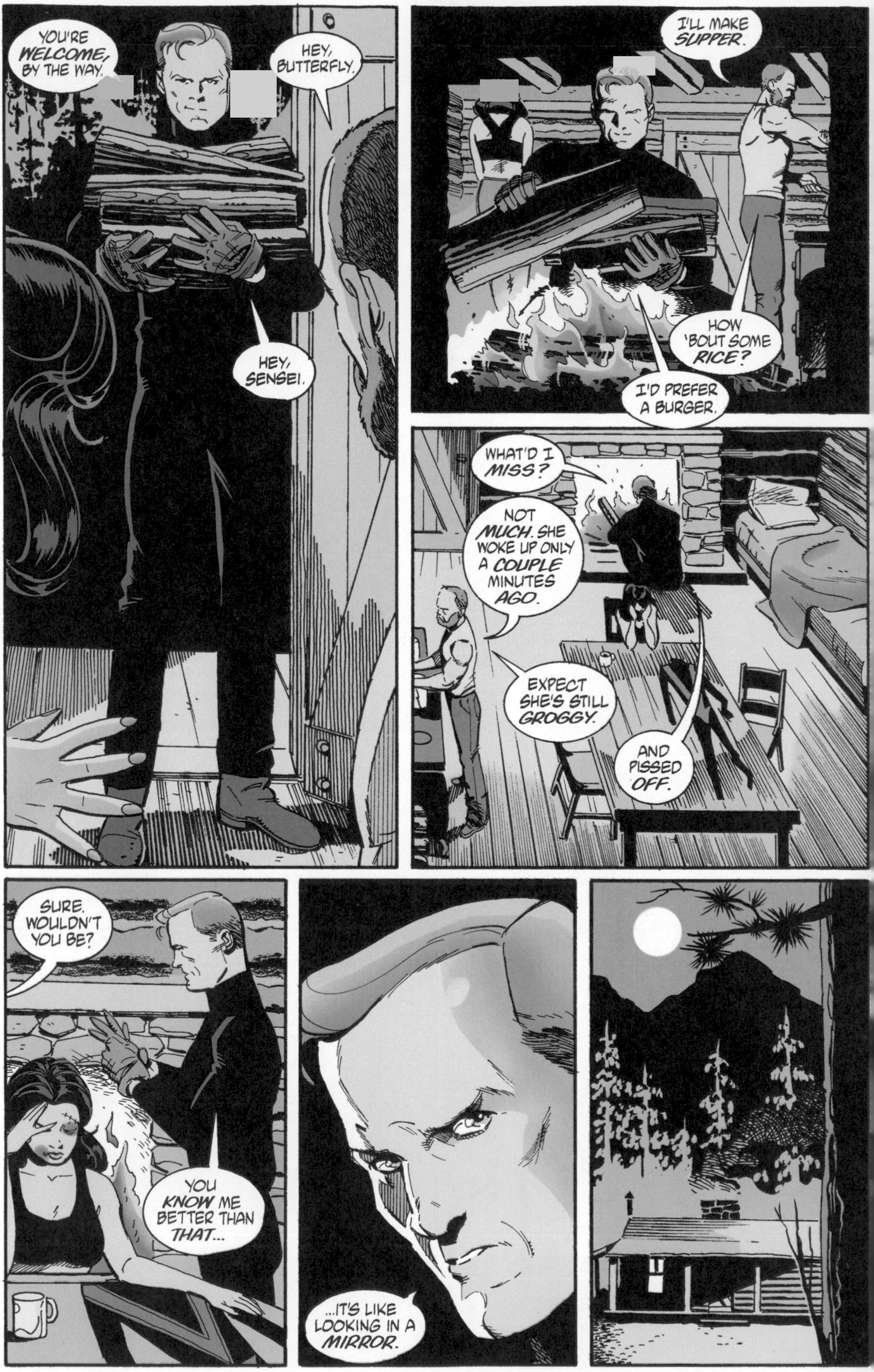
YOU'RE WELCOME, BY THE WAY.
HEY, BUTTERFLY.
HEY, SENSEI.
I'LL MAKE SUPPER.
HOW 'BOUT SOME RICE?
I'D PREFER A BURGER.
WHAT'D I MISS?
NOT MUCH. SHE WOKE UP ONLY A COUPLE MINUTES AGO.
EXPECT SHE'S STILL GROGGY.
AND PISSED OFF.
SURE. WOULDN'T YOU BE?
YOU KNOW ME BETTER THAN THAT...
...IT'S LIKE LOOKING IN A MIRROR.

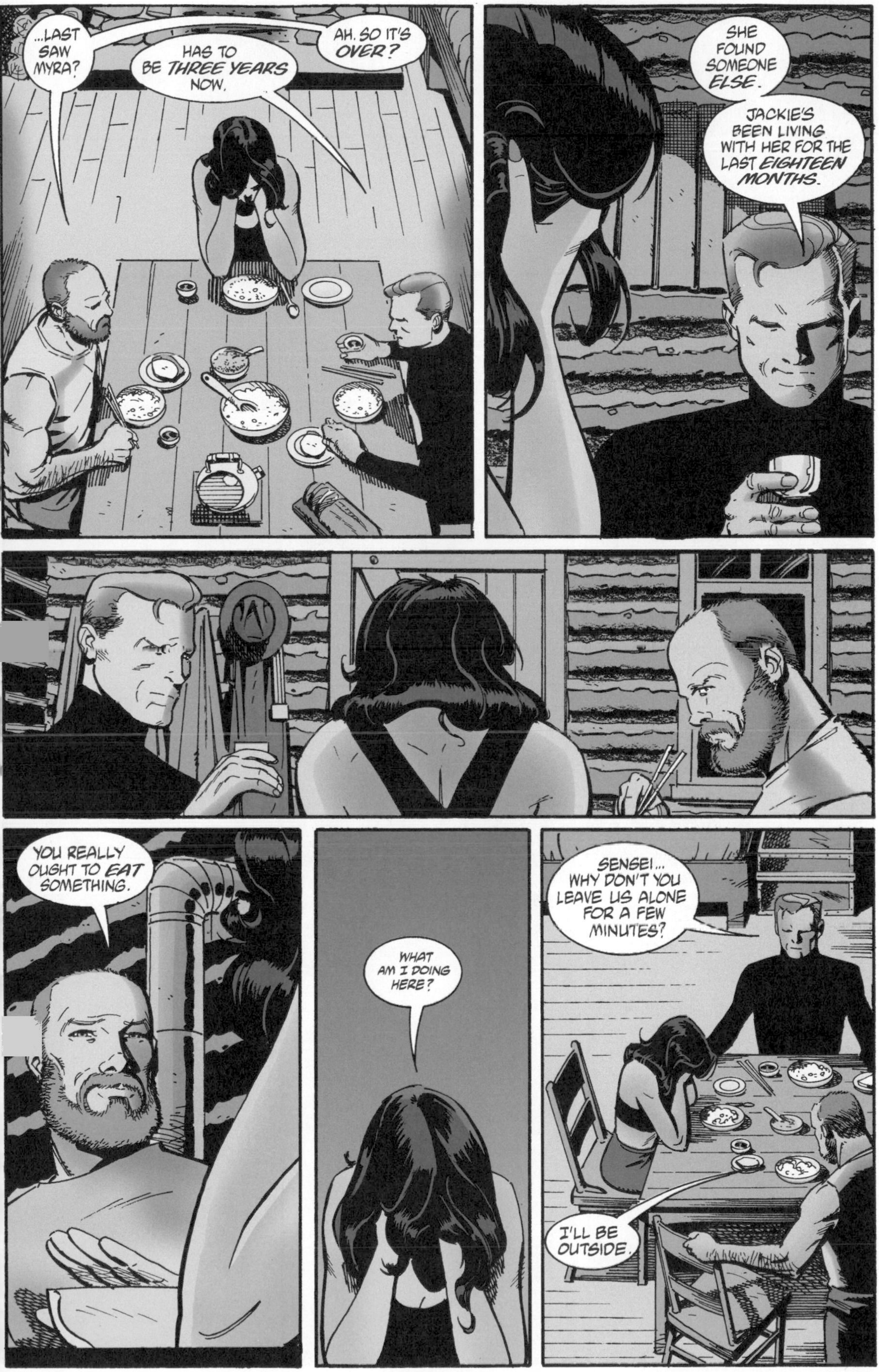
...LAST SAW MYRA?
HAS TO BE THREE YEARS NOW.
AH. SO IT'S OVER?
SHE FOUND SOMEONE ELSE.
JACKIE'S BEEN LIVING WITH HER FOR THE LAST EIGHTEEN MONTHS.
YOU REALLY OUGHT TO EAT SOMETHING.
WHAT AM I DOING HERE?
SENSEI... WHY DON'T YOU LEAVE US ALONE FOR A FEW MINUTES?
I'LL BE OUTSIDE.

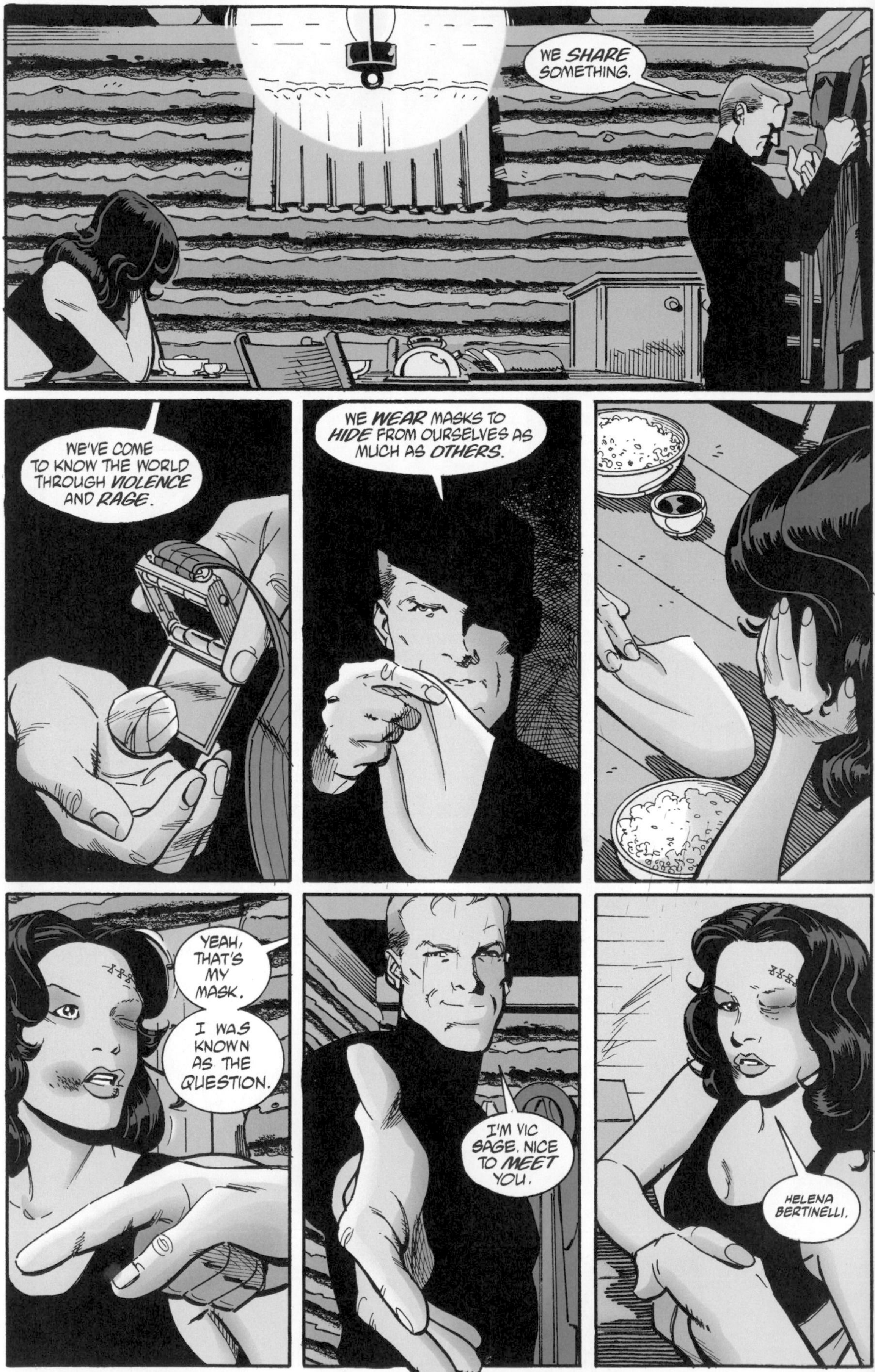
WE SHARE SOMETHING.
WE'VE COME TO KNOW THE WORLD THROUGH VIOLENCE AND RAGE.
WE WEAR MASKS TO HIDE FROM OURSELVES AS MUCH AS OTHERS.
YEAH, THAT'S MY MASK.
I WAS KNOWN AS THE QUESTION.
I'M VIC SAGE. NICE TO MEET YOU.
HELENA BERTINELLI.

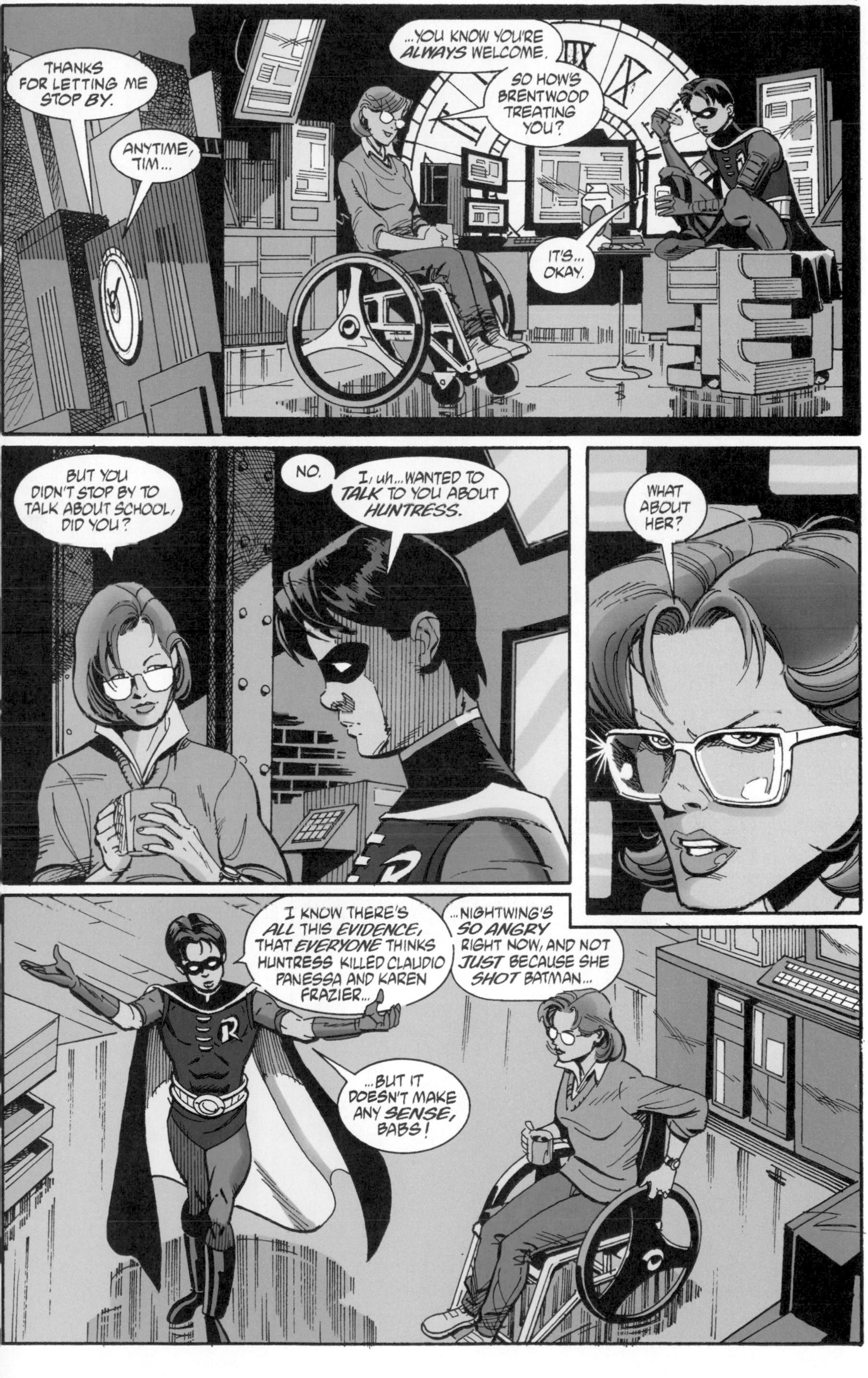
THANKS FOR LETTING ME STOP BY.
ANYTIME, TIM...
...YOU KNOW YOU'RE ALWAYS WELCOME.
SO HOW'S BRENTWOOD TREATING YOU?
IT'S... OKAY.
BUT YOU DIDN'T STOP BY TO TALK ABOUT SCHOOL, DID YOU?
NO.
I, uh...WANTED TO TALK TO YOU ABOUT HUNTRESS.
WHAT ABOUT HER?
I KNOW THERE'S ALL THIS EVIDENCE, THAT EVERYONE THINKS HUNTRESS KILLED CLAUDIO PANESSA AND KAREN FRAZIER...
...NIGHTWING'S SO ANGRY RIGHT NOW, AND NOT JUST BECAUSE SHE SHOT BATMAN...
...BUT IT DOESN'T MAKE ANY SENSE, BABS!

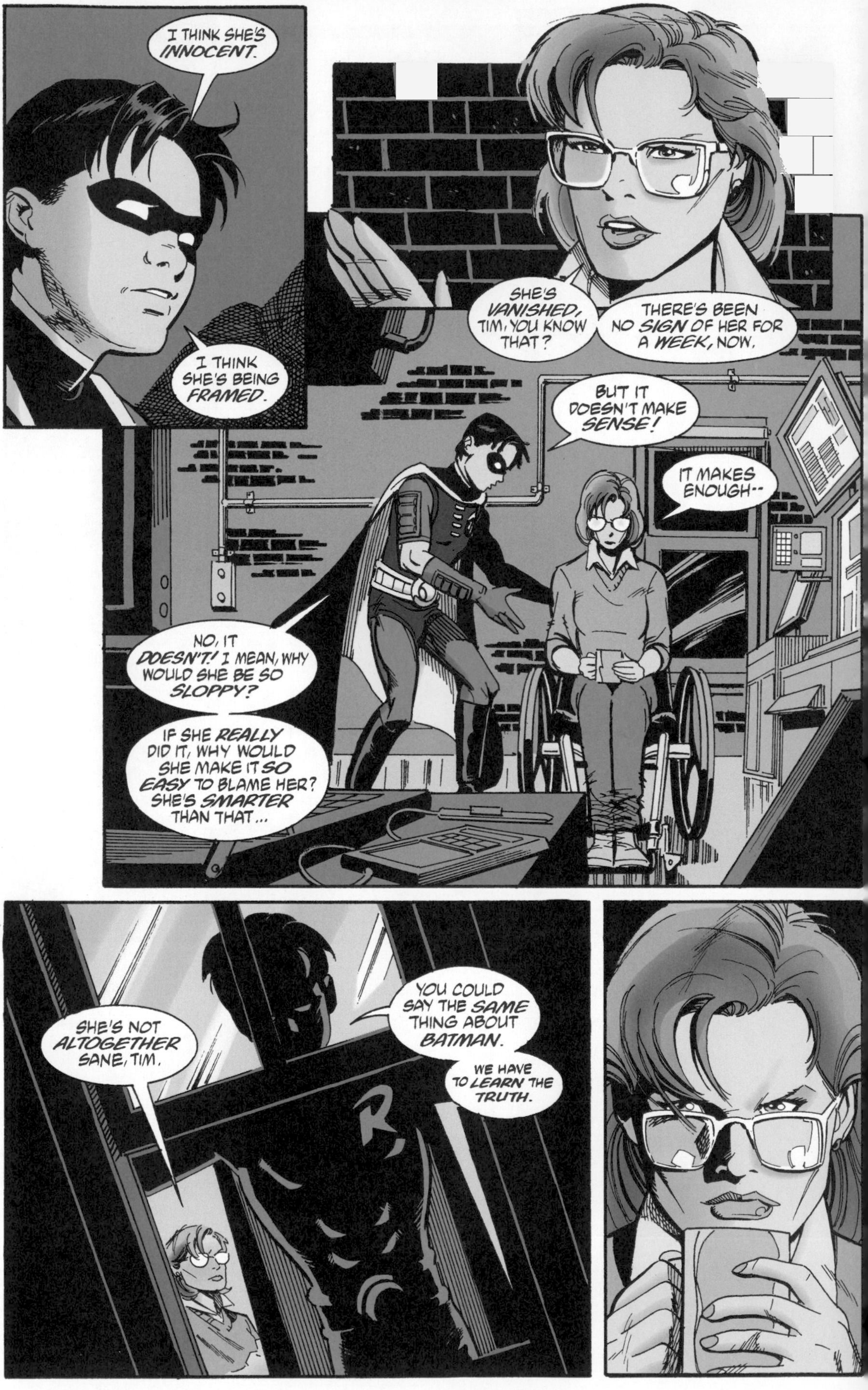
I THINK SHE'S INNOCENT.
I THINK SHE'S BEING FRAMED.
SHE'S VANISHED, TIM, YOU KNOW THAT?
THERE'S BEEN NO SIGN OF HER FOR A WEEK, NOW.
BUT IT DOESN'T MAKE SENSE!
IT MAKES ENOUGH--
NO, IT DOESN'T! I MEAN, WHY WOULD SHE BE SO SLOPPY?
IF SHE REALLY DID IT, WHY WOULD SHE MAKE IT SO EASY TO BLAME HER? SHE'S SMARTER THAN THAT...
SHE'S NOT ALTOGETHER SANE, TIM.
YOU COULD SAY THE SAME THING ABOUT BATMAN.
WE HAVE TO LEARN THE TRUTH.

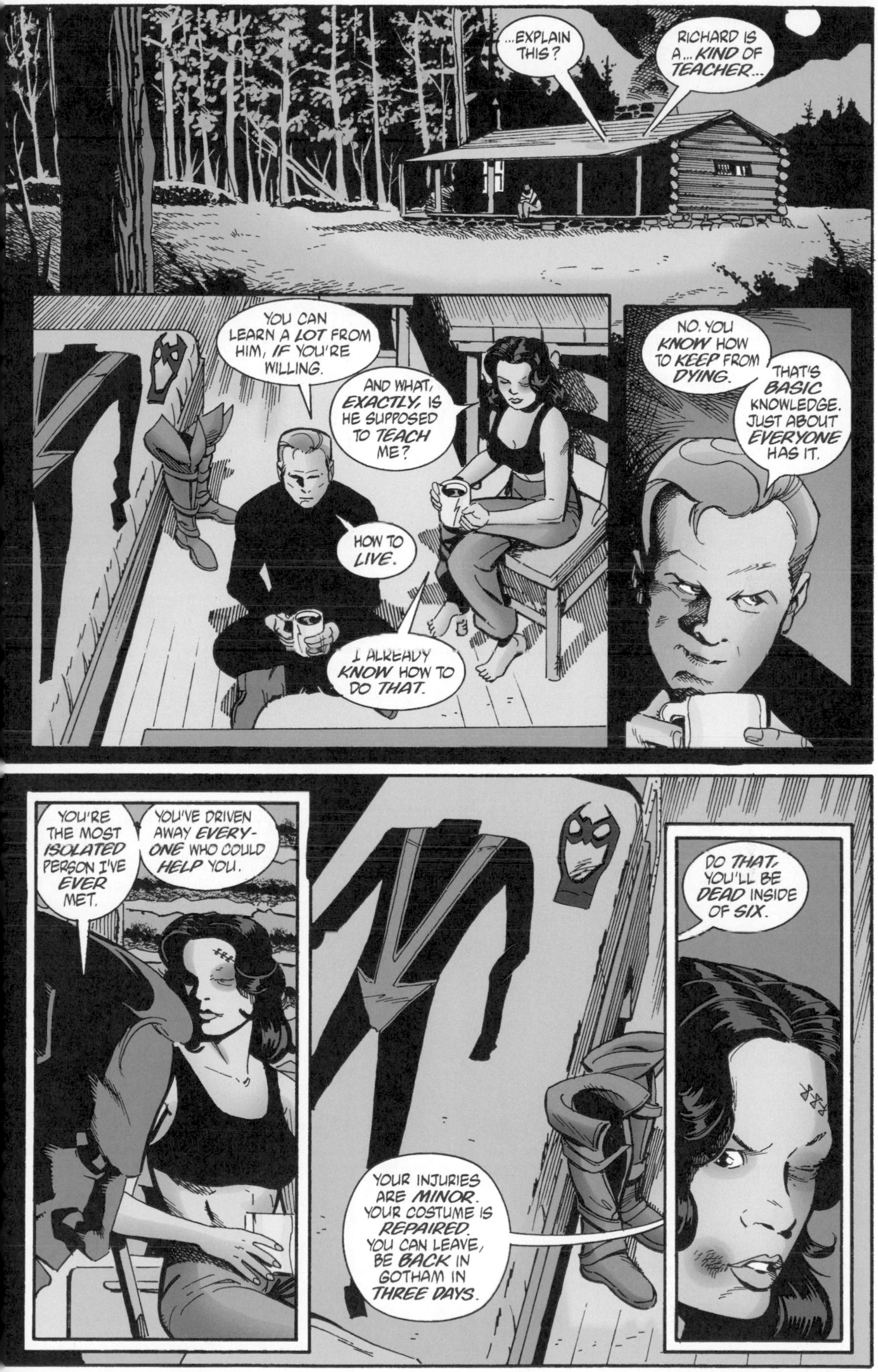
...EXPLAIN THIS?
RICHARD IS A... KIND OF TEACHER...
YOU CAN LEARN A LOT FROM HIM, IF YOU'RE WILLING.
AND WHAT, EXACTLY, IS HE SUPPOSED TO TEACH ME?
HOW TO LIVE.
I ALREADY KNOW HOW TO DO THAT.
NO. YOU KNOW HOW TO KEEP FROM DYING.
THAT'S BASIC KNOWLEDGE. JUST ABOUT EVERYONE HAS IT.
YOU'RE THE MOST ISOLATED PERSON I'VE EVER MET.
YOU'VE DRIVEN AWAY EVERY-ONE WHO COULD HELP YOU.
YOUR INJURIES ARE MINOR. YOUR COSTUME IS REPAIRED. YOU CAN LEAVE, BE BACK IN GOTHAM IN THREE DAYS.
DO THAT, YOU'LL BE DEAD INSIDE OF SIX.

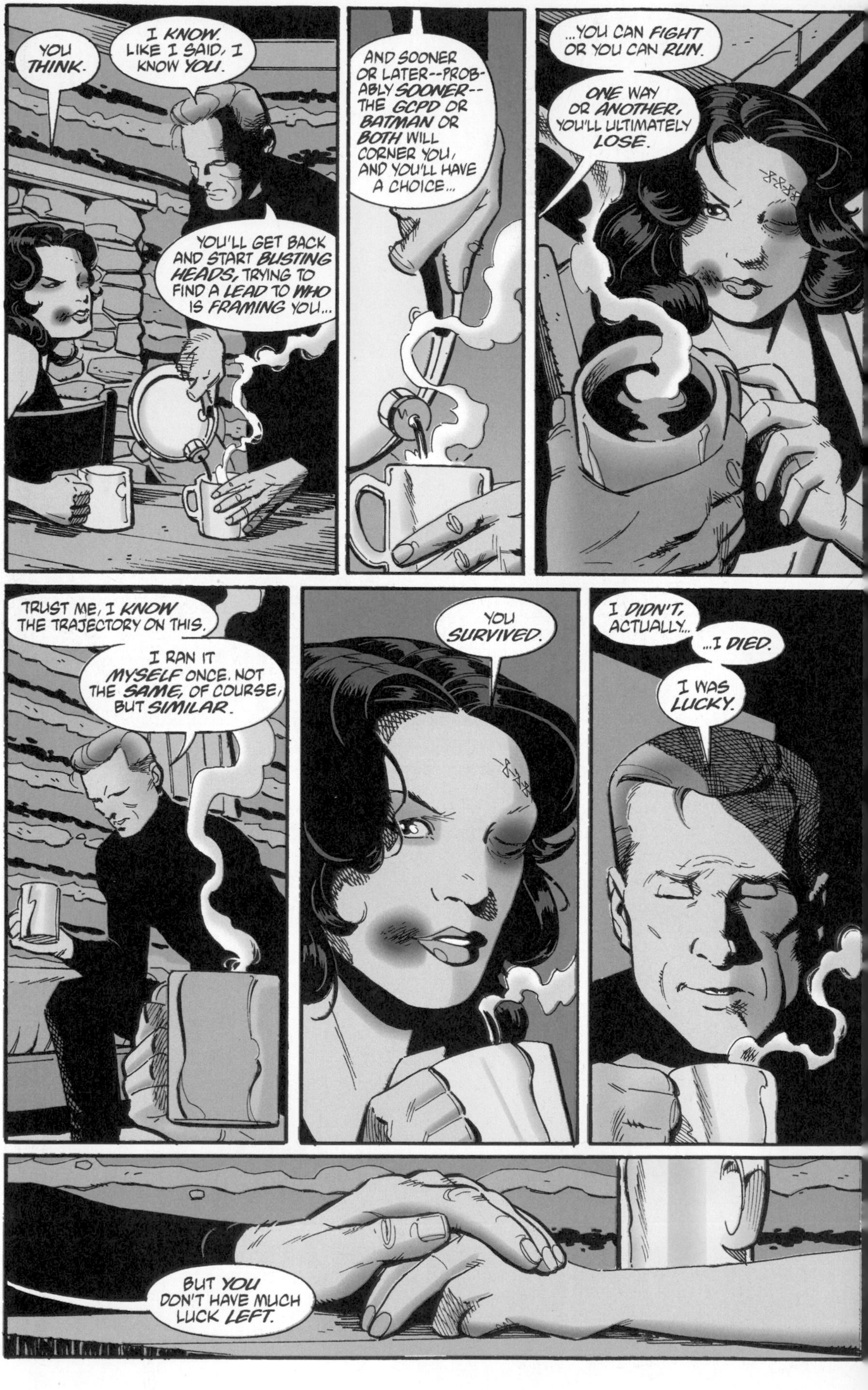
YOU THINK.
I KNOW. LIKE I SAID, I KNOW YOU.
YOU'LL GET BACK AND START BUSTING HEADS, TRYING TO FIND A LEAD TO WHO IS FRAMING YOU...
AND SOONER OR LATER--PROBABLY SOONER-- THE GCPD OR BATMAN OR BOTH WILL CORNER YOU, AND YOU'LL HAVE A CHOICE...
...YOU CAN FIGHT OR YOU CAN RUN.
ONE WAY OR ANOTHER, YOU'LL ULTIMATELY LOSE.
TRUST ME, I KNOW THE TRAJECTORY ON THIS.
I RAN IT MYSELF ONCE. NOT THE SAME, OF COURSE, BUT SIMILAR.
YOU SURVIVED.
I DIDN'T, ACTUALLY...
...I DIED.
I WAS LUCKY.
BUT YOU DON'T HAVE MUCH LUCK LEFT.

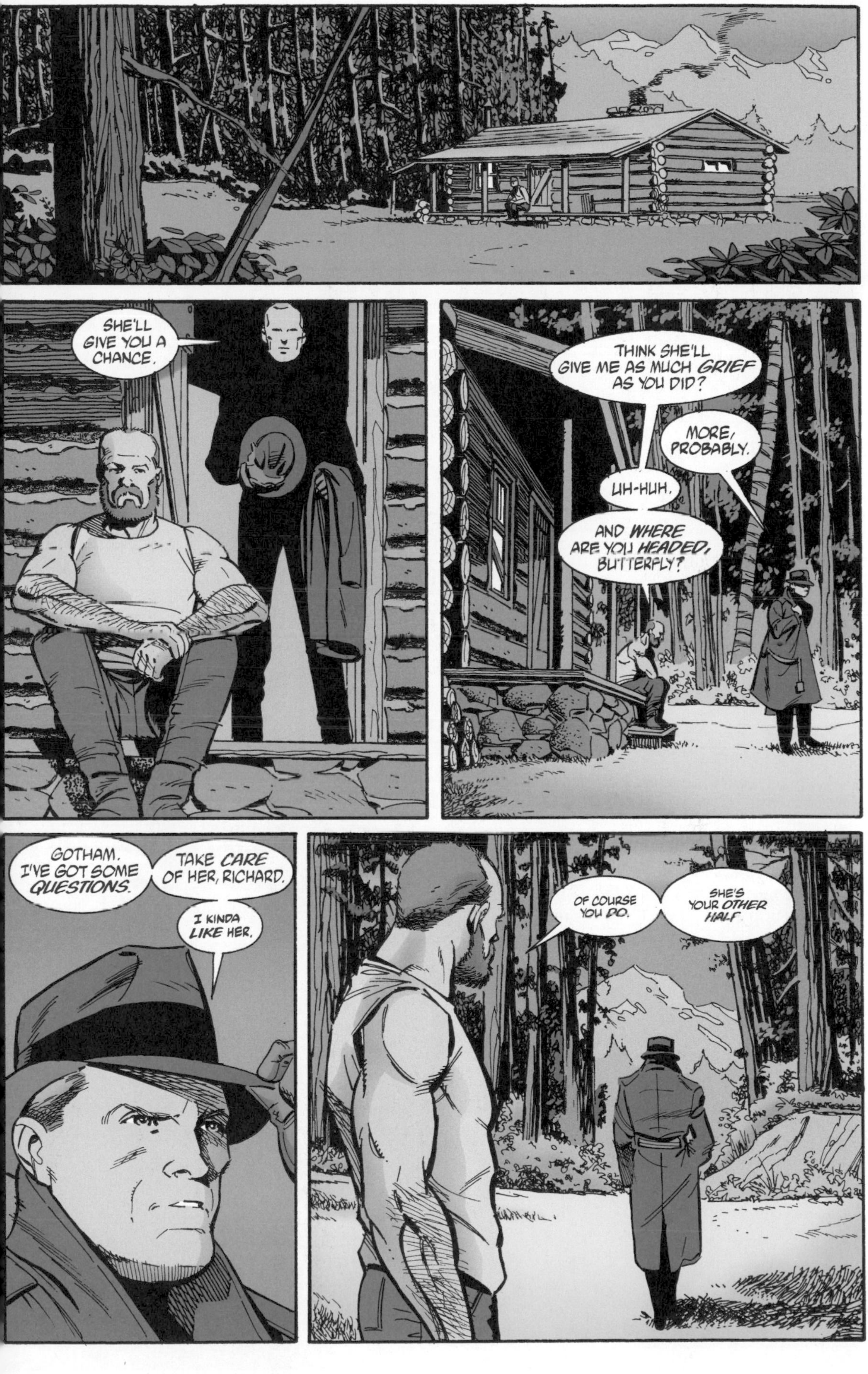
SHE'LL GIVE YOU A CHANCE.
THINK SHE'LL GIVE ME AS MUCH GRIEF AS YOU DID?
MORE, PROBABLY.
UH-HUH.
AND WHERE ARE YOU HEADED, BUTTERFLY?
GOTHAM. I'VE GOT SOME QUESTIONS.
TAKE CARE OF HER, RICHARD.
I KINDA LIKE HER.
OF COURSE YOU DO.
SHE'S YOUR OTHER HALF.

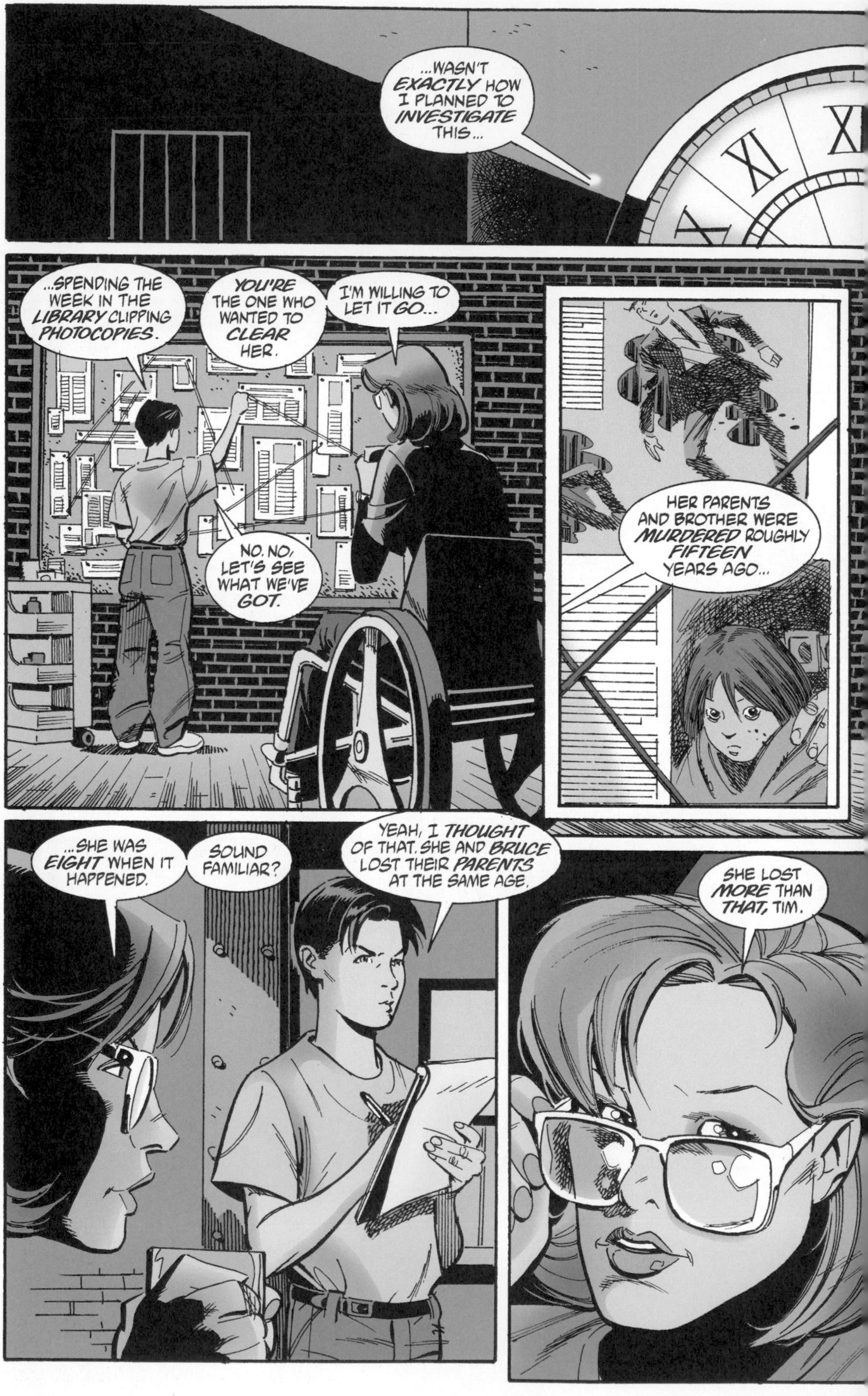
...WASN'T EXACTLY HOW I PLANNED TO INVESTIGATE THIS...
...SPENDING THE WEEK IN THE LIBRARY CLIPPING PHOTOCOPIES.
YOU'RE THE ONE WHO WANTED TO CLEAR HER.
I'M WILLING TO LET IT GO...
NO. NO, LET'S SEE WHAT WE'VE GOT.
HER PARENTS AND BROTHER WERE MURDERED ROUGHLY FIFTEEN YEARS AGO...
...SHE WAS EIGHT WHEN IT HAPPENED.
SOUND FAMILIAR?
YEAH, I THOUGHT OF THAT. SHE AND BRUCE LOST THEIR PARENTS AT THE SAME AGE.
SHE LOST MORE THAN THAT, TIM.

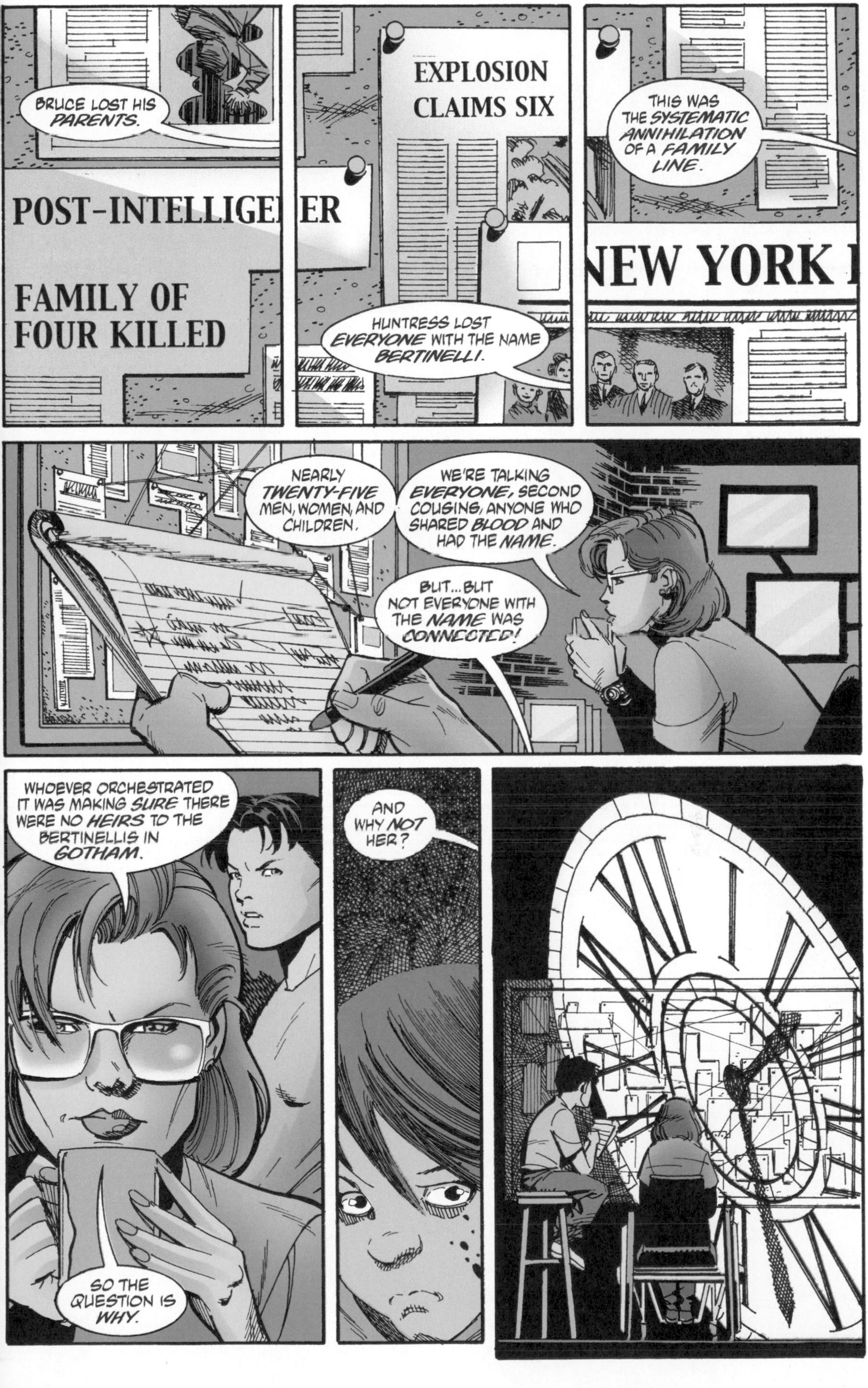

BRUCE LOST HIS PARENTS.
POST-INTELLIGE ER
FAMILY OF FOUR KILLED
EXPLOSION CLAIMS SIX
HUNTRESS LOST EVERYONE WITH THE NAME BERTINELLI.
THIS WAS THE SYSTEMATIC ANNIHILATION OF A FAMILY LINE.
NEW YORK
NEARLY TWENTY-FIVE MEN, WOMEN, AND CHILDREN.
WE'RE TALKING EVERYONE, SECOND COUSINS, ANYONE WHO SHARED BLOOD AND HAD THE NAME.
BUT...BUT NOT EVERYONE WITH THE NAME WAS CONNECTED!
WHOEVER ORCHESTRATED IT WAS MAKING SURE THERE WERE NO HEIRS TO THE BERTINELLIS IN GOTHAM.
SO THE QUESTION IS WHY.
AND WHY NOT HER?

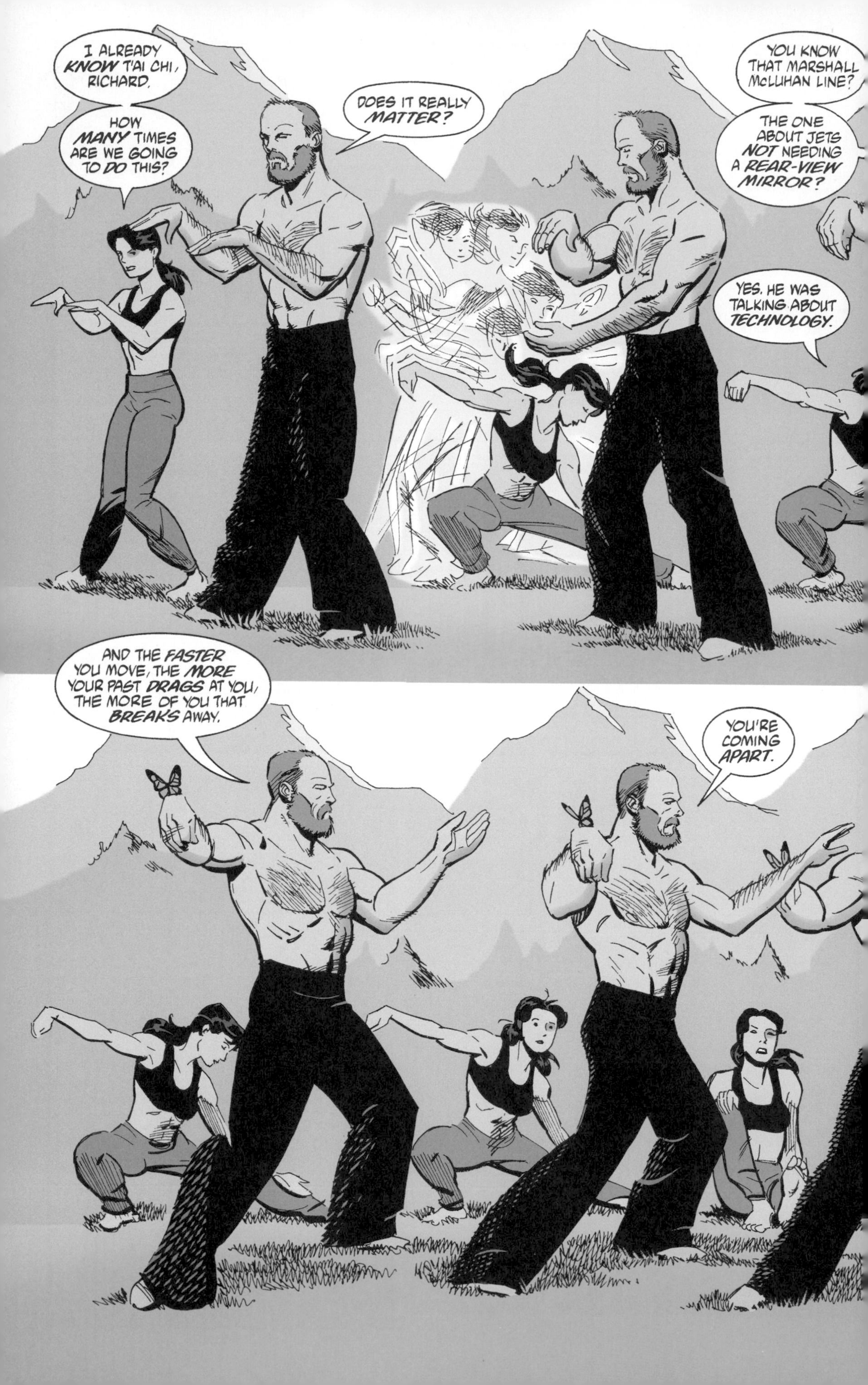
I ALREADY KNOW T'AI CHI, RICHARD.
HOW MANY TIMES ARE WE GOING TO DO THIS?
DOES IT REALLY MATTER?
YOU KNOW THAT MARSHALL McLUHAN LINE?
THE ONE ABOUT JETS NOT NEEDING A REAR-VIEW MIRROR?
YES. HE WAS TALKING ABOUT TECHNOLOGY.
AND THE FASTER YOU MOVE, THE MORE YOUR PAST DRAGS AT YOU, THE MORE OF YOU THAT BREAKS AWAY.
YOU'RE COMING APART.

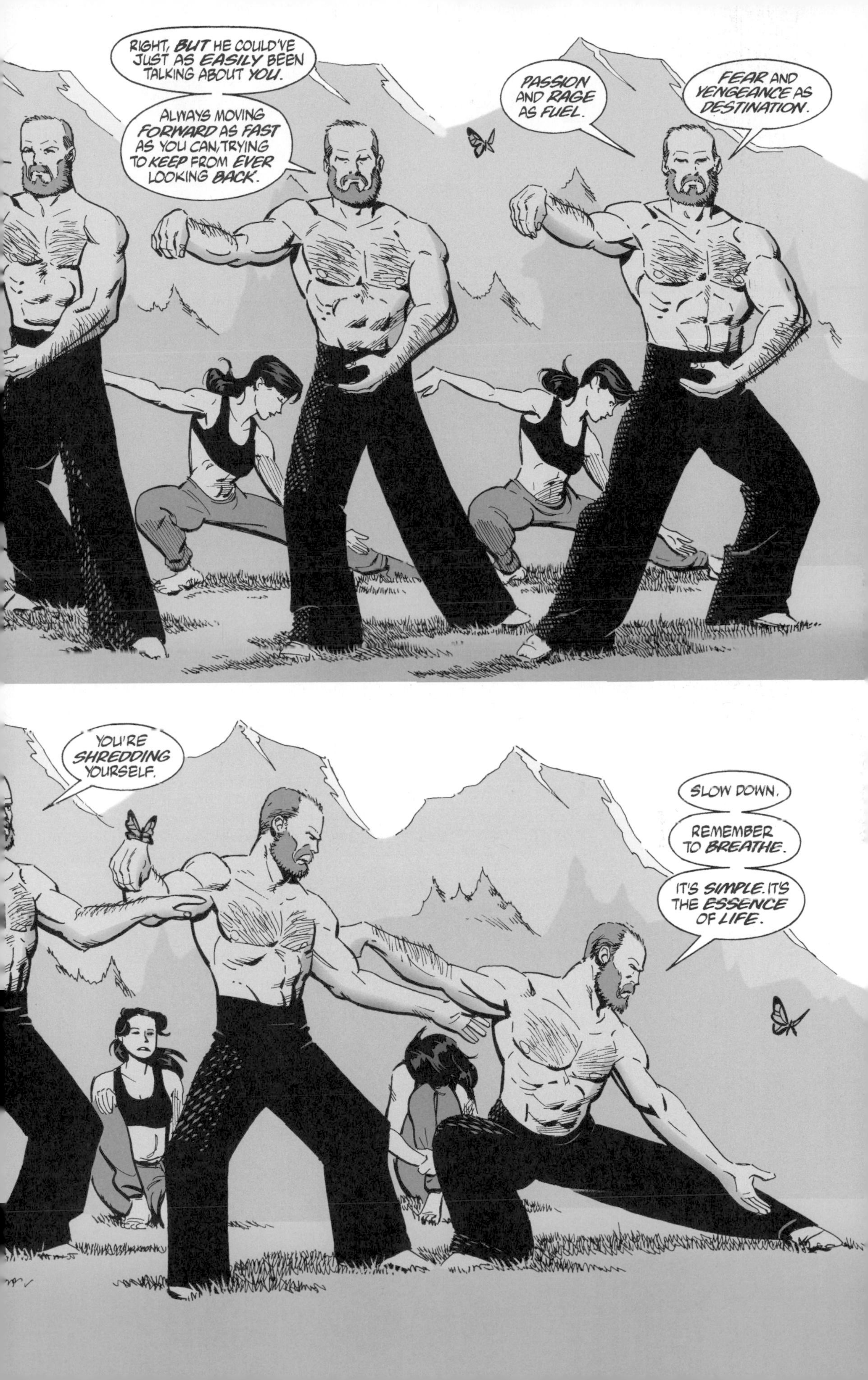
RIGHT, BUT HE COULD'VE JUST AS EASILY BEEN TALKING ABOUT YOU.
ALWAYS MOVING FORWARD AS FAST AS YOU CAN, TRYING TO KEEP FROM EVER LOOKING BACK.
PASSION AND RAGE AS FUEL.
FEAR AND VENGEANCE AS DESTINATION.
YOU'RE SHREDDING YOURSELF.
SLOW DOWN.
REMEMBER TO BREATHE.
IT'S SIMPLE. IT'S THE ESSENCE OF LIFE.

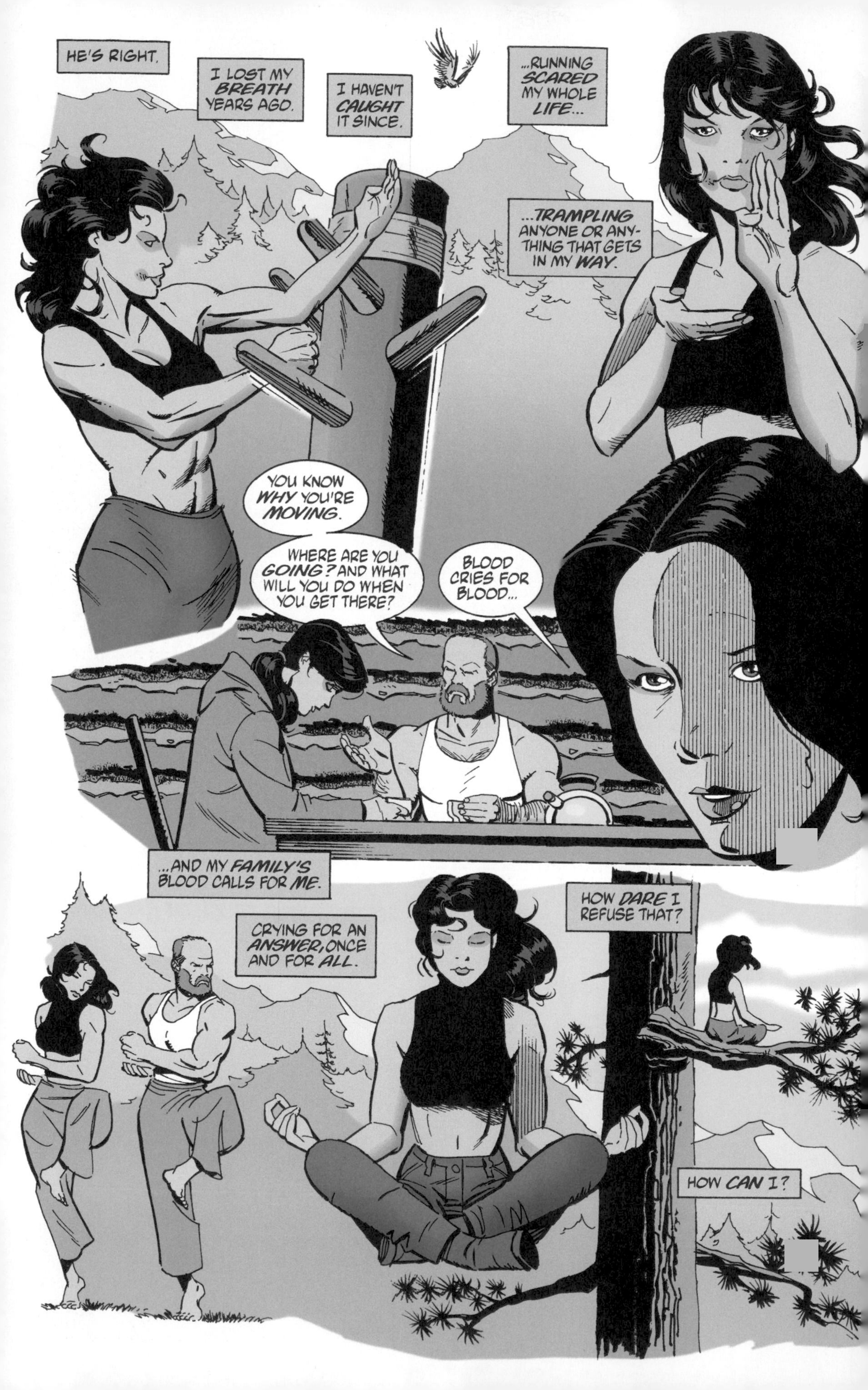
HE'S RIGHT.
I LOST MY BREATH YEARS AGO.
I HAVEN'T CAUGHT IT SINCE.
...RUNNING SCARED MY WHOLE LIFE...
...TRAMPLING ANYONE OR ANYTHING THAT GETS IN MY WAY.
YOU KNOW WHY YOU'RE MOVING.
WHERE ARE YOU GOING? AND WHAT WILL YOU DO WHEN YOU GET THERE?
BLOOD CRIES FOR BLOOD...
...AND MY FAMILY'S BLOOD CALLS FOR ME.
CRYING FOR AN ANSWER, ONCE AND FOR ALL.
HOW DARE I REFUSE THAT?
HOW CAN I?

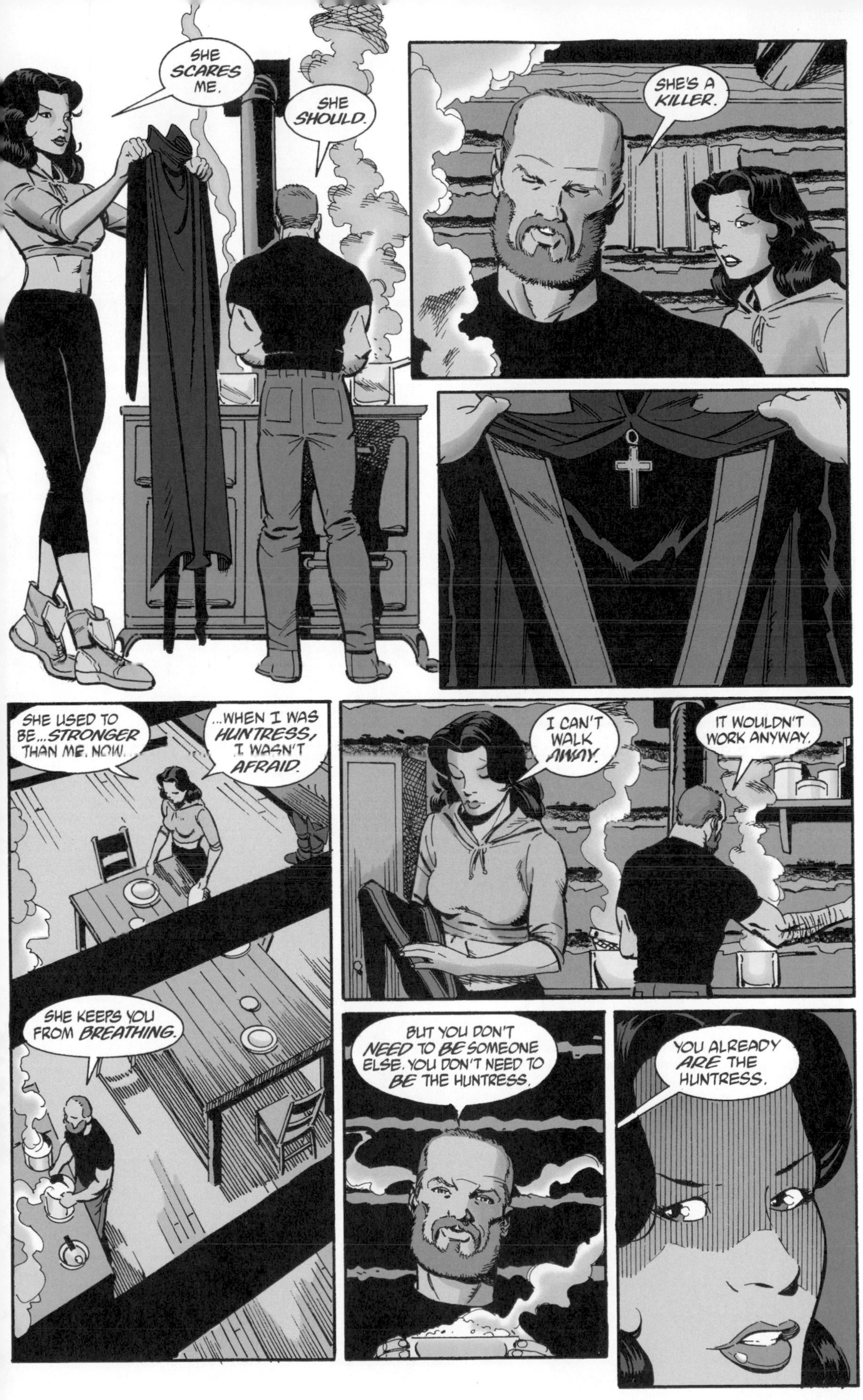
SHE SCARES ME.
SHE SHOULD.
SHE'S A KILLER.
SHE USED TO BE...STRONGER THAN ME. NOW...
...WHEN I WAS HUNTRESS, I WASN'T AFRAID.
I CAN'T WALK AWAY.
IT WOULDN'T WORK ANYWAY.
SHE KEEPS YOU FROM BREATHING.
BUT YOU DON'T NEED TO BE SOMEONE ELSE. YOU DON'T NEED TO BE THE HUNTRESS.
YOU ALREADY ARE THE HUNTRESS.

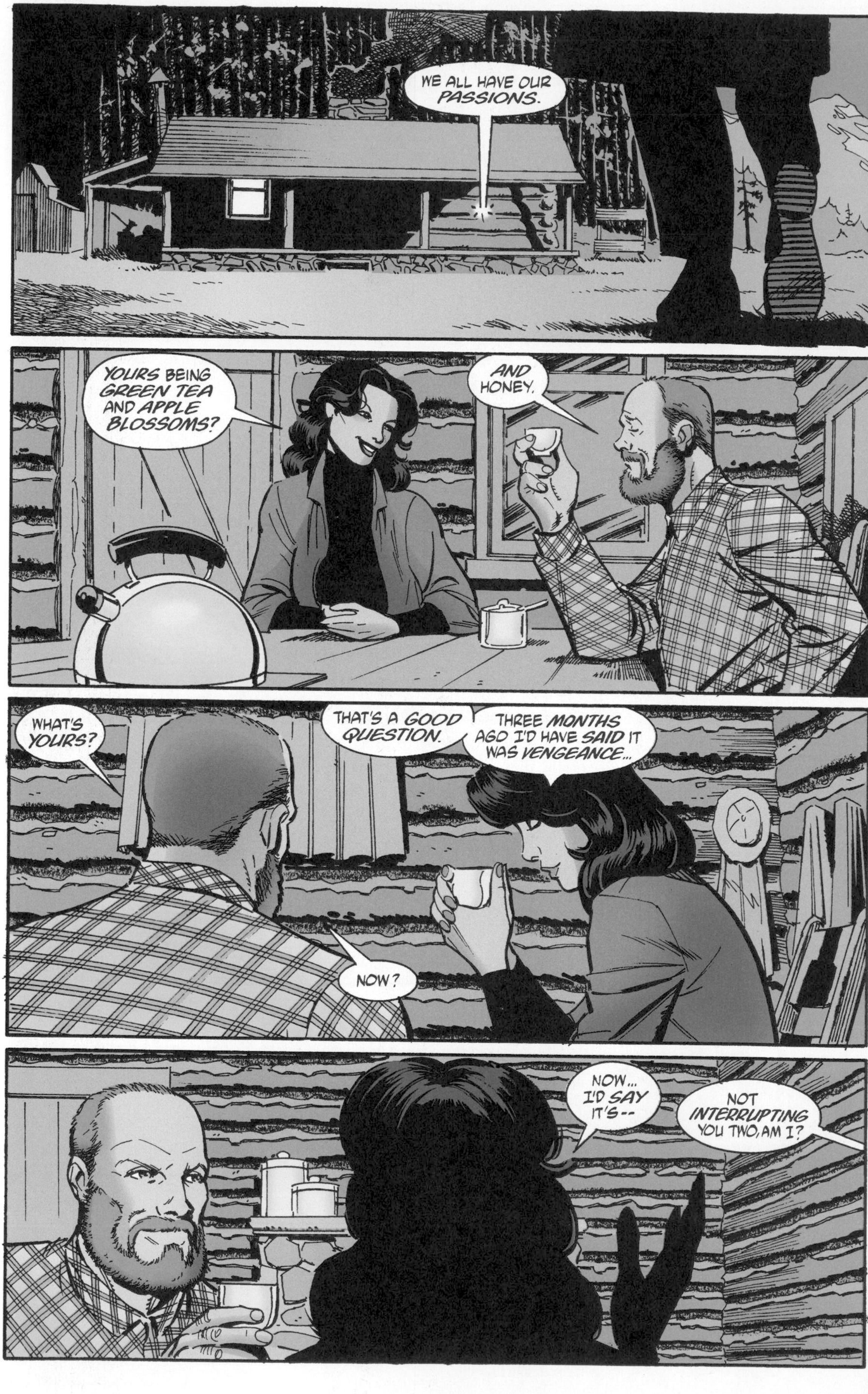
WE ALL HAVE OUR PASSIONS.
YOURS BEING GREEN TEA AND APPLE BLOSSOMS?
AND HONEY.
WHAT'S YOURS?
THAT'S A GOOD QUESTION.
THREE MONTHS AGO I'D HAVE SAID IT WAS VENGEANCE...
NOW?
NOW... I'D SAY IT'S--
NOT INTERRUPTING YOU TWO, AM I?

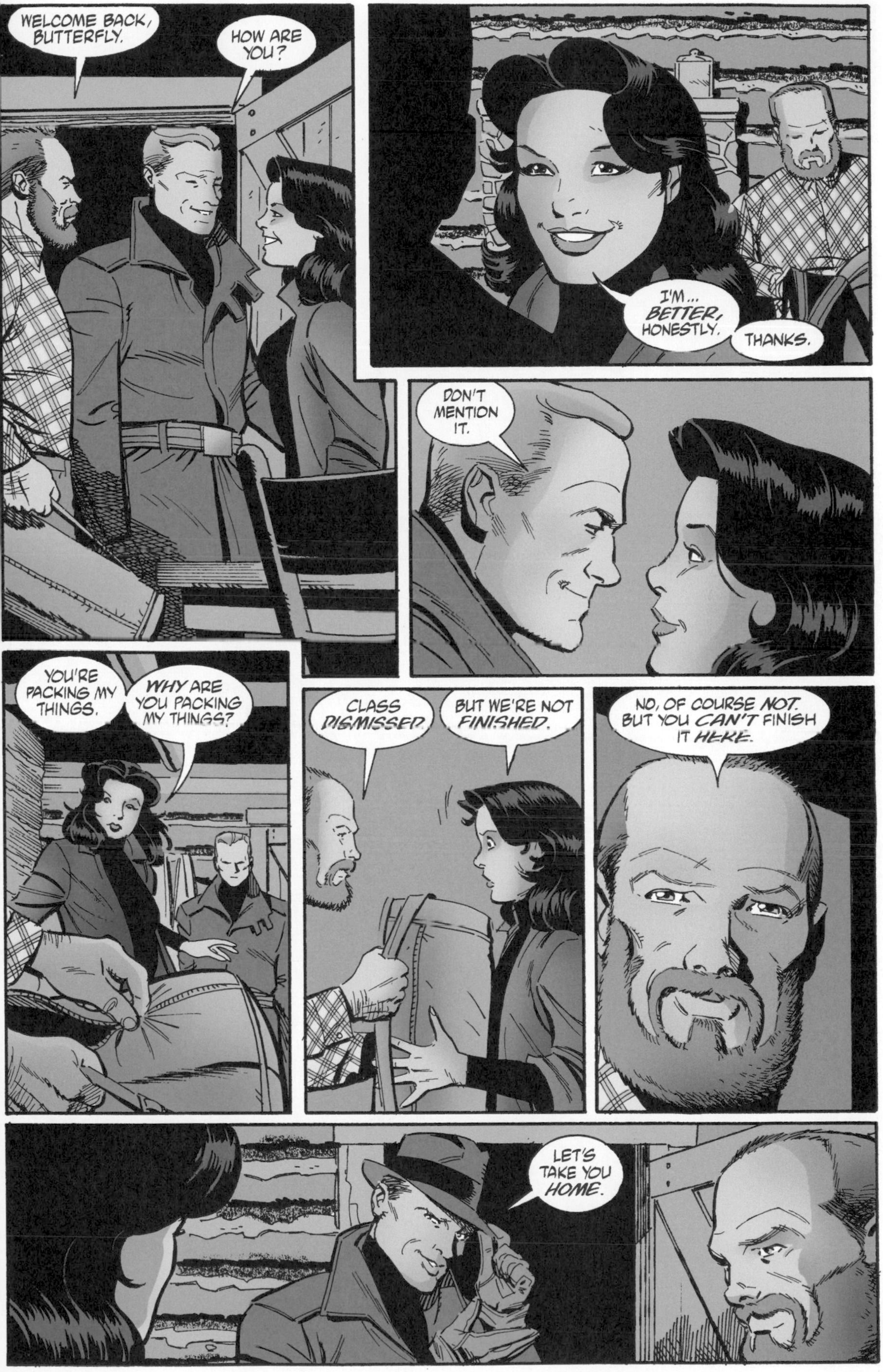
WELCOME BACK, BUTTERFLY.
HOW ARE YOU?
I'M... BETTER, HONESTLY.
THANKS.
DON'T MENTION IT.
YOU'RE PACKING MY THINGS.
WHY ARE YOU PACKING MY THINGS?
CLASS DISMISSED.
BUT WE'RE NOT FINISHED.
NO, OF COURSE NOT. BUT YOU CAN'T FINISH IT HERE.
LET'S TAKE YOU HOME.

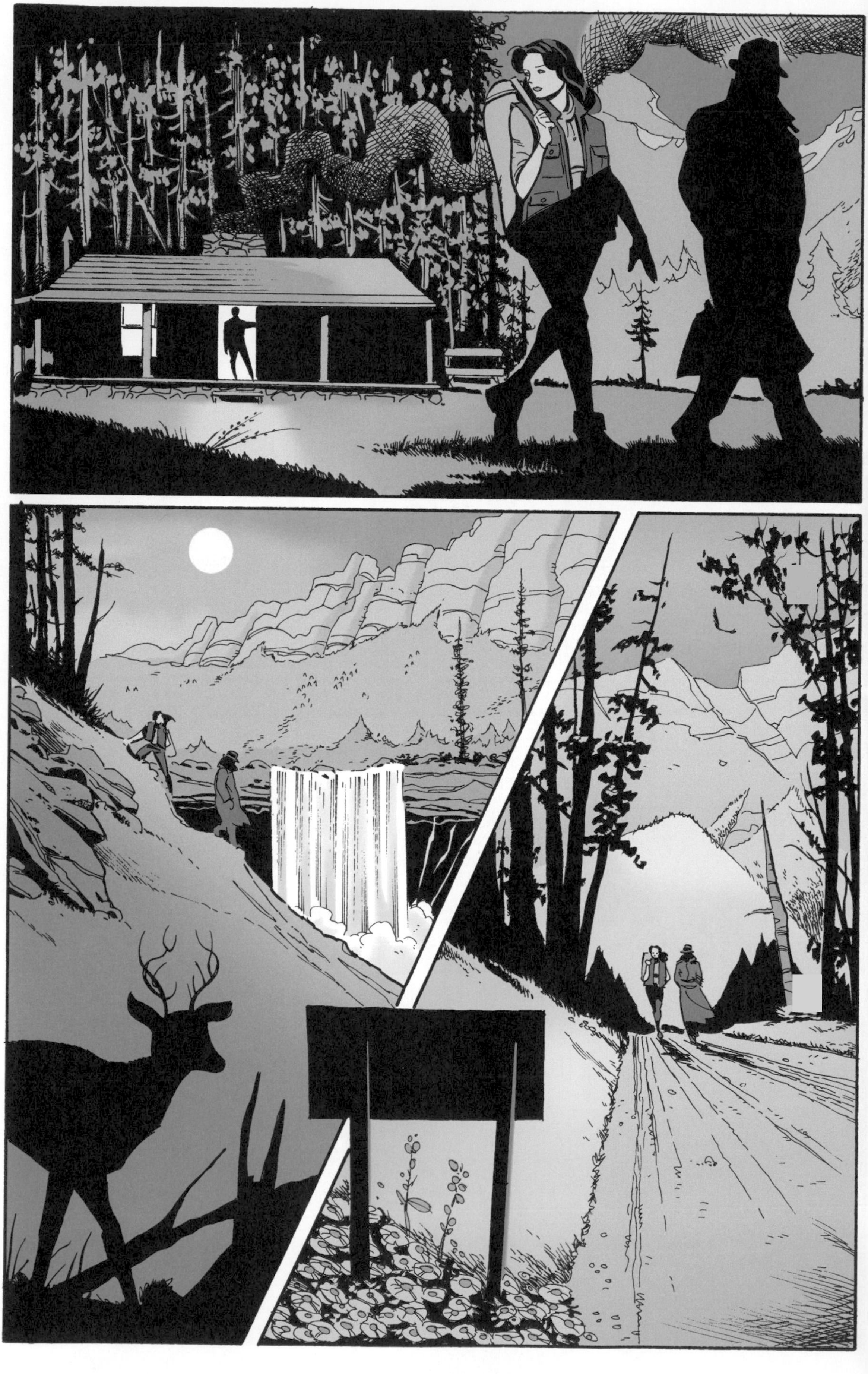

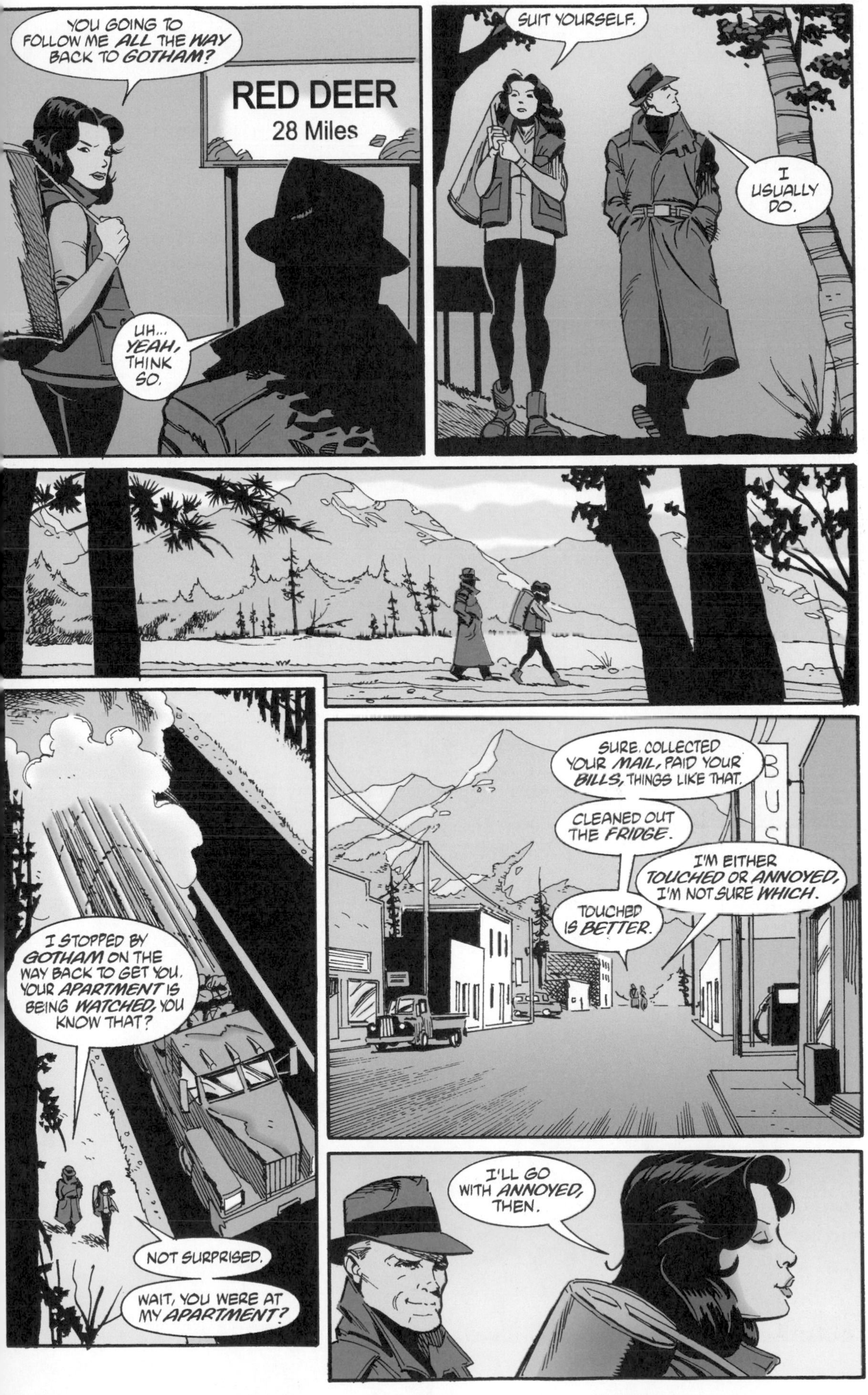
YOU GOING TO FOLLOW ME ALL THE WAY BACK TO GOTHAM?
RED DEER
28 Miles
UH... YEAH, THINK SO.
SUIT YOURSELF.
I USUALLY DO.
I STOPPED BY GOTHAM ON THE WAY BACK TO GET YOU. YOUR APARTMENT IS BEING WATCHED, YOU KNOW THAT?
NOT SURPRISED.
WAIT, YOU WERE AT MY APARTMENT?
SURE. COLLECTED YOUR MAIL, PAID YOUR BILLS, THINGS LIKE THAT.
CLEANED OUT THE FRIDGE.
I'M EITHER TOUCHED OR ANNOYED, I'M NOT SURE WHICH.
TOUCHED IS BETTER.
BUS
I'LL GO WITH ANNOYED, THEN.

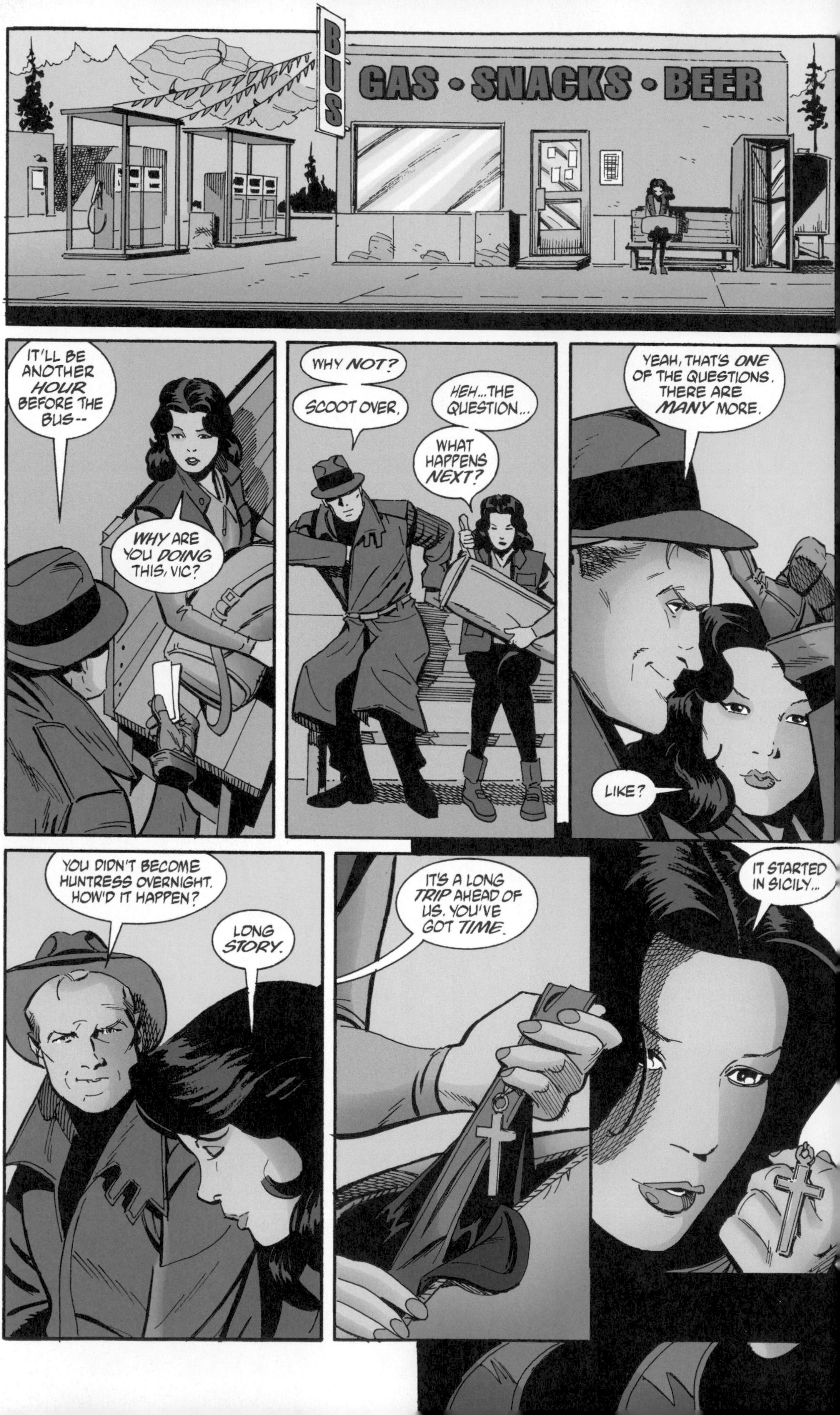
BUS
GAS • SNACKS • BEER
IT'LL BE ANOTHER HOUR BEFORE THE BUS--
WHY ARE YOU DOING THIS, VIC?
WHY NOT?
SCOOT OVER.
HEH...THE QUESTION...
WHAT HAPPENS NEXT?
YEAH, THAT'S ONE OF THE QUESTIONS. THERE ARE MANY MORE.
LIKE?
YOU DIDN'T BECOME HUNTRESS OVERNIGHT. HOW'D IT HAPPEN?
LONG STORY.
IT'S A LONG TRIP AHEAD OF US. YOU'VE GOT TIME.
IT STARTED IN SICILY...

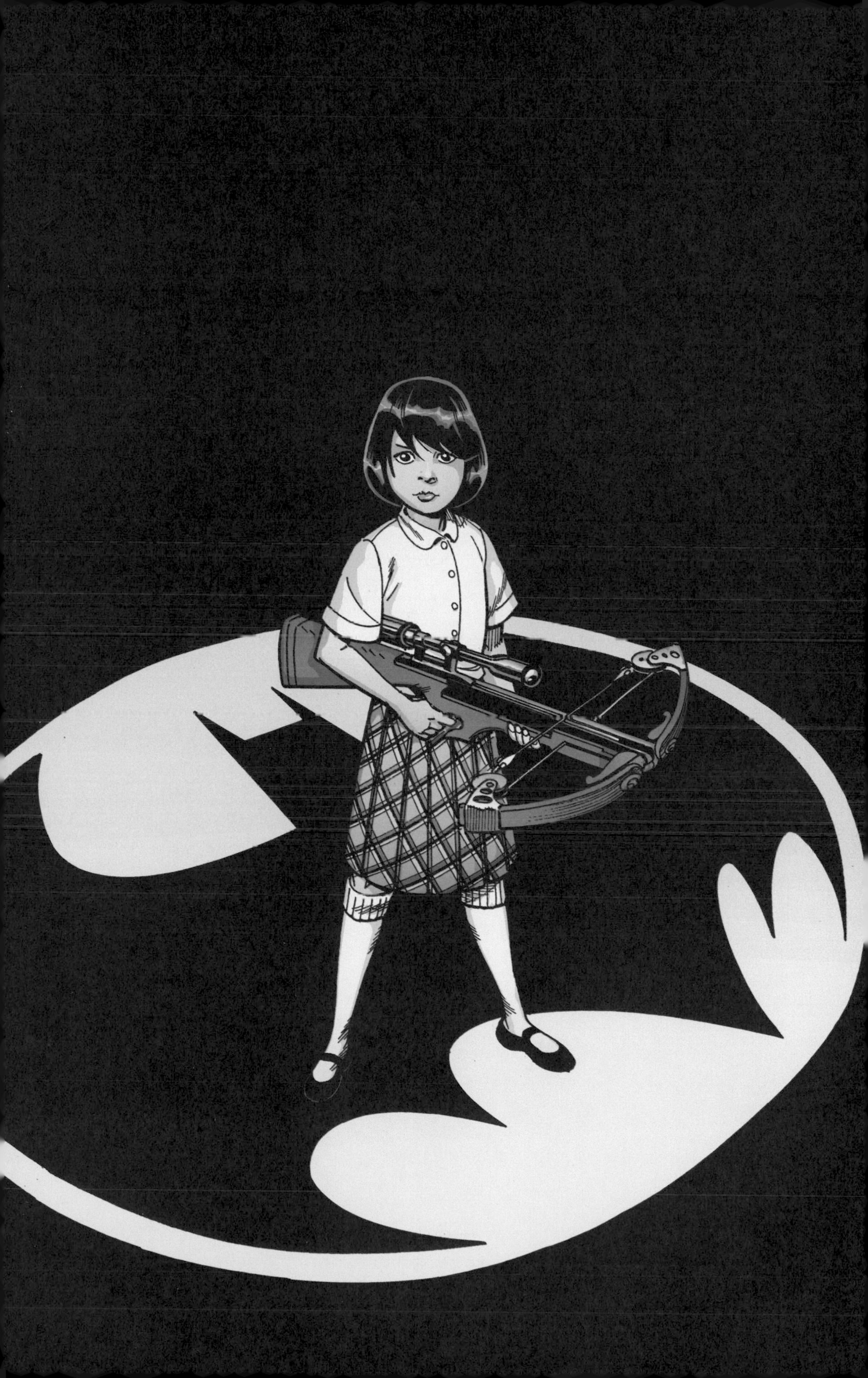

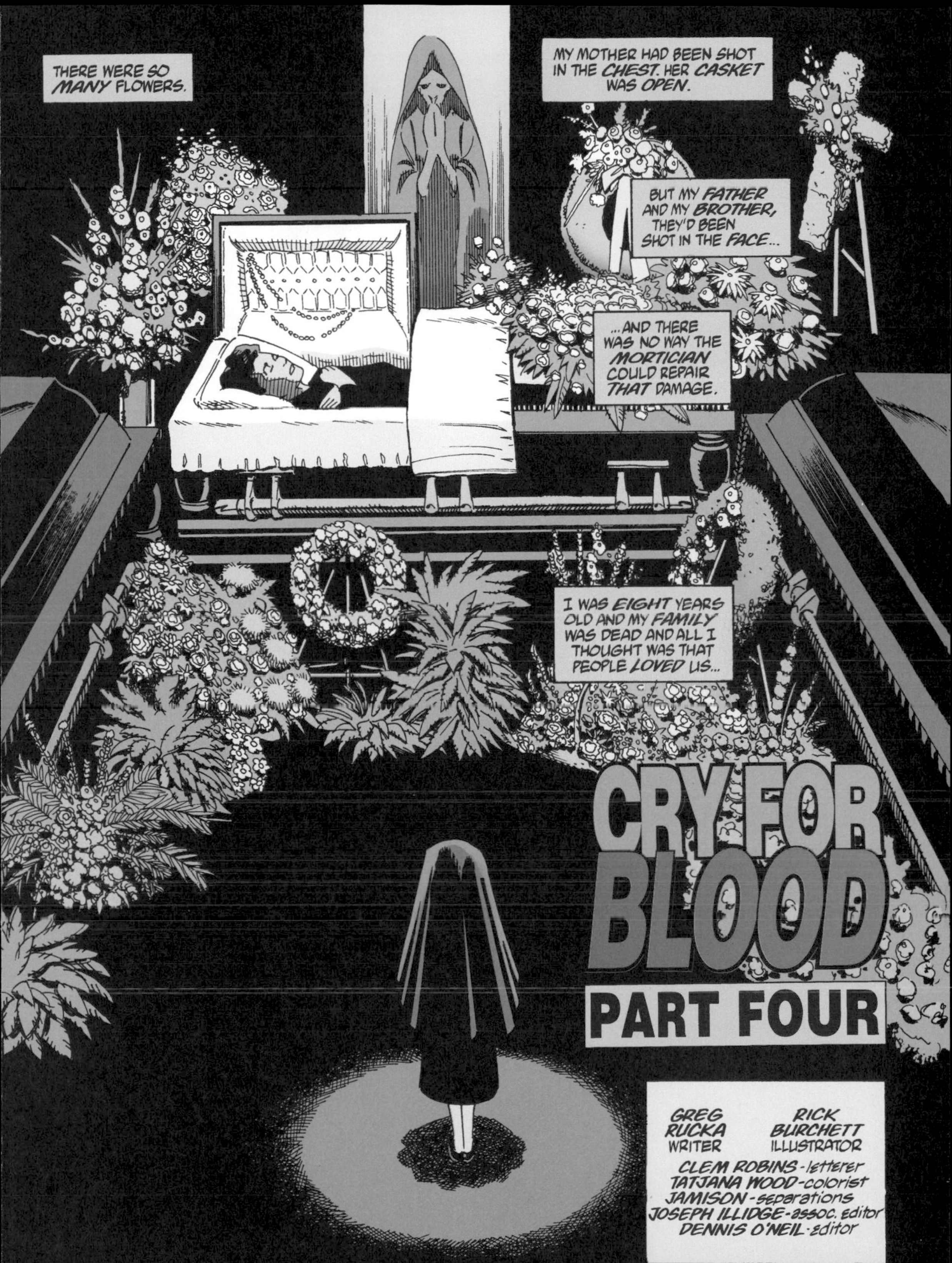
THERE WERE SO MANY FLOWERS.
MY MOTHER HAD BEEN SHOT IN THE CHEST. HER CASKET WAS OPEN.
BUT MY FATHER AND MY BROTHER, THEY'D BEEN SHOT IN THE FACE...
...AND THERE WAS NO WAY THE MORTICIAN COULD REPAIR THAT DAMAGE.
I WAS EIGHT YEARS OLD AND MY FAMILY WAS DEAD AND ALL I THOUGHT WAS THAT PEOPLE LOVED US...
CRY FOR BLOOD
PART FOUR
GREG RUCKA WRITER
RICK BURCHETT ILLUSTRATOR
CLEM ROBINS - letterer
TATJANA WOOD - colorist
JAMISON - separations
JOSEPH ILLIDGE - assoc. editor
DENNIS O'NEIL - editor

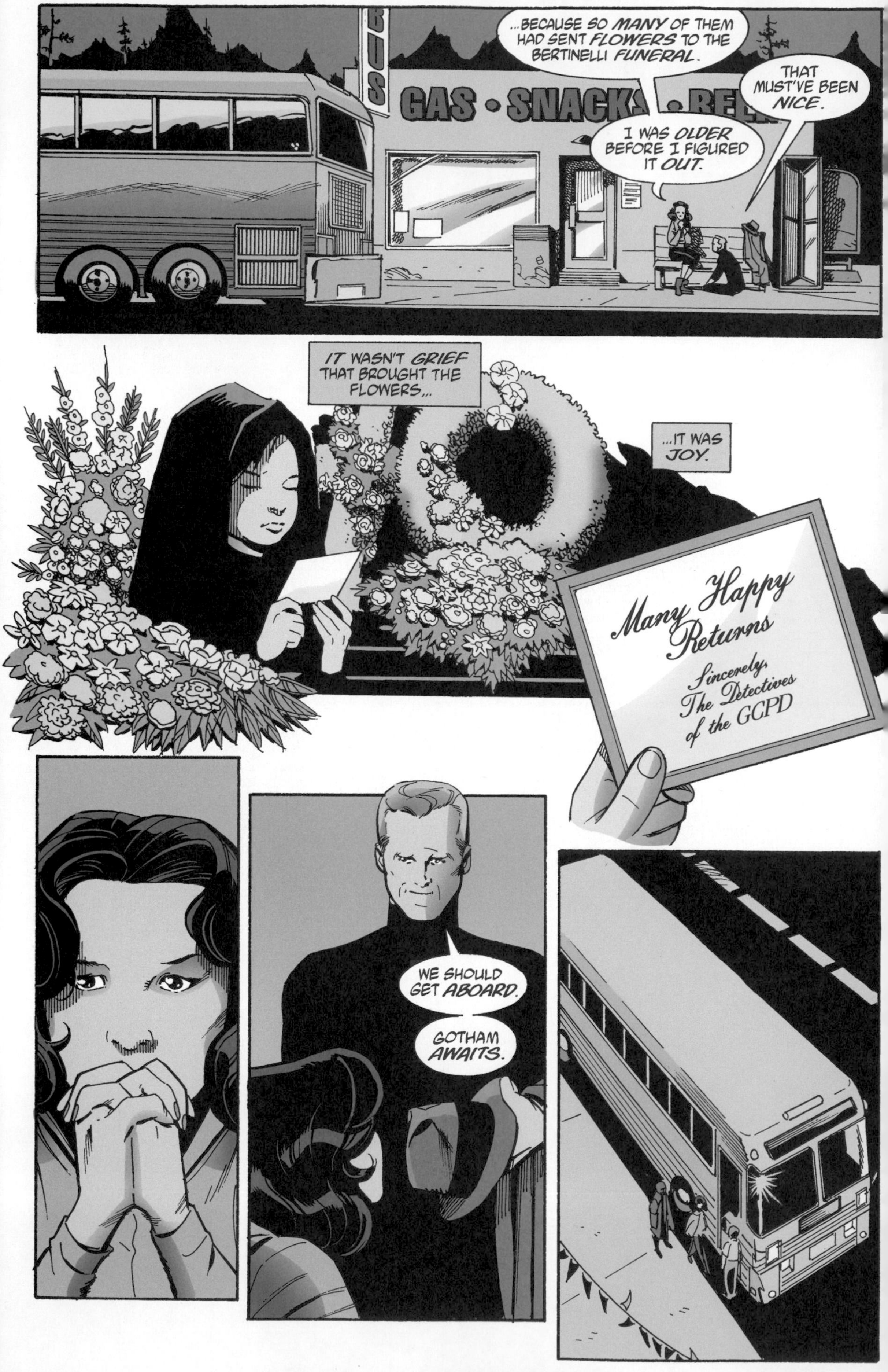

...BECAUSE SO MANY OF THEM HAD SENT FLOWERS TO THE BERTINELLI FUNERAL.
I WAS OLDER BEFORE I FIGURED IT OUT.
THAT MUST'VE BEEN NICE.
BUS
GAS • SNACKS • BEER
IT WASN'T GRIEF THAT BROUGHT THE FLOWERS...
...IT WAS JOY.
Many Happy Returns
Sincerely, The Detectives of the GCPD
WE SHOULD GET ABOARD.
GOTHAM AWAITS.

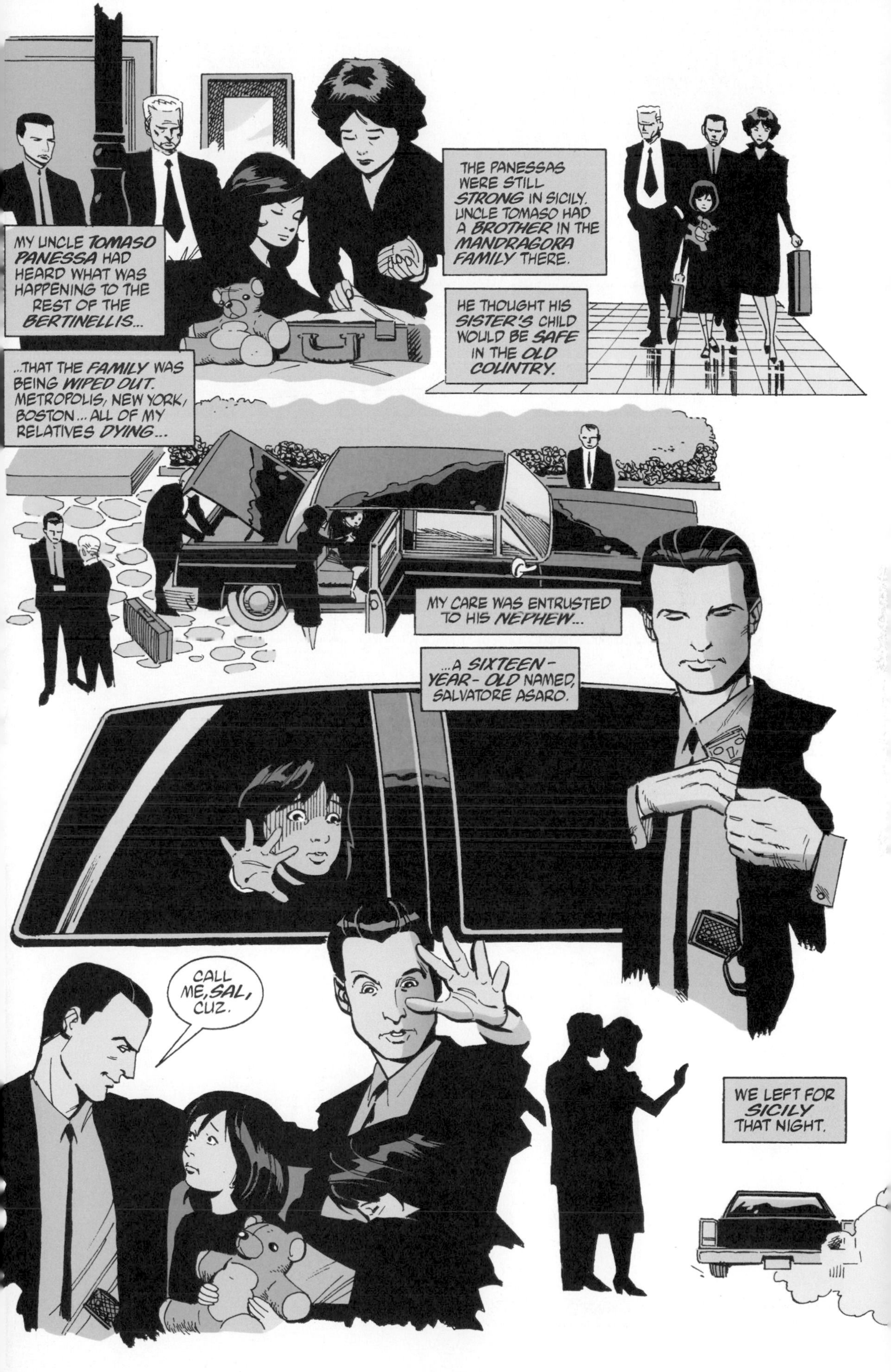
MY UNCLE TOMASO PANESSA HAD HEARD WHAT WAS HAPPENING TO THE REST OF THE BERTINELLIS...
...THAT THE FAMILY WAS BEING WIPED OUT. METROPOLIS, NEW YORK, BOSTON... ALL OF MY RELATIVES DYING...
THE PANESSAS WERE STILL STRONG IN SICILY. UNCLE TOMASO HAD A BROTHER IN THE MANDRAGORA FAMILY THERE.
HE THOUGHT HIS SISTER'S CHILD WOULD BE SAFE IN THE OLD COUNTRY.
MY CARE WAS ENTRUSTED TO HIS NEPHEW...
...A SIXTEEN-YEAR-OLD NAMED, SALVATORE ASARO.
CALL ME, SAL, CUZ.
WE LEFT FOR SICILY THAT NIGHT.

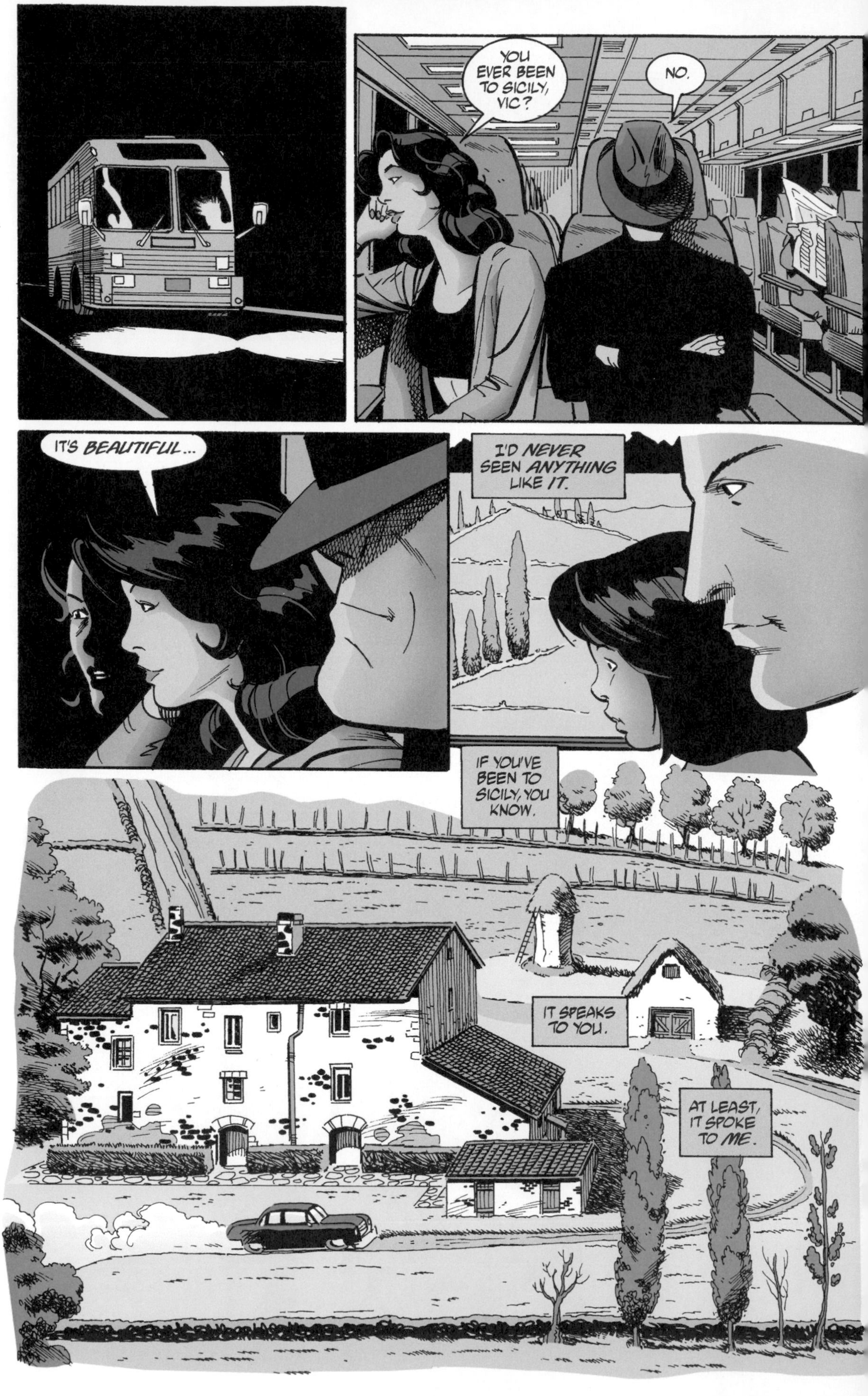

YOU EVER BEEN TO SICILY, VIC?
NO.
IT'S BEAUTIFUL...
I'D NEVER SEEN ANYTHING LIKE IT.
IF YOU'VE BEEN TO SICILY, YOU KNOW.
IT SPEAKS TO YOU.
AT LEAST, IT SPOKE TO ME.

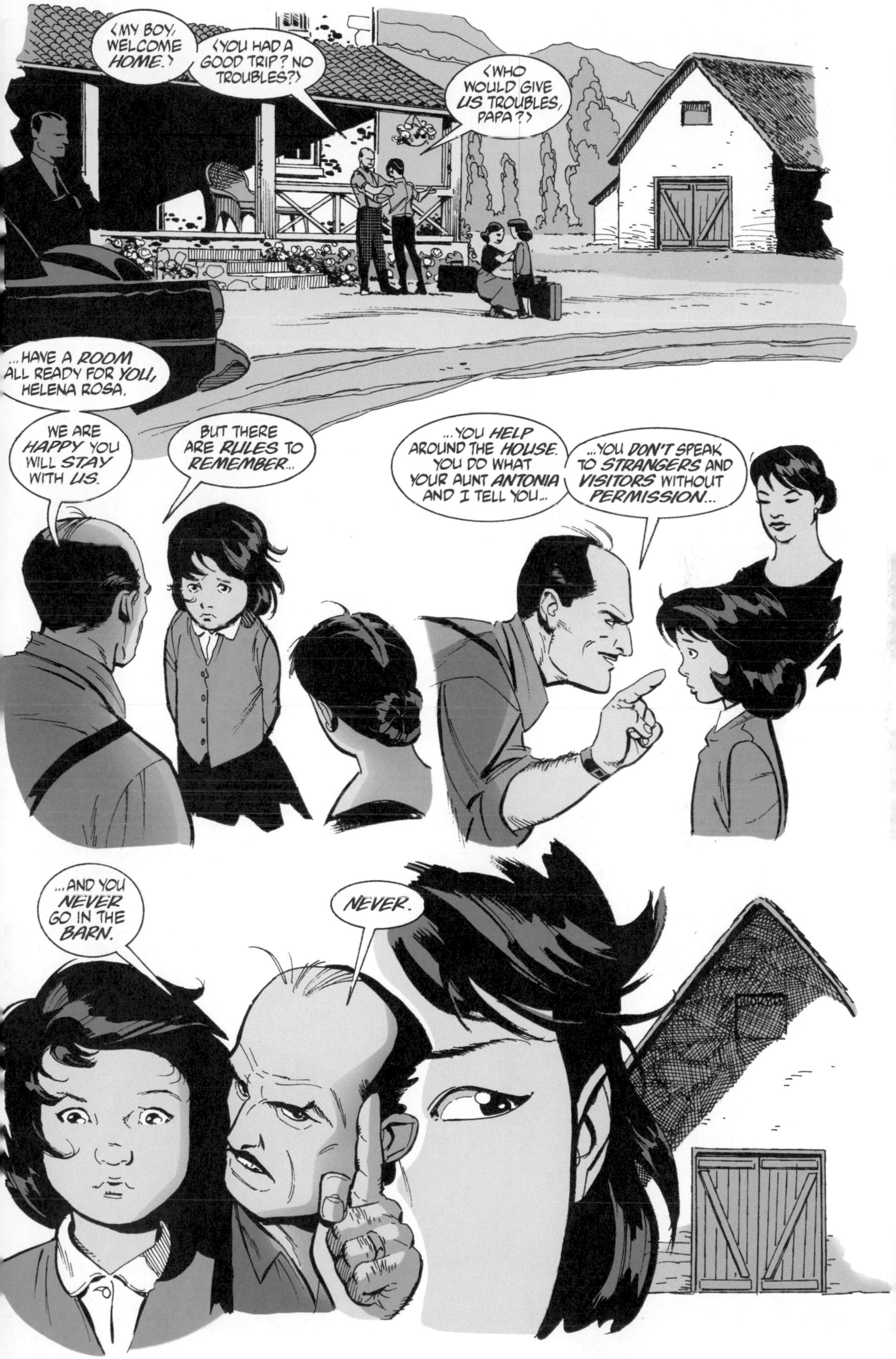
<MY BOY, WELCOME HOME.>
<YOU HAD A GOOD TRIP? NO TROUBLES?>
<WHO WOULD GIVE US TROUBLES, PAPA?>
...HAVE A ROOM ALL READY FOR YOU, HELENA ROSA.
WE ARE HAPPY YOU WILL STAY WITH US.
BUT THERE ARE RULES TO REMEMBER...
...YOU HELP AROUND THE HOUSE. YOU DO WHAT YOUR AUNT ANTONIA AND I TELL YOU...
...YOU DON'T SPEAK TO STRANGERS AND VISITORS WITHOUT PERMISSION...
...AND YOU NEVER GO IN THE BARN.
NEVER.

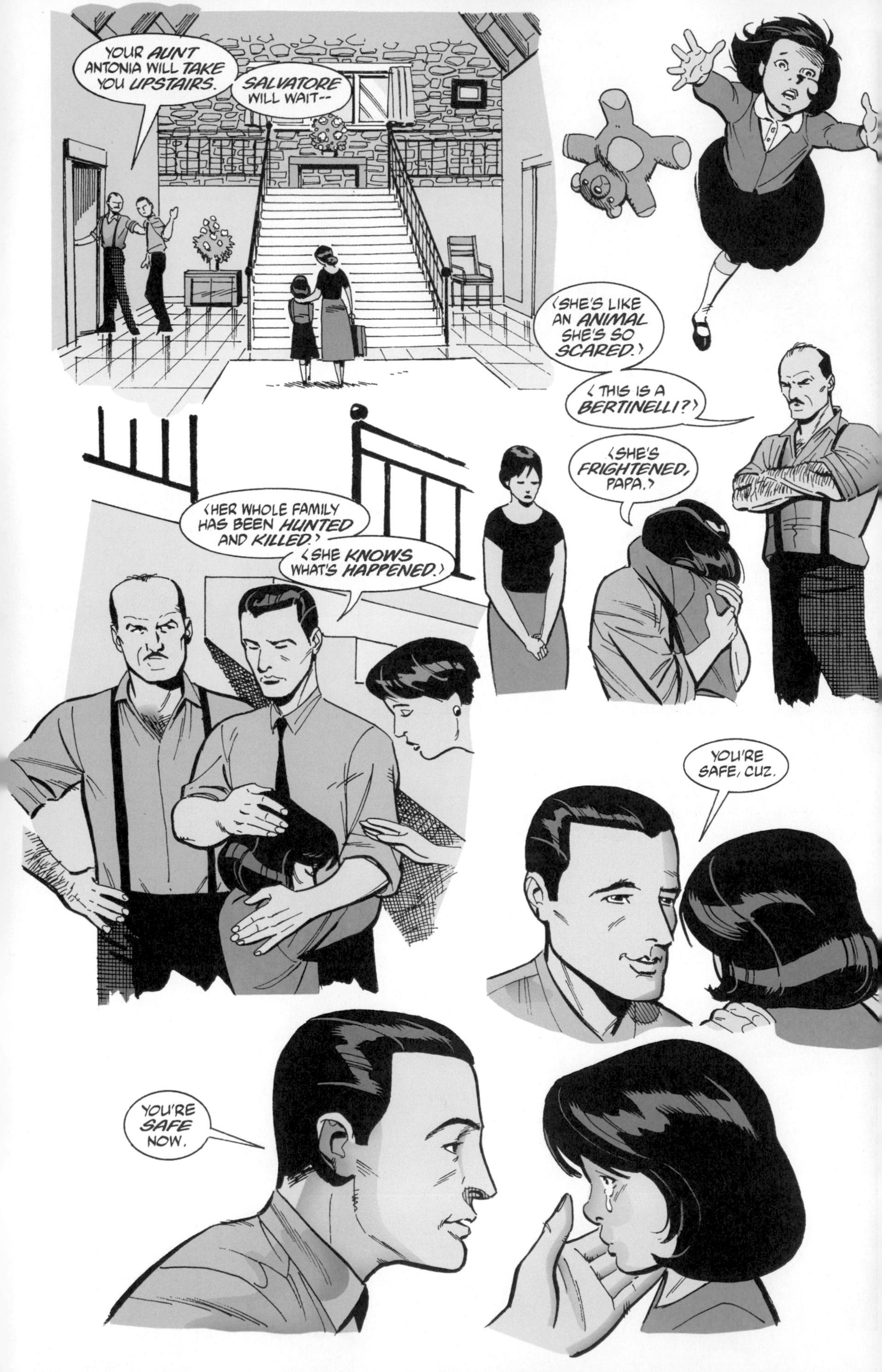
YOUR AUNT ANTONIA WILL TAKE YOU UPSTAIRS.
SALVATORE WILL WAIT--
‹SHE'S LIKE AN ANIMAL SHE'S SO SCARED.›
‹THIS IS A BERTINELLI?›
‹SHE'S FRIGHTENED, PAPA.›
‹HER WHOLE FAMILY HAS BEEN HUNTED AND KILLED.›
‹SHE KNOWS WHAT'S HAPPENED.›
YOU'RE SAFE, CUZ.
YOU'RE SAFE NOW.

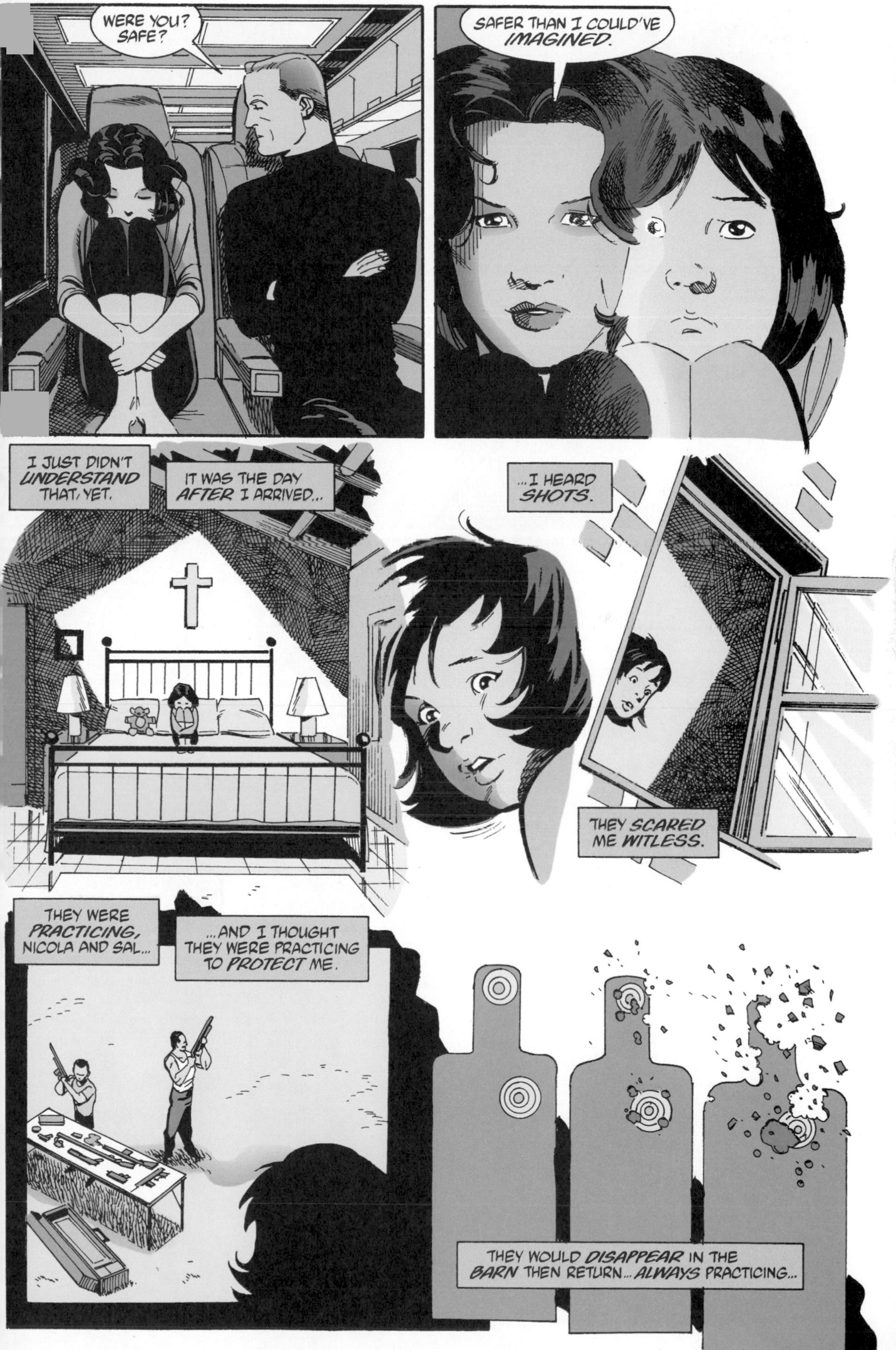

WERE YOU? SAFE?
SAFER THAN I COULD'VE IMAGINED.
I JUST DIDN'T UNDERSTAND THAT, YET.
IT WAS THE DAY AFTER I ARRIVED...
...I HEARD SHOTS.
THEY SCARED ME WITLESS.
THEY WERE PRACTICING, NICOLA AND SAL...
...AND I THOUGHT THEY WERE PRACTICING TO PROTECT ME.
THEY WOULD DISAPPEAR IN THE BARN THEN RETURN... ALWAYS PRACTICING...

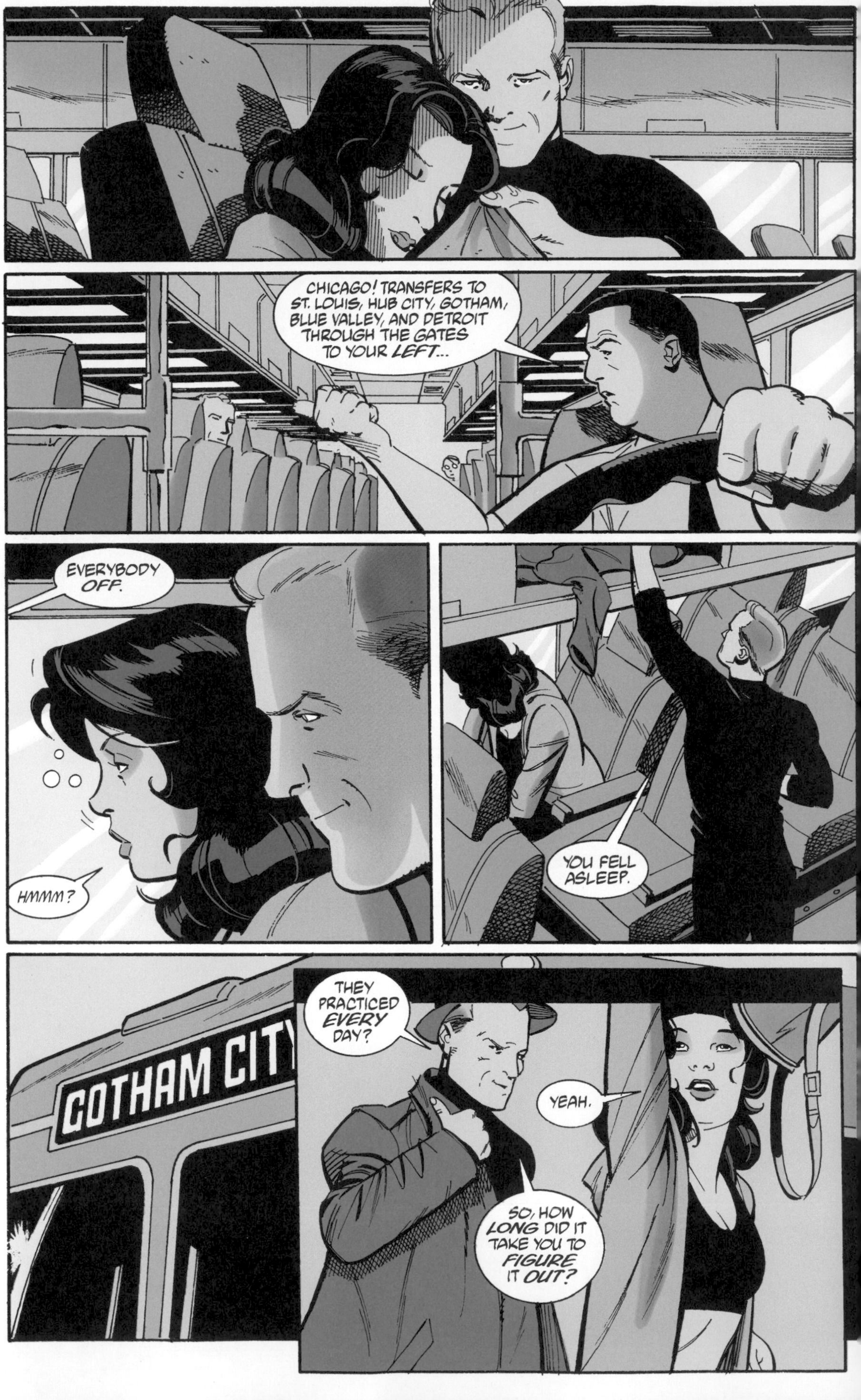
CHICAGO! TRANSFERS TO ST. LOUIS, HUB CITY, GOTHAM, BLUE VALLEY, AND DETROIT THROUGH THE GATES TO YOUR LEFT...
EVERYBODY OFF.
HMMM?
YOU FELL ASLEEP.
GOTHAM CITY
THEY PRACTICED EVERY DAY?
YEAH.
SO, HOW LONG DID IT TAKE YOU TO FIGURE IT OUT?

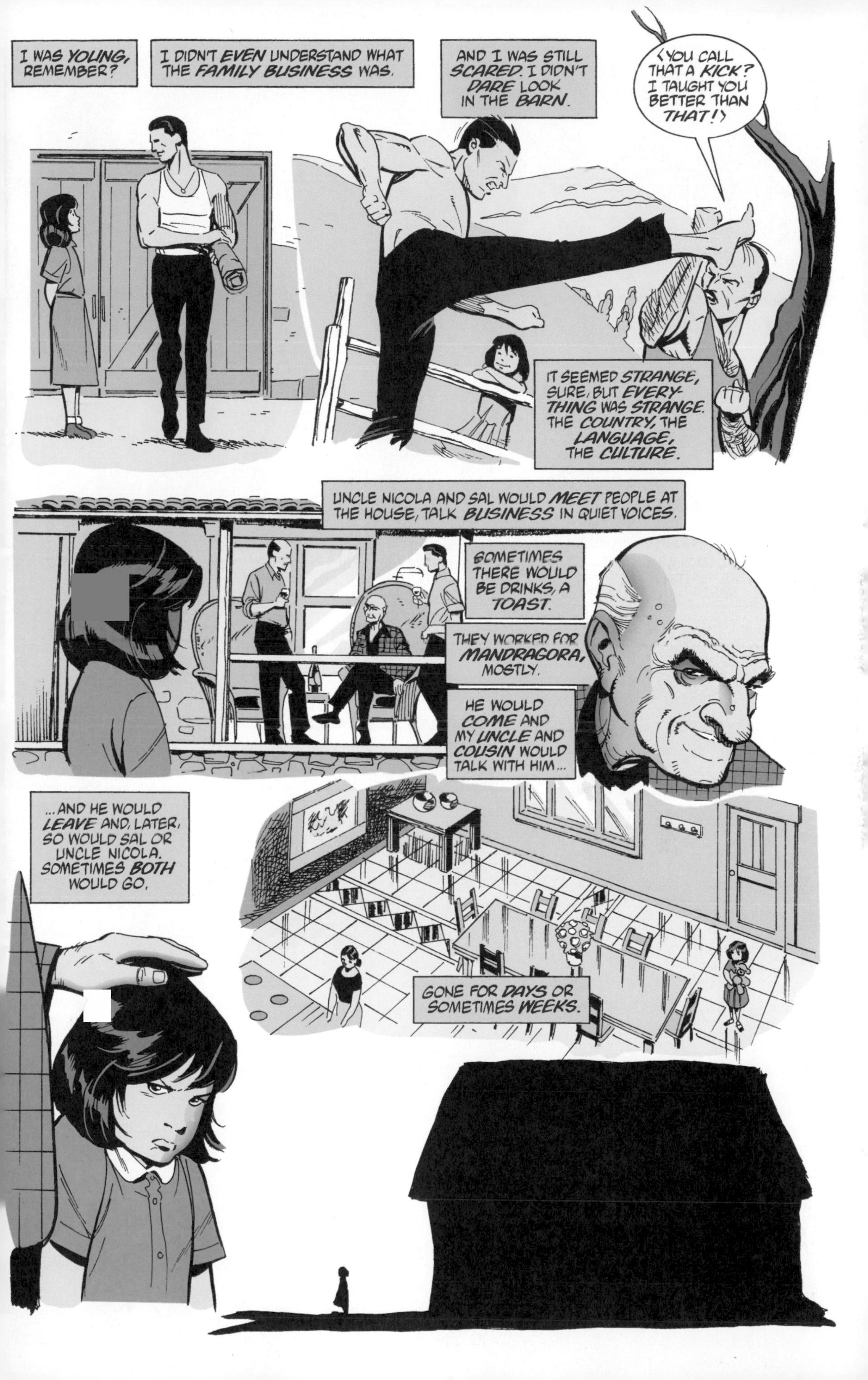
I WAS YOUNG, REMEMBER?
I DIDN'T EVEN UNDERSTAND WHAT THE FAMILY BUSINESS WAS.
AND I WAS STILL SCARED. I DIDN'T DARE LOOK IN THE BARN.
‹YOU CALL THAT A KICK? I TAUGHT YOU BETTER THAN THAT!›
IT SEEMED STRANGE, SURE, BUT EVERY-THING WAS STRANGE. THE COUNTRY, THE LANGUAGE, THE CULTURE.
UNCLE NICOLA AND SAL WOULD MEET PEOPLE AT THE HOUSE, TALK BUSINESS IN QUIET VOICES.
SOMETIMES THERE WOULD BE DRINKS, A TOAST.
THEY WORKED FOR MANDRAGORA, MOSTLY.
HE WOULD COME AND MY UNCLE AND COUSIN WOULD TALK WITH HIM...
...AND HE WOULD LEAVE AND, LATER, SO WOULD SAL OR UNCLE NICOLA. SOMETIMES BOTH WOULD GO.
GONE FOR DAYS OR SOMETIMES WEEKS.

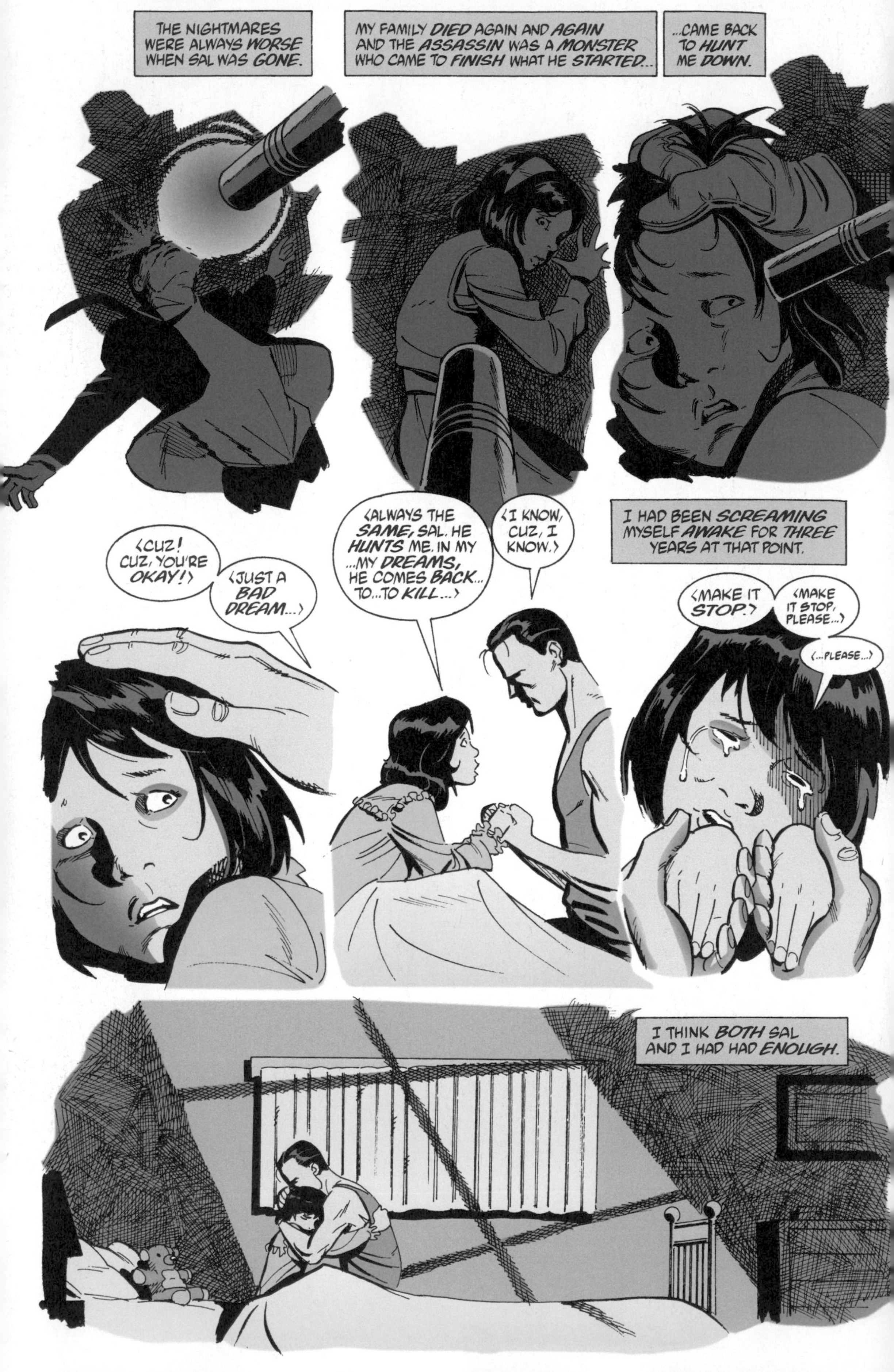
THE NIGHTMARES WERE ALWAYS WORSE WHEN SAL WAS GONE.
MY FAMILY DIED AGAIN AND AGAIN AND THE ASSASSIN WAS A MONSTER WHO CAME TO FINISH WHAT HE STARTED...
...CAME BACK TO HUNT ME DOWN.
‹CUZ! CUZ, YOU'RE OKAY!›
‹JUST A BAD DREAM...›
‹ALWAYS THE SAME, SAL. HE HUNTS ME. IN MY ...MY DREAMS, HE COMES BACK... TO...TO KILL...›
‹I KNOW, CUZ, I KNOW.›
I HAD BEEN SCREAMING MYSELF AWAKE FOR THREE YEARS AT THAT POINT.
‹MAKE IT STOP.›
‹MAKE IT STOP, PLEASE...›
‹...PLEASE...›
I THINK BOTH SAL AND I HAD HAD ENOUGH.

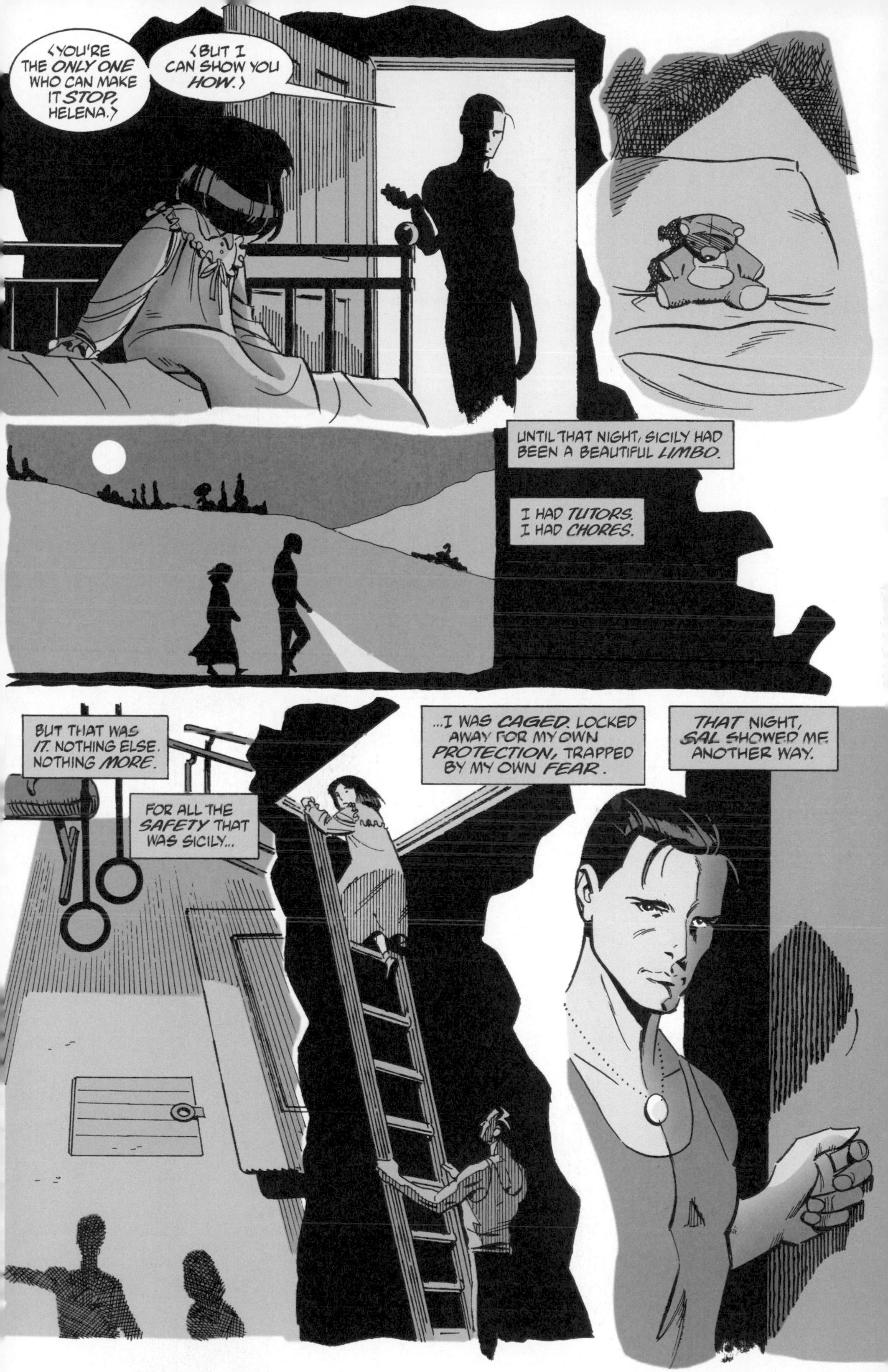
‹YOU'RE THE ONLY ONE WHO CAN MAKE IT STOP, HELENA.›
‹BUT I CAN SHOW YOU HOW.›
UNTIL THAT NIGHT, SICILY HAD BEEN A BEAUTIFUL LIMBO.
I HAD TUTORS. I HAD CHORES.
BUT THAT WAS IT. NOTHING ELSE. NOTHING MORE.
FOR ALL THE SAFETY THAT WAS SICILY...
...I WAS CAGED. LOCKED AWAY FOR MY OWN PROTECTION, TRAPPED BY MY OWN FEAR.
THAT NIGHT, SAL SHOWED ME ANOTHER WAY.

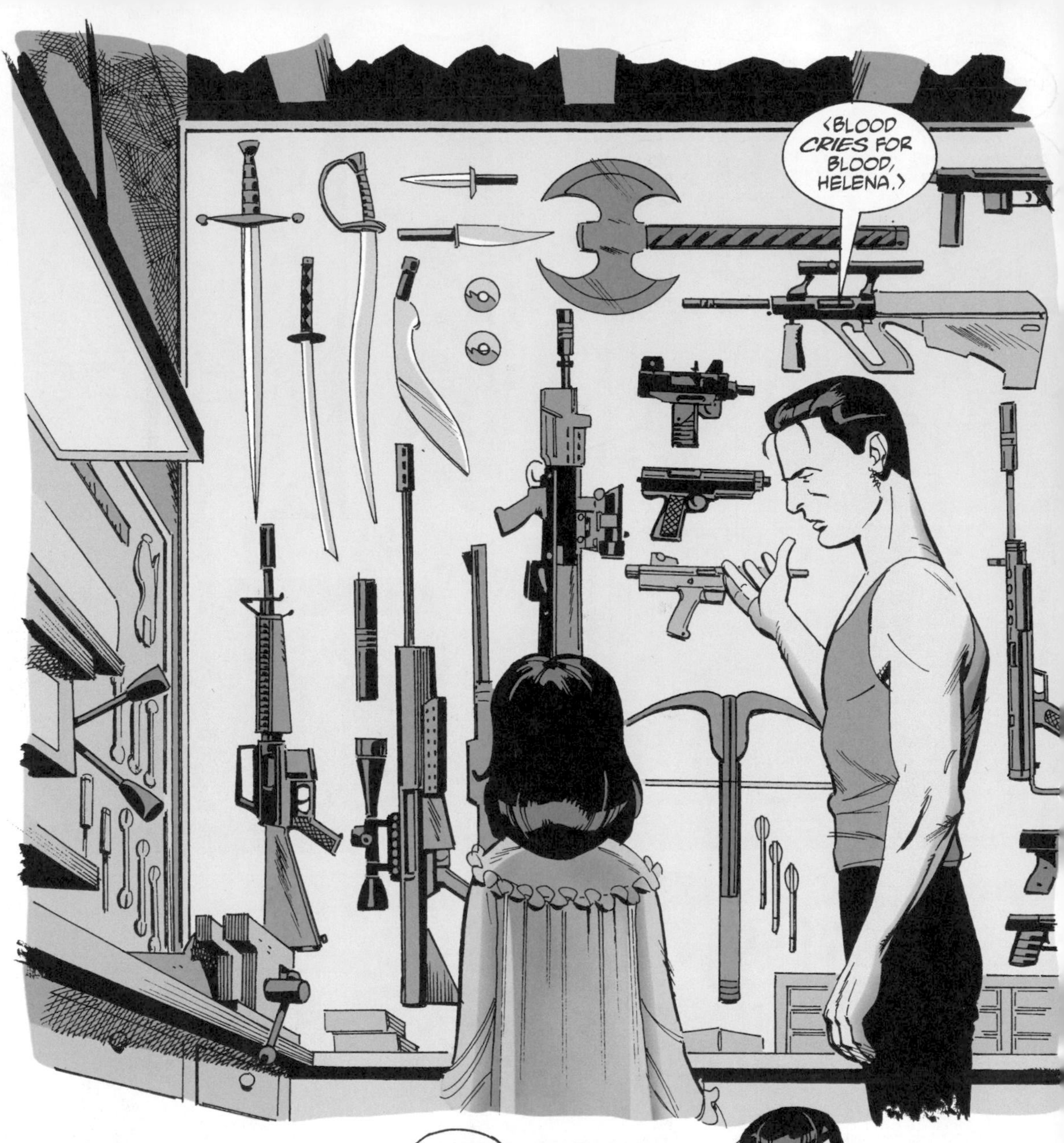
<BLOOD CRIES FOR BLOOD, HELENA.>

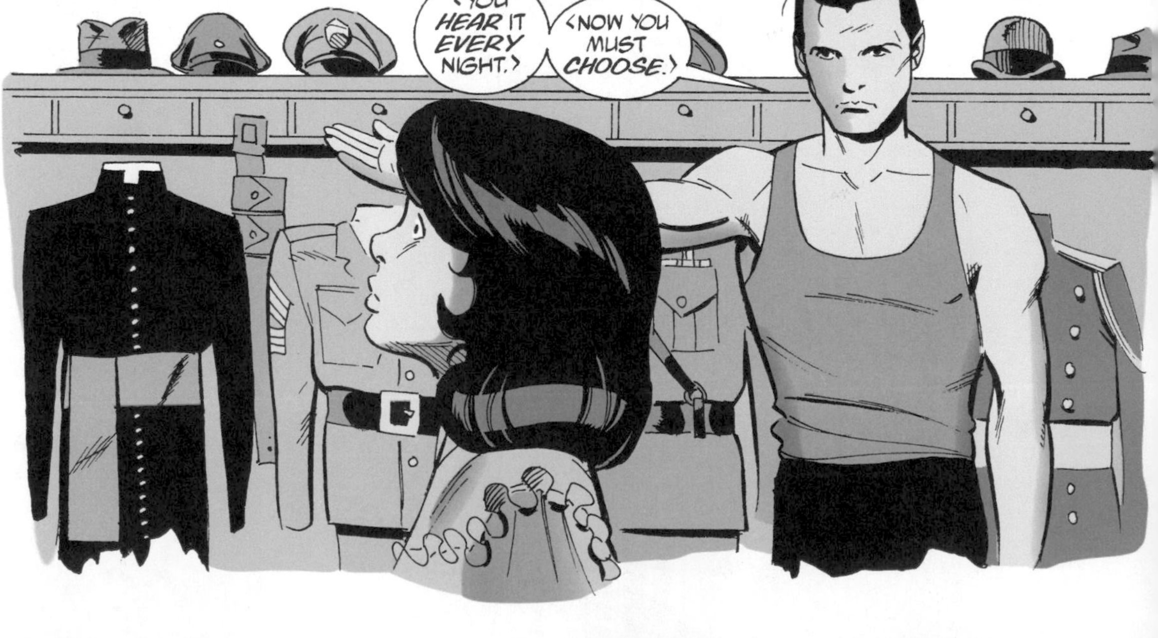
<YOU HEAR IT EVERY NIGHT.>
<NOW YOU MUST CHOOSE.>

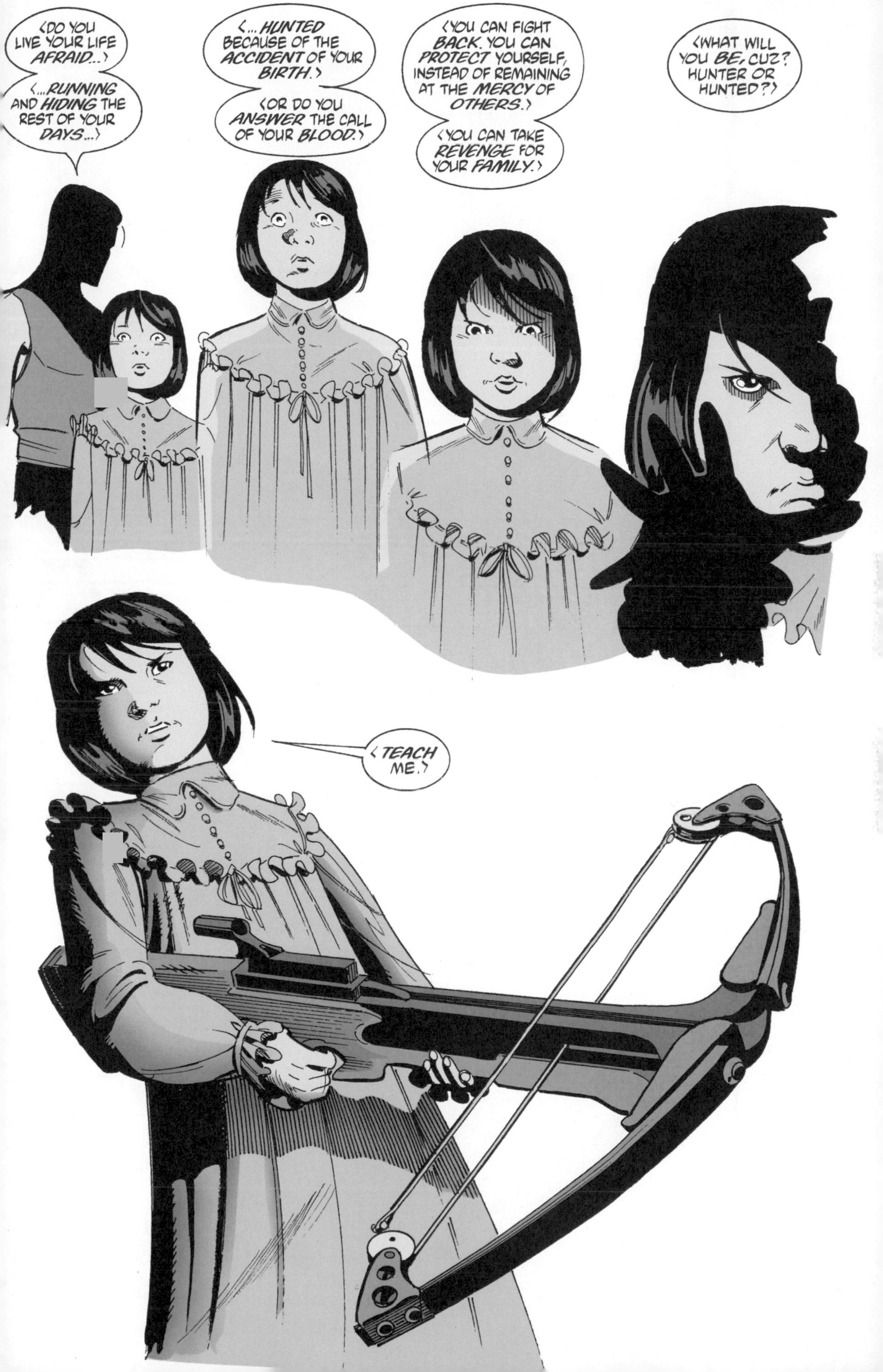
‹DO YOU LIVE YOUR LIFE AFRAID...›
‹...RUNNING AND HIDING THE REST OF YOUR DAYS...›
‹...HUNTED BECAUSE OF THE ACCIDENT OF YOUR BIRTH.›
‹OR DO YOU ANSWER THE CALL OF YOUR BLOOD.›
‹YOU CAN FIGHT BACK. YOU CAN PROTECT YOURSELF, INSTEAD OF REMAINING AT THE MERCY OF OTHERS.›
‹YOU CAN TAKE REVENGE FOR YOUR FAMILY.›
‹WHAT WILL YOU BE, CUZ? HUNTER OR HUNTED?›
‹TEACH ME.›

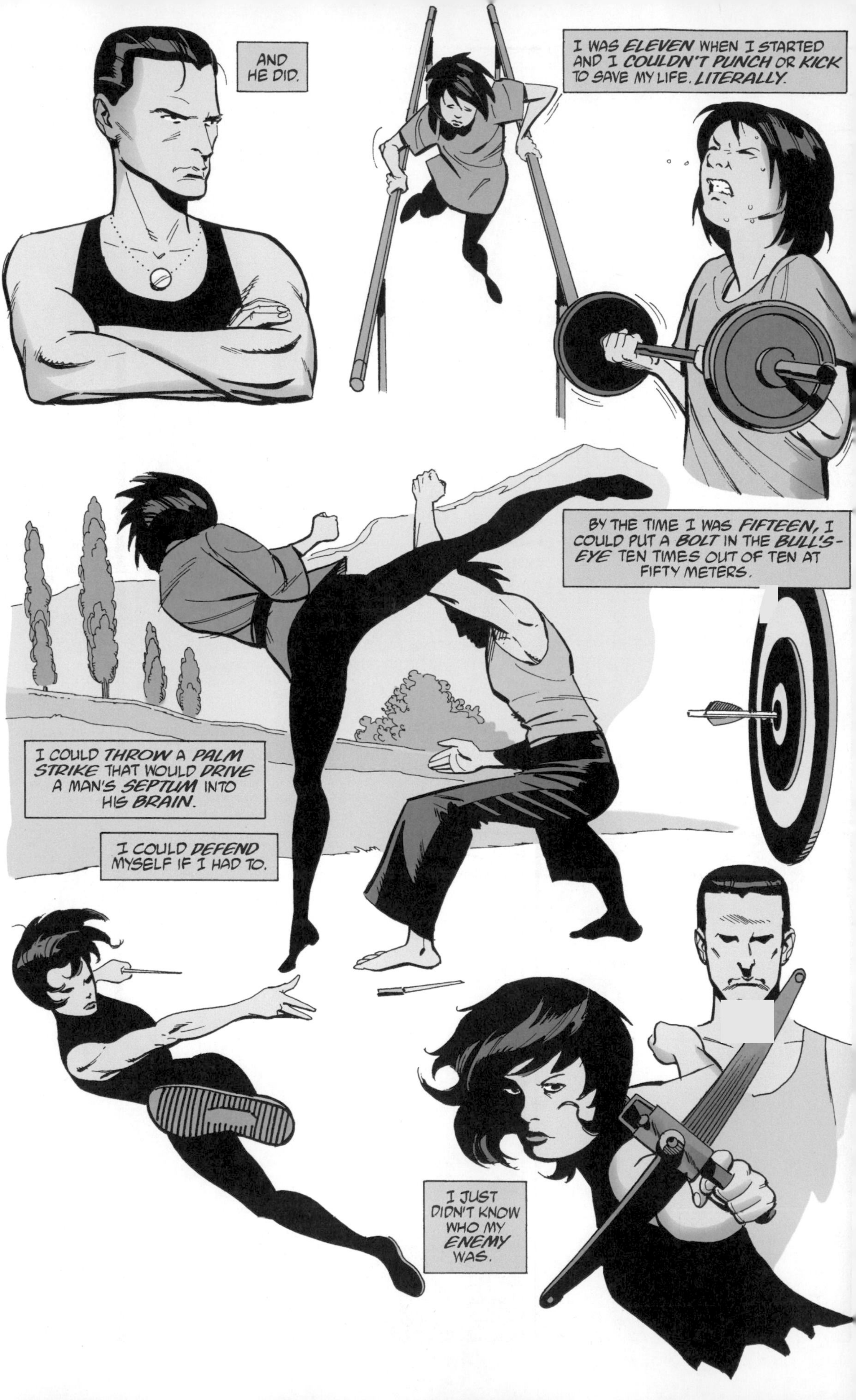
AND HE DID.
I WAS ELEVEN WHEN I STARTED AND I COULDN'T PUNCH OR KICK TO SAVE MY LIFE. LITERALLY.
BY THE TIME I WAS FIFTEEN, I COULD PUT A BOLT IN THE BULL'S-EYE TEN TIMES OUT OF TEN AT FIFTY METERS.
I COULD THROW A PALM STRIKE THAT WOULD DRIVE A MAN'S SEPTUM INTO HIS BRAIN.
I COULD DEFEND MYSELF IF I HAD TO.
I JUST DIDN'T KNOW WHO MY ENEMY WAS.

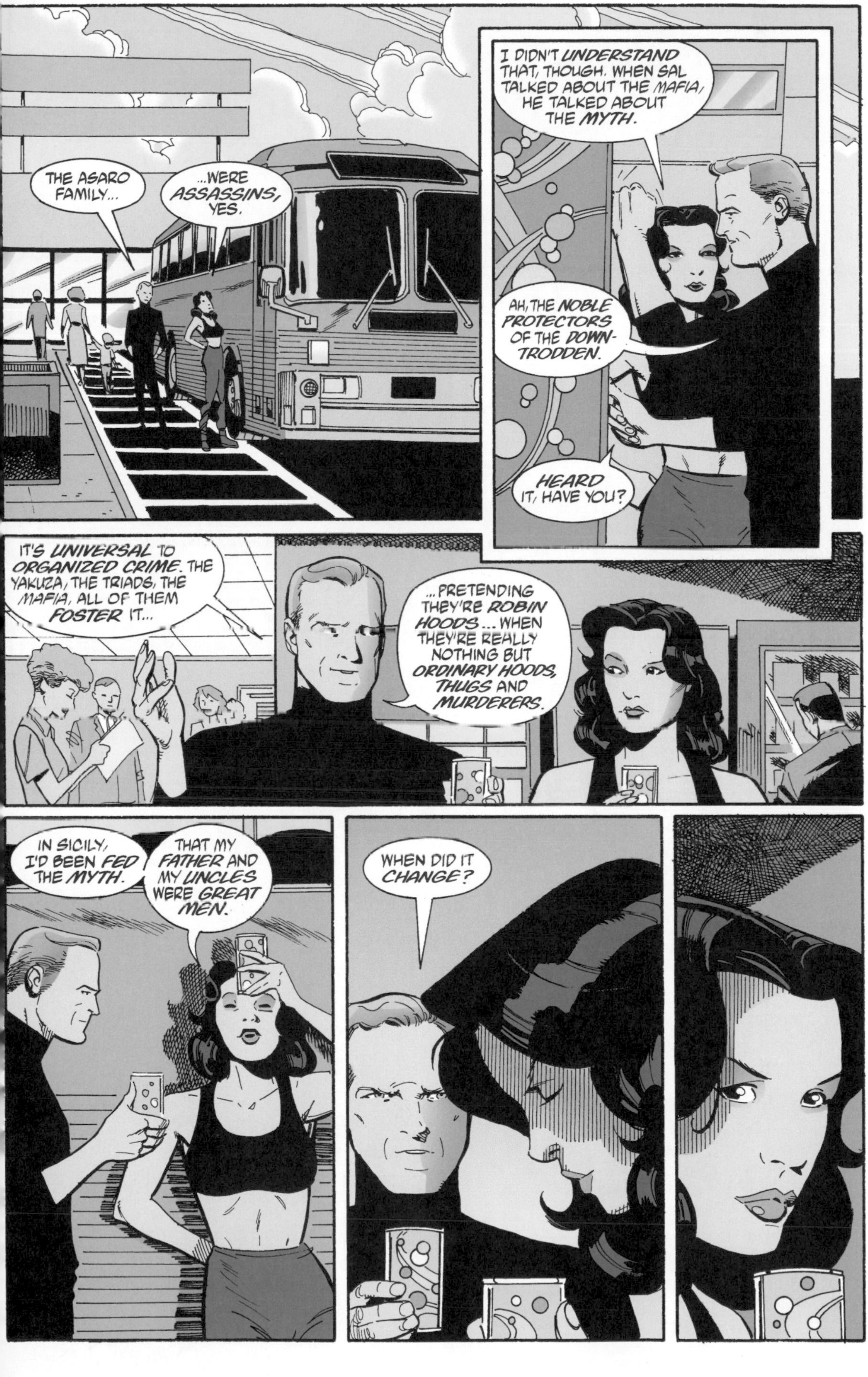
THE ASARO FAMILY...
...WERE ASSASSINS, YES.
I DIDN'T UNDERSTAND THAT, THOUGH. WHEN SAL TALKED ABOUT THE MAFIA, HE TALKED ABOUT THE MYTH.
AH, THE NOBLE PROTECTORS OF THE DOWN-TRODDEN.
HEARD IT, HAVE YOU?
IT'S UNIVERSAL TO ORGANIZED CRIME. THE YAKUZA, THE TRIADS, THE MAFIA, ALL OF THEM FOSTER IT...
...PRETENDING THEY'RE ROBIN HOODS... WHEN THEY'RE REALLY NOTHING BUT ORDINARY HOODS, THUGS AND MURDERERS.
IN SICILY, I'D BEEN FED THE MYTH.
THAT MY FATHER AND MY UNCLES WERE GREAT MEN.
WHEN DID IT CHANGE?

WHEN THE *POLICE* CAME, UNCLE COLI AND SAL *DIDN'T* FIGHT.

THEY THOUGHT IT WAS *NOTHING*. AFTER ALL, THE MAFIA HAD BEEN *UNTOUCHABLE* FOR *HUNDREDS* OF YEARS.

THEY WERE *WRONG*.

THE ITALIAN GOVERNMENT WAS *CRACKING DOWN* ON THE *MAFIA*, AND THIS TIME THEY WEREN'T *FOOLING*.

THERE WERE *HUNDREDS* OF *ARRESTS*. THE *TRIALS* WERE *INTERNATIONAL NEWS*.

ANTONIA SENT ME TO *BOARDING SCHOOL* IN *EUROPE*, KEEPING ME OUT OF THE *WAY* WHILE HER *HUSBAND* AND *SON* WERE TRIED AS *MASS MURDERERS*.

BUT I *SAW* THE *NEWS*.

FAMILY OF HITMEN
TIMES

Palermo — Nicola Asaro and son Salvadore were indicted on eighteen separate counts of murder yesterday as the Italian Government's "maxi-trial" against the Sicilian *Mafia* entered its eighth week. If convicted, father and son could serve multiple life sentences. In a series of court appearances before a ——— magistrate, Asa—— innocenc—— of——

I *READ* THE STORIES.

THEN I READ *MORE*.

AND *MORE*.

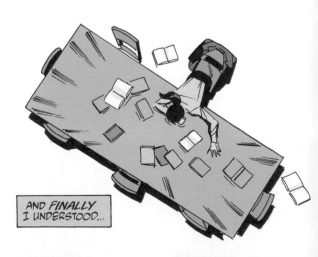

AND *FINALLY* I UNDERSTOOD...

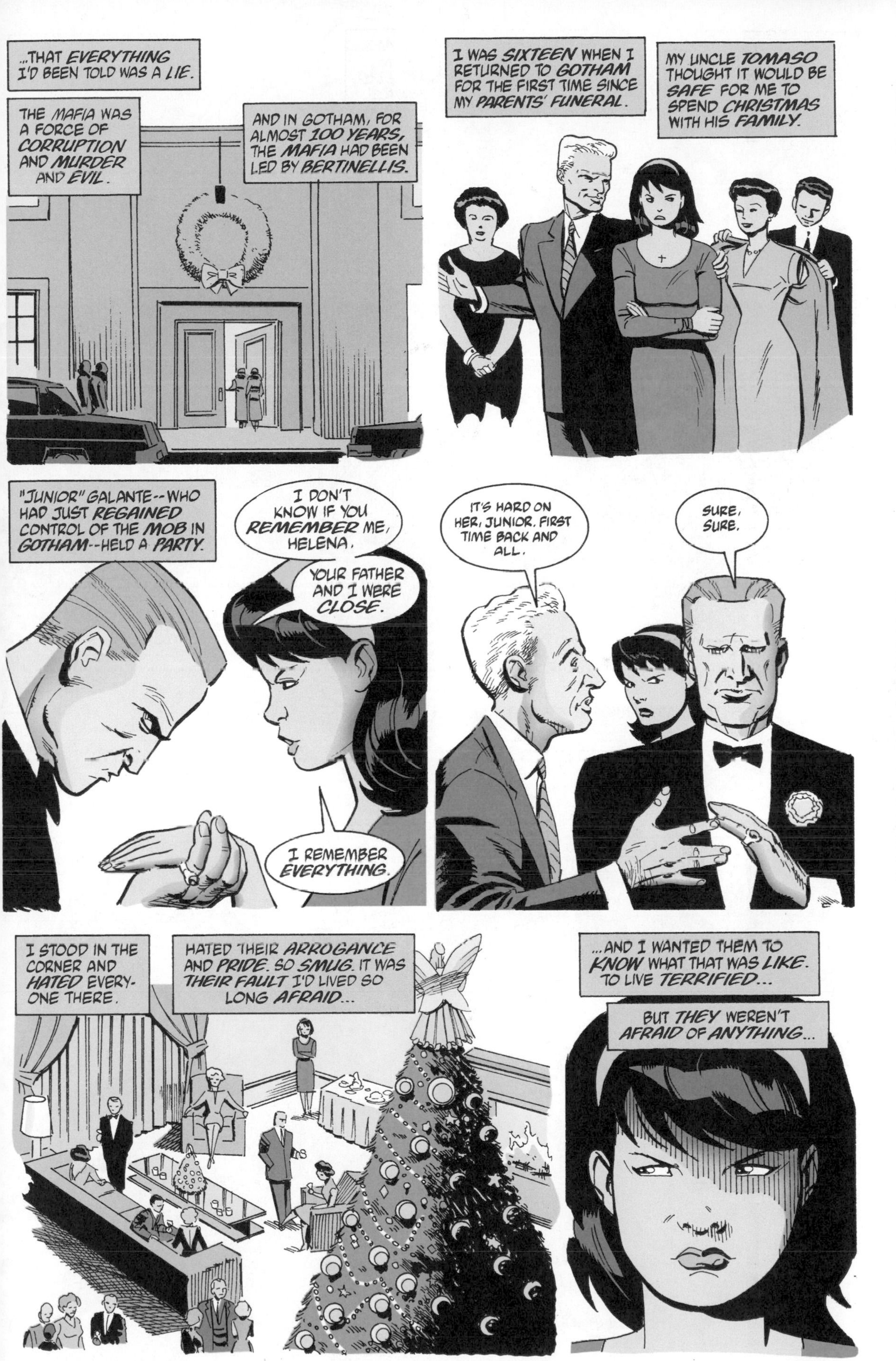
...THAT EVERYTHING I'D BEEN TOLD WAS A LIE.
THE MAFIA WAS A FORCE OF CORRUPTION AND MURDER AND EVIL.
AND IN GOTHAM, FOR ALMOST 100 YEARS, THE MAFIA HAD BEEN LED BY BERTINELLIS.
I WAS SIXTEEN WHEN I RETURNED TO GOTHAM FOR THE FIRST TIME SINCE MY PARENTS' FUNERAL.
MY UNCLE TOMASO THOUGHT IT WOULD BE SAFE FOR ME TO SPEND CHRISTMAS WITH HIS FAMILY.
"JUNIOR" GALANTE--WHO HAD JUST REGAINED CONTROL OF THE MOB IN GOTHAM--HELD A PARTY.
I DON'T KNOW IF YOU REMEMBER ME, HELENA.
YOUR FATHER AND I WERE CLOSE.
I REMEMBER EVERYTHING.
IT'S HARD ON HER, JUNIOR. FIRST TIME BACK AND ALL.
SURE, SURE.
I STOOD IN THE CORNER AND HATED EVERY-ONE THERE.
HATED THEIR ARROGANCE AND PRIDE. SO SMUG. IT WAS THEIR FAULT I'D LIVED SO LONG AFRAID...
...AND I WANTED THEM TO KNOW WHAT THAT WAS LIKE. TO LIVE TERRIFIED...
BUT THEY WEREN'T AFRAID OF ANYTHING...

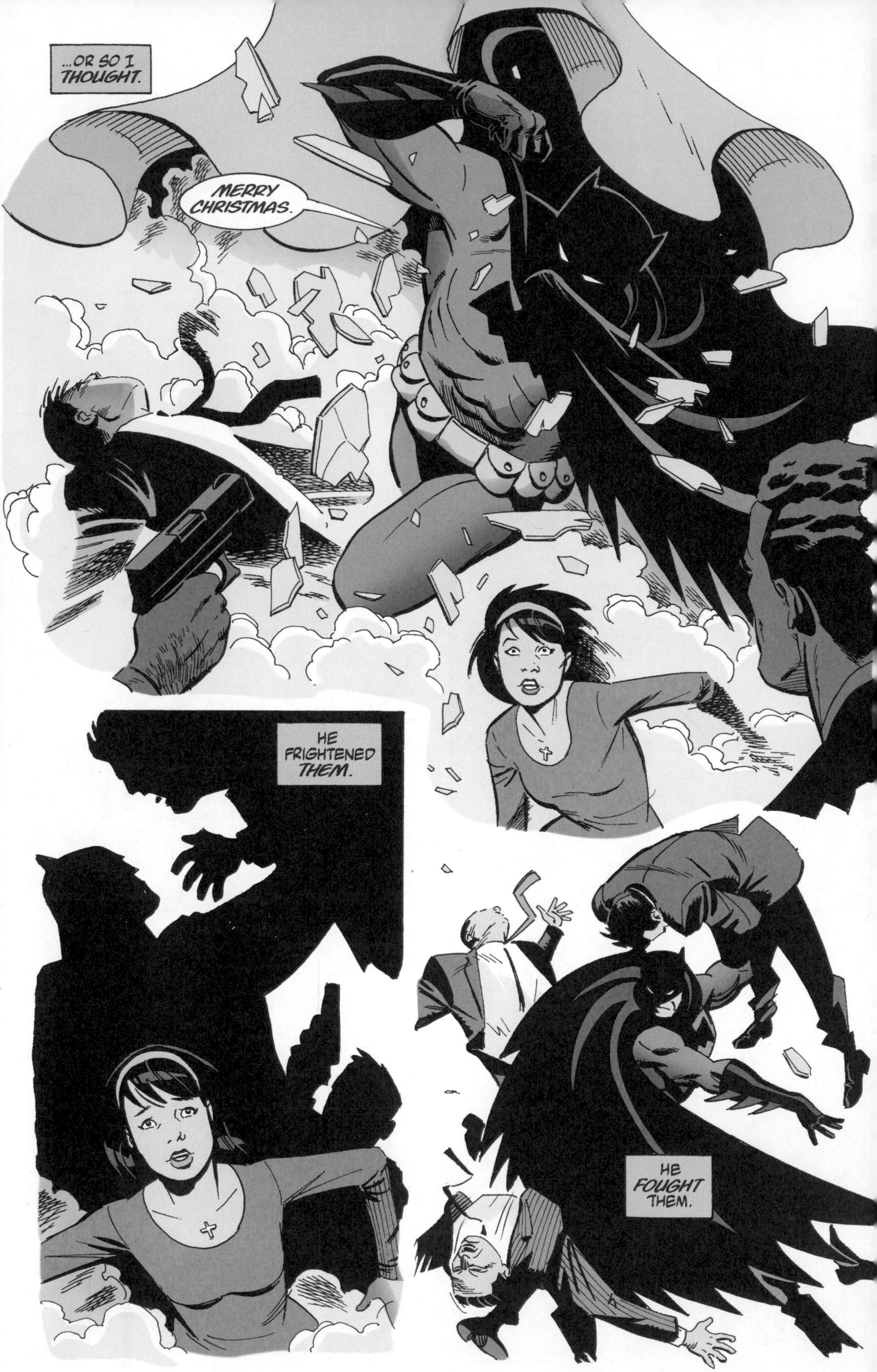
...OR SO I THOUGHT.
MERRY CHRISTMAS.
HE FRIGHTENED THEM.
HE FOUGHT THEM.

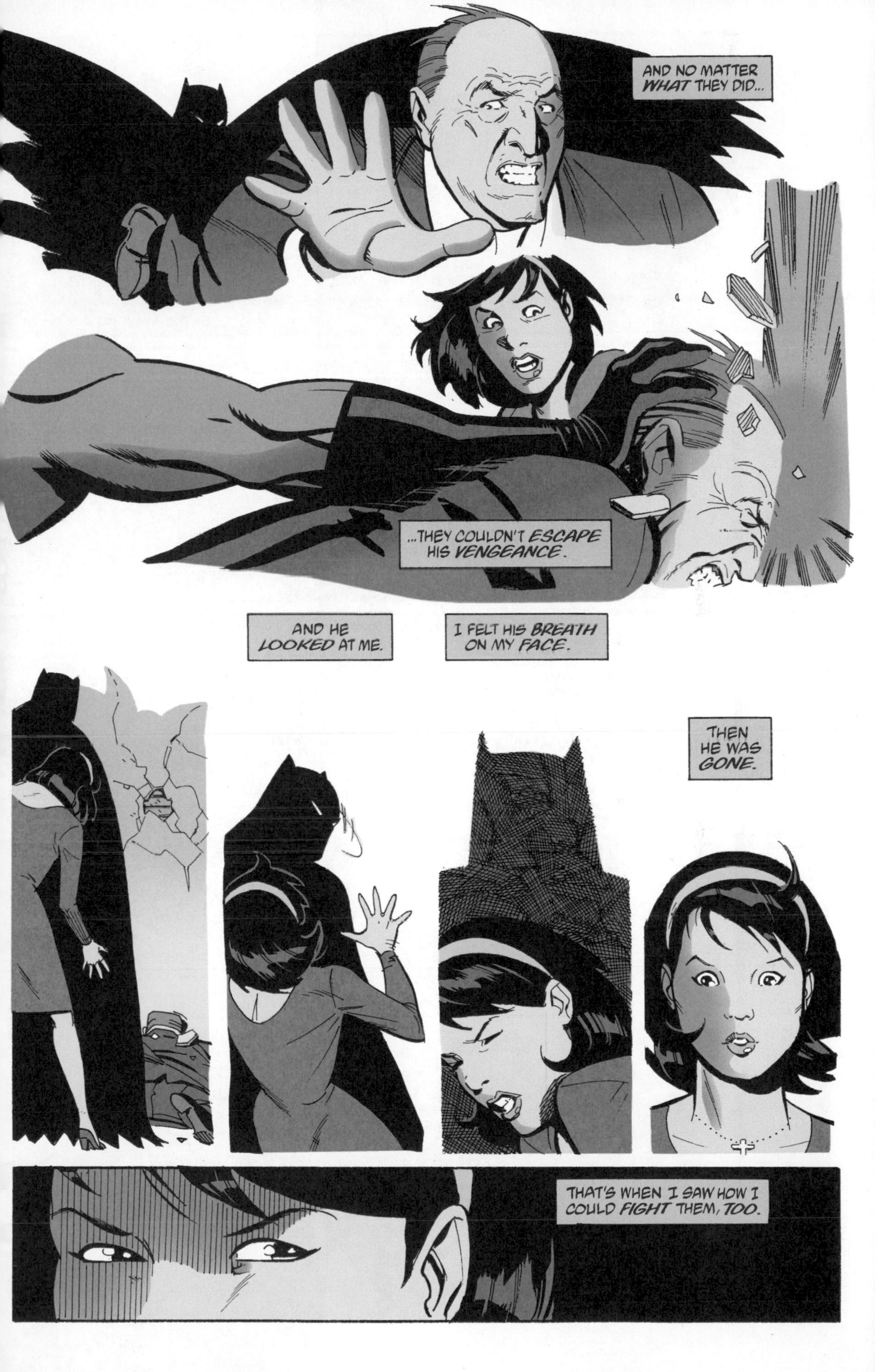
AND NO MATTER WHAT THEY DID...
...THEY COULDN'T ESCAPE HIS VENGEANCE.
AND HE LOOKED AT ME.
I FELT HIS BREATH ON MY FACE.
THEN HE WAS GONE.
THAT'S WHEN I SAW HOW I COULD FIGHT THEM, TOO.

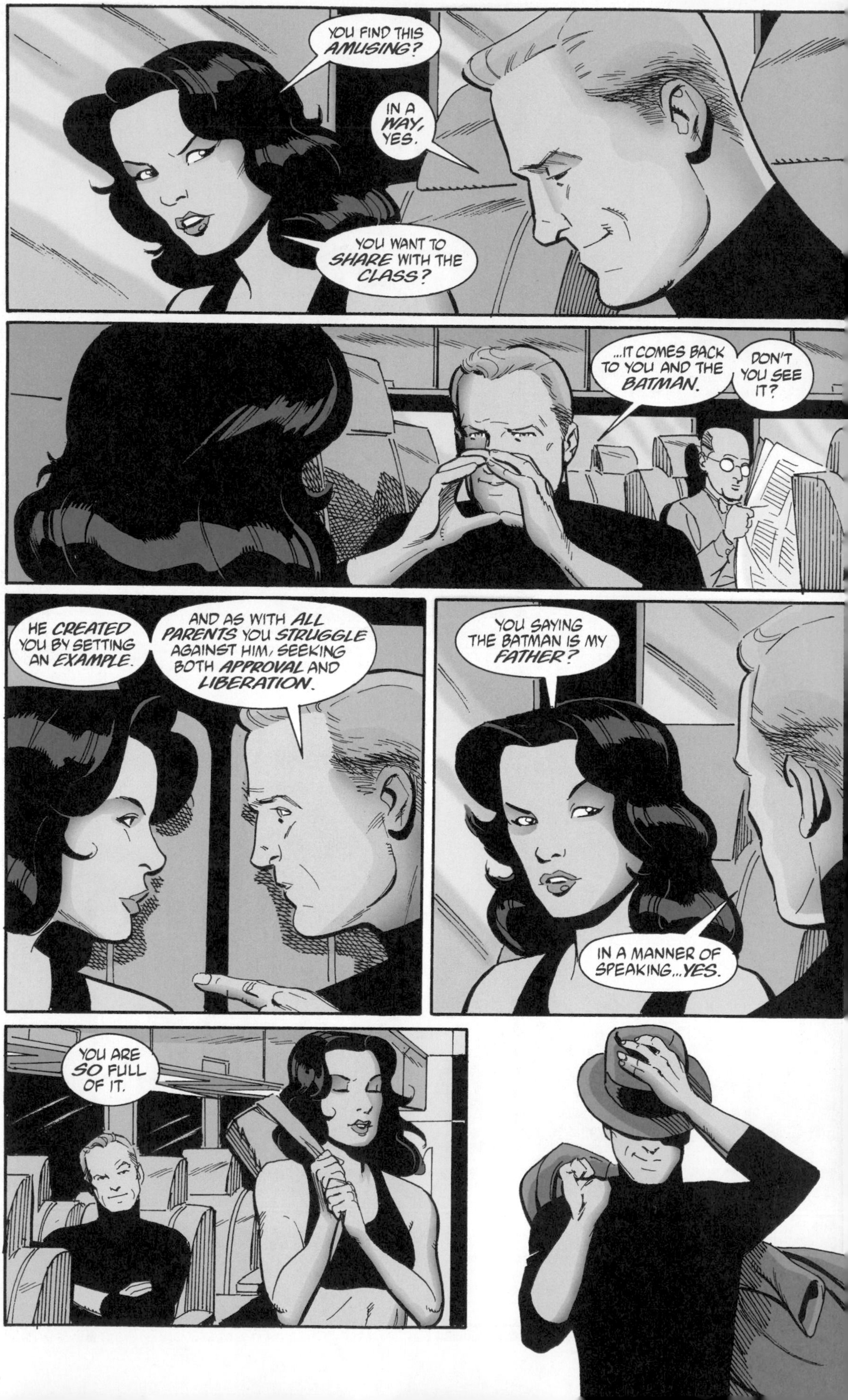
YOU FIND THIS AMUSING?
IN A WAY, YES.
YOU WANT TO SHARE WITH THE CLASS?
...IT COMES BACK TO YOU AND THE BATMAN.
DON'T YOU SEE IT?
HE CREATED YOU BY SETTING AN EXAMPLE.
AND AS WITH ALL PARENTS YOU STRUGGLE AGAINST HIM, SEEKING BOTH APPROVAL AND LIBERATION.
YOU SAYING THE BATMAN IS MY FATHER?
IN A MANNER OF SPEAKING...YES.
YOU ARE SO FULL OF IT.

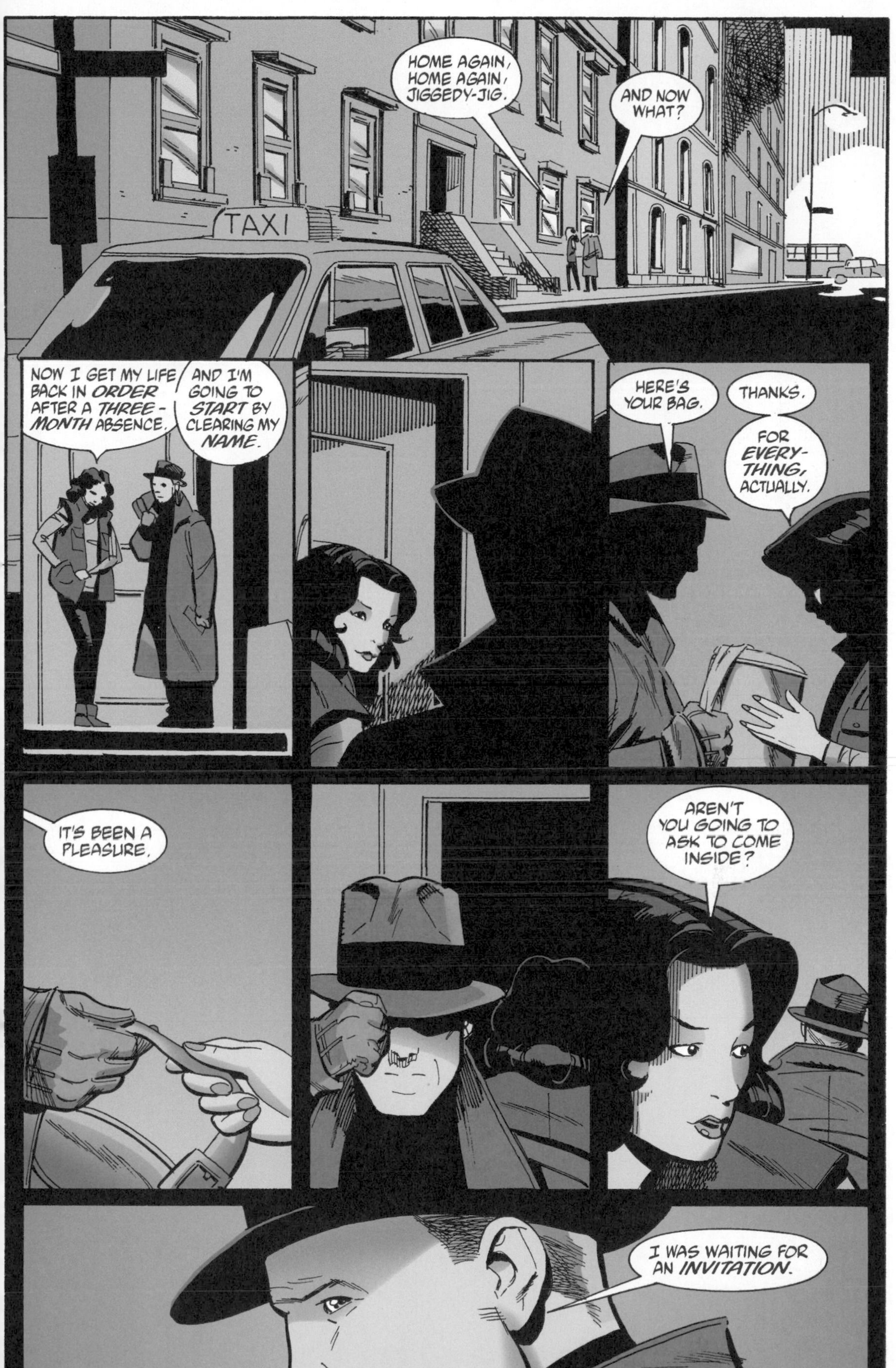

TAXI
HOME AGAIN, HOME AGAIN, JIGGEDY-JIG.
AND NOW WHAT?
NOW I GET MY LIFE BACK IN *ORDER* AFTER A *THREE-MONTH* ABSENCE.
AND I'M GOING TO *START* BY CLEARING MY *NAME*.
HERE'S YOUR BAG.
THANKS.
FOR *EVERYTHING*, ACTUALLY.
IT'S BEEN A PLEASURE.
AREN'T YOU GOING TO ASK TO COME INSIDE?
I WAS WAITING FOR AN *INVITATION*.

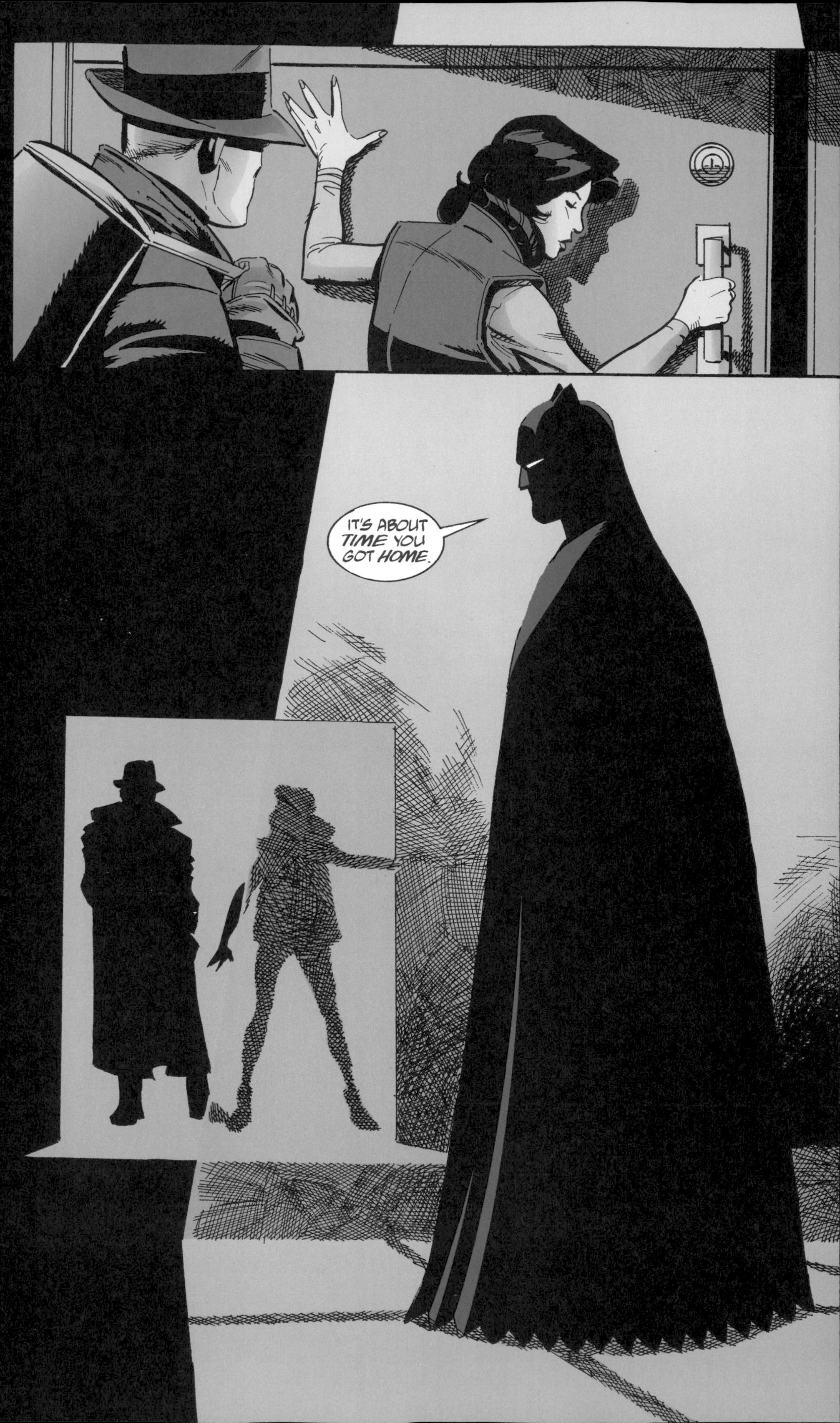
IT'S ABOUT TIME YOU GOT HOME.

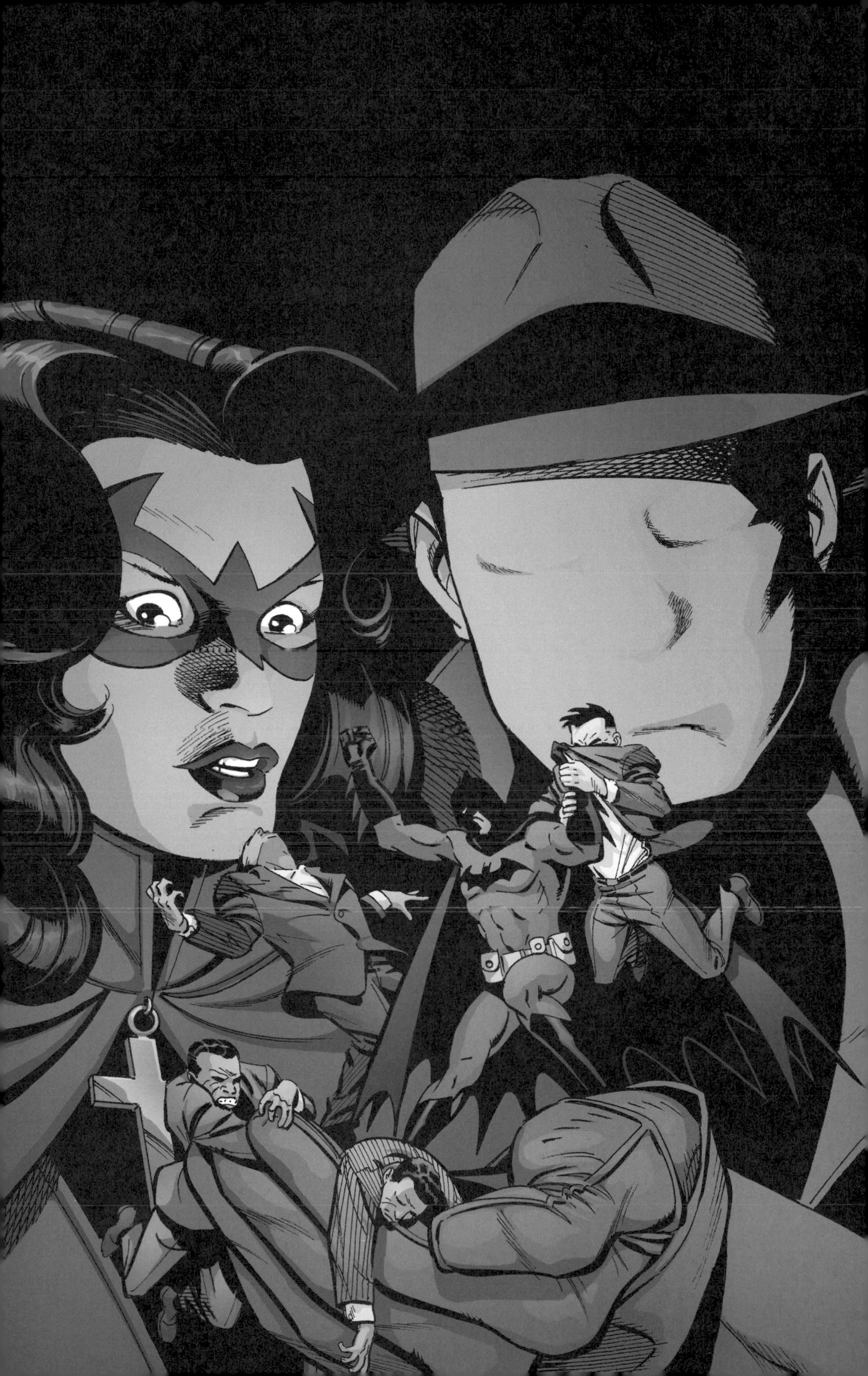

I'VE BEEN *GONE* FROM GOTHAM FOR *THREE MONTHS*.

I LEFT IN A *HURRY* BECAUSE I WAS WANTED FOR *MURDER*.

FIGURED I'D HAVE A LOT TO DEAL WITH WHEN I GOT BACK HOME--

--CLEANING OUT THE FRIDGE, PAYING OVER-DUE BILLS, THINGS LIKE THAT--

WHERE HAVE YOU BEEN?

--BUT I SURE DIDN'T EXPECT *THIS*.

CRY FOR BLOOD

PART FIVE

GREG RUCKA	RICK BURCHETT	TERRY BEATTY	CLEM ROBINS	TATJANA WOOD	JAMISON	JOE ILLIDGE	DENNIS O'NEIL
WRITER	PENCILLER	INKER	LETTERER	COLORIST	SEPARATIONS	ASSOCIATE	EDITOR

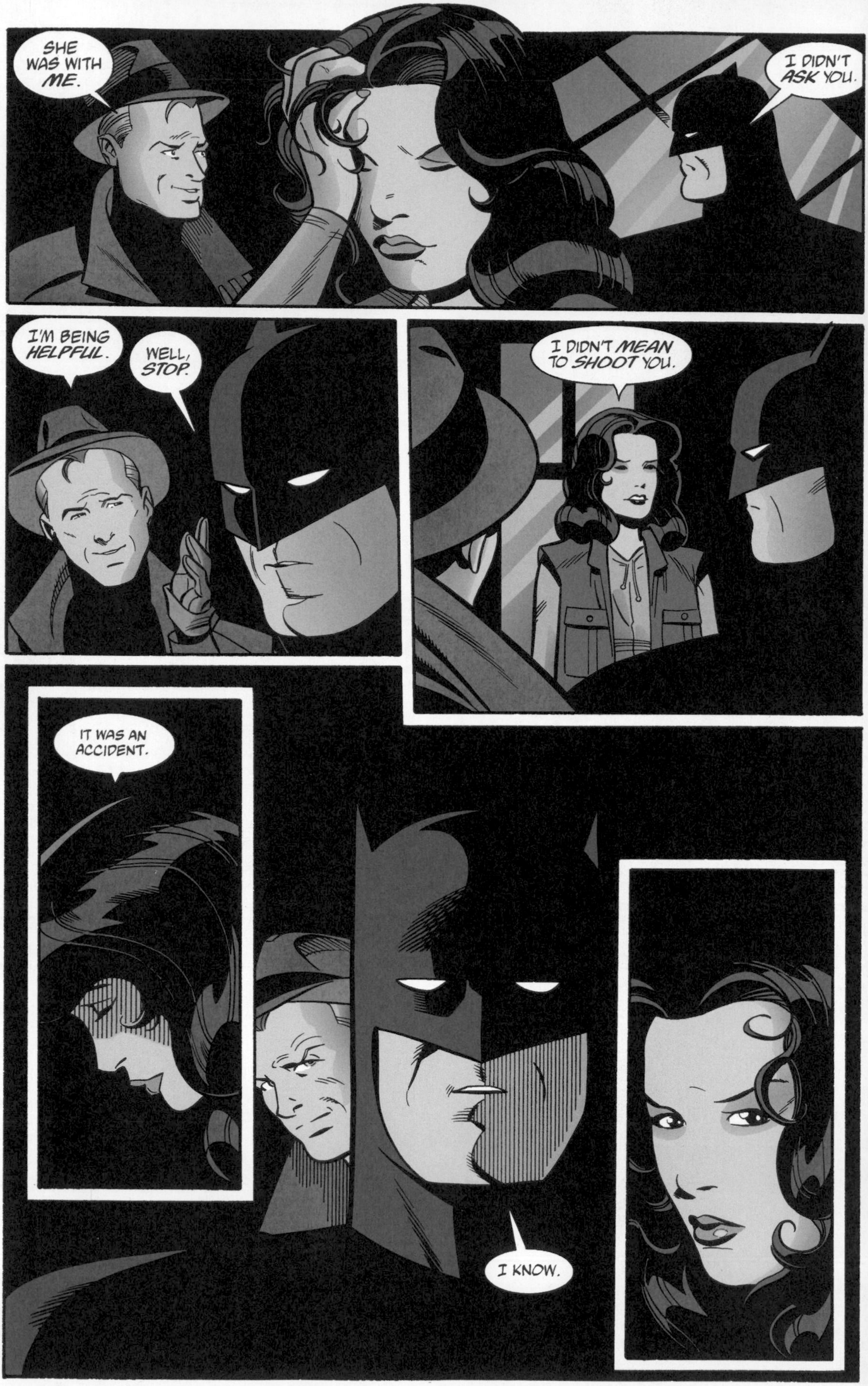
SHE WAS WITH ME.
I DIDN'T ASK YOU.
I'M BEING HELPFUL.
WELL, STOP.
I DIDN'T MEAN TO SHOOT YOU.
IT WAS AN ACCIDENT.
I KNOW.

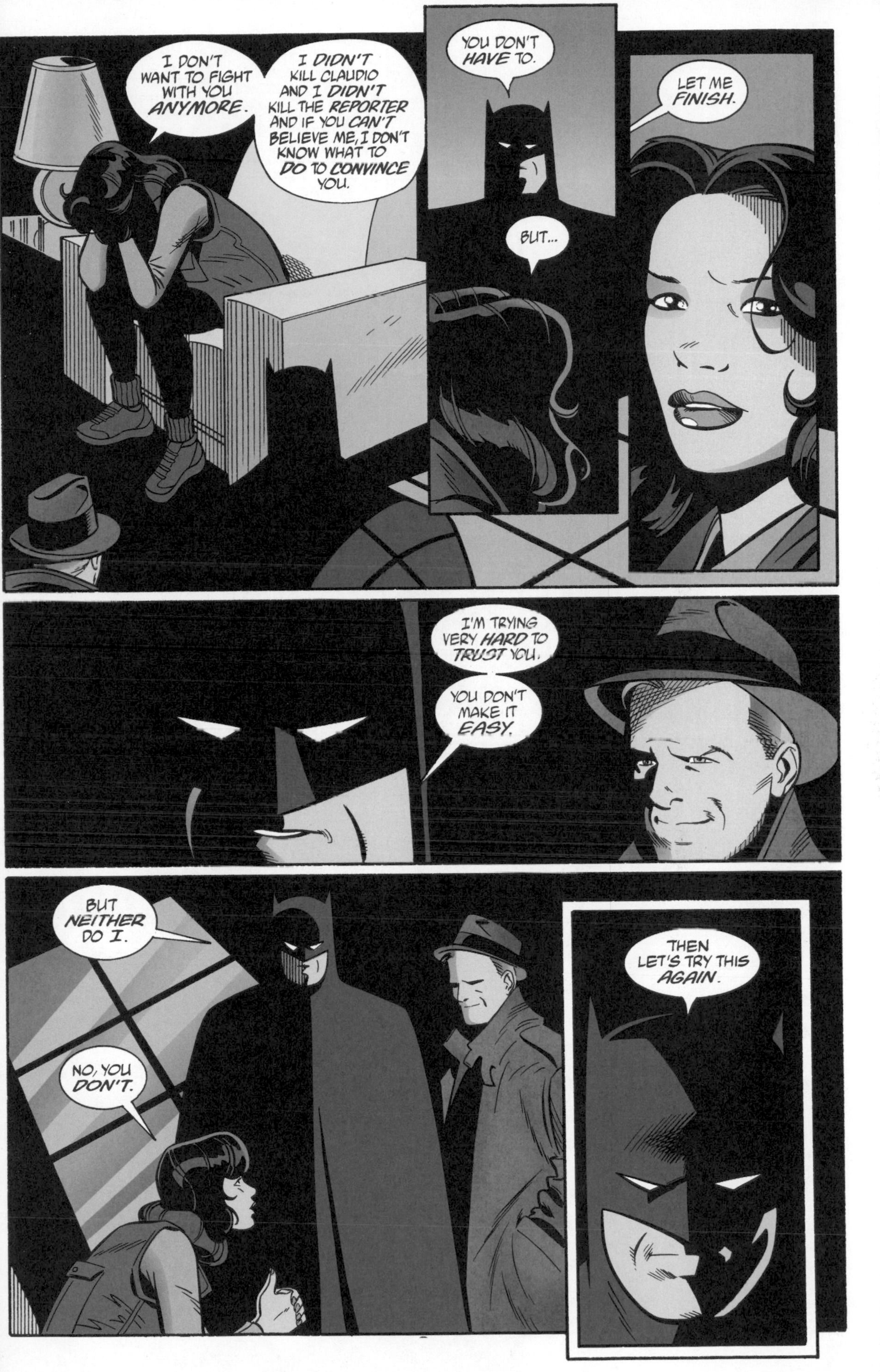
I DON'T WANT TO FIGHT WITH YOU ANYMORE.
I DIDN'T KILL CLAUDIO AND I DIDN'T KILL THE REPORTER AND IF YOU CAN'T BELIEVE ME, I DON'T KNOW WHAT TO DO TO CONVINCE YOU.
YOU DON'T HAVE TO.
BUT...
LET ME FINISH.
I'M TRYING VERY HARD TO TRUST YOU.
YOU DON'T MAKE IT EASY.
BUT NEITHER DO I.
NO, YOU DON'T.
THEN LET'S TRY THIS AGAIN.

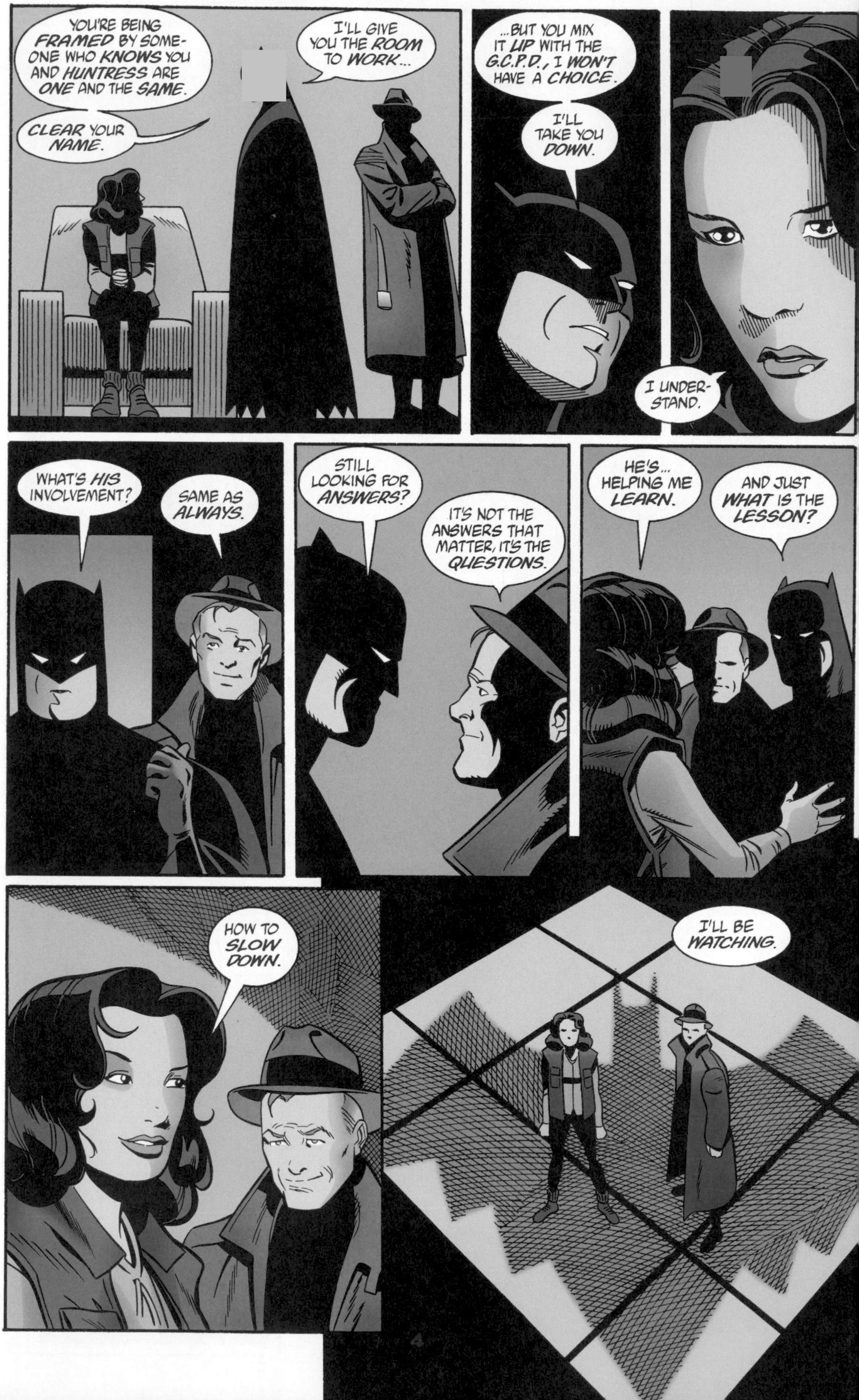
YOU'RE BEING FRAMED BY SOME-ONE WHO KNOWS YOU AND HUNTRESS ARE ONE AND THE SAME.
CLEAR YOUR NAME.
I'LL GIVE YOU THE ROOM TO WORK...
...BUT YOU MIX IT UP WITH THE G.C.P.D., I WON'T HAVE A CHOICE.
I'LL TAKE YOU DOWN.
I UNDER-STAND.
WHAT'S HIS INVOLVEMENT?
SAME AS ALWAYS.
STILL LOOKING FOR ANSWERS?
IT'S NOT THE ANSWERS THAT MATTER, IT'S THE QUESTIONS.
HE'S... HELPING ME LEARN.
AND JUST WHAT IS THE LESSON?
HOW TO SLOW DOWN.
I'LL BE WATCHING.

FAMILY'S ALWAYS EMBARRASSING, HUH?

WILL YOU STOP WITH THAT ALREADY?

I AM NOT A MEMBER OF HIS BAT-FAMILY. HE'S ALREADY GOT TWO "KIDS" AS IT IS...

...AND NIGHTWING AND I--

TOO MUCH INFORMATION.

OOH, DON'T WANT TO HEAR THAT PART, HUH?

ONLY IF YOU REALLY WANT TO TELL ME ABOUT IT.

NOT REALLY.

IT'S OVER AND DONE. ANYWAY...

...IT WAS A MISTAKE...

UH-HUH.

...BAD FOR BOTH OF US...

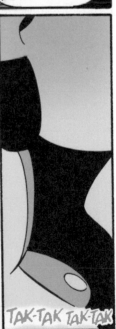

TAK-TAK TAK-TAK

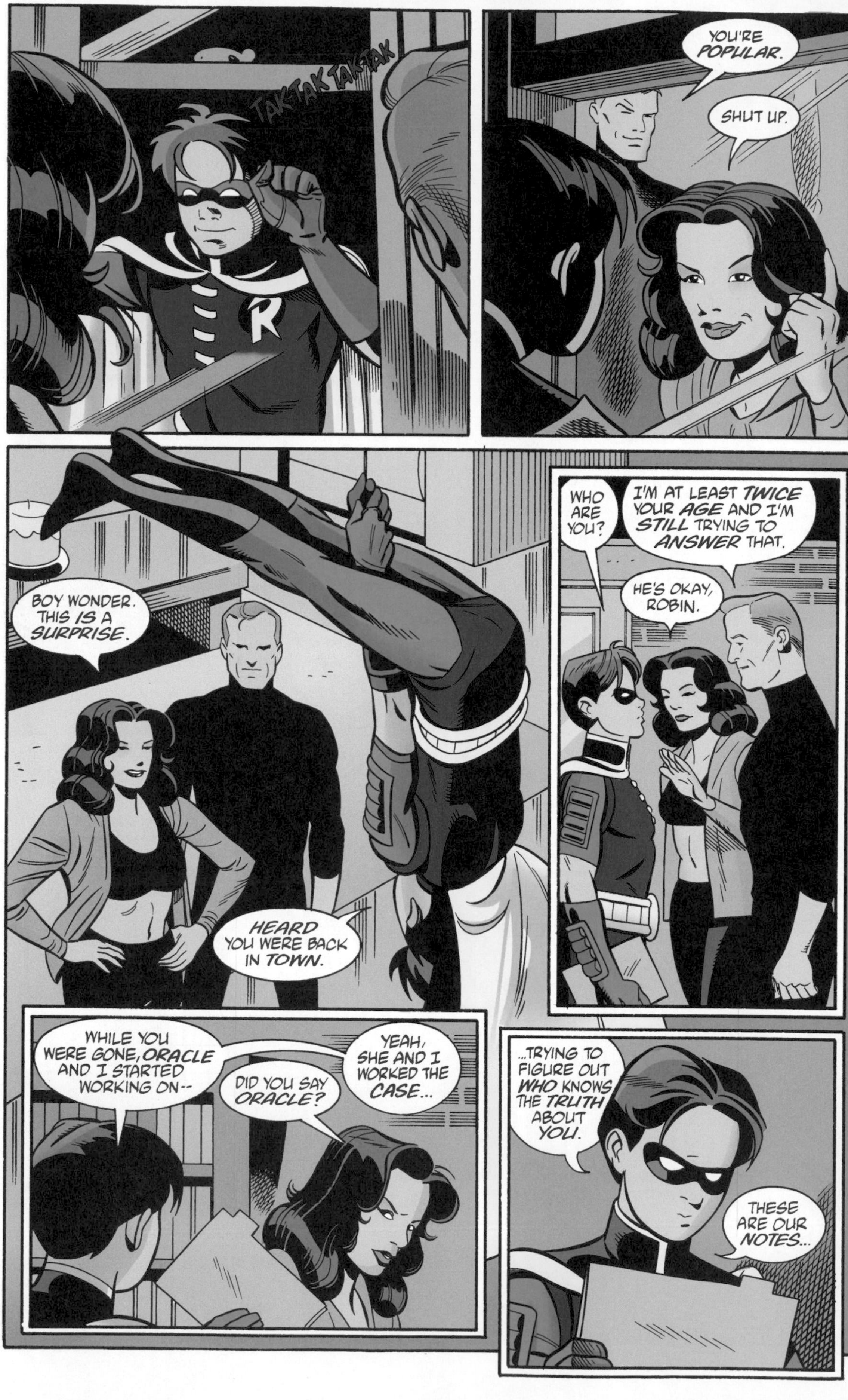
TAKTAK TAKTAK
YOU'RE POPULAR.
SHUT UP.
BOY WONDER. THIS IS A SURPRISE.
HEARD YOU WERE BACK IN TOWN.
WHO ARE YOU?
I'M AT LEAST TWICE YOUR AGE AND I'M STILL TRYING TO ANSWER THAT.
HE'S OKAY, ROBIN.
WHILE YOU WERE GONE, ORACLE AND I STARTED WORKING ON--
DID YOU SAY ORACLE?
YEAH, SHE AND I WORKED THE CASE...
...TRYING TO FIGURE OUT WHO KNOWS THE TRUTH ABOUT YOU.
THESE ARE OUR NOTES...

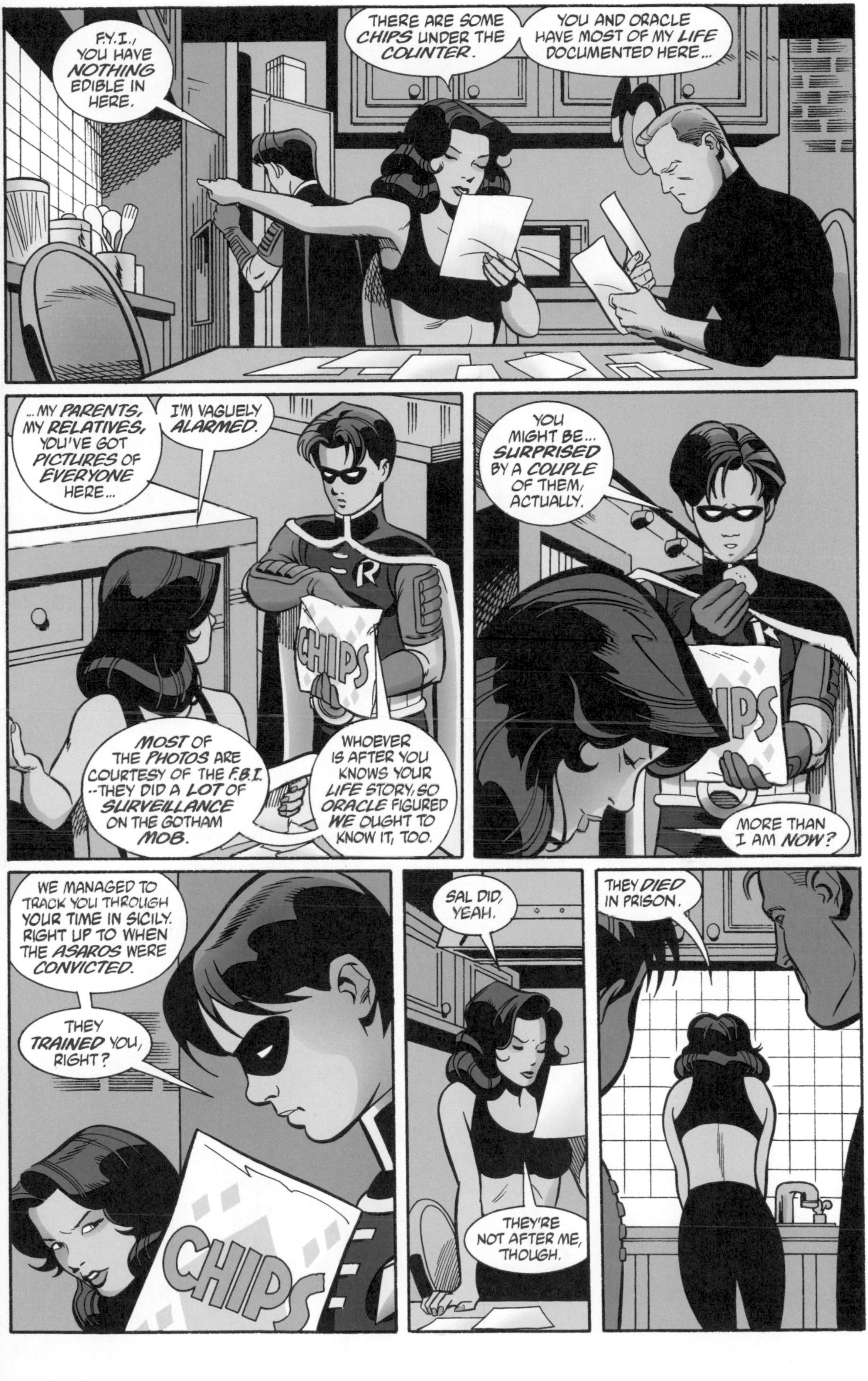
F.Y.I., YOU HAVE NOTHING EDIBLE IN HERE.
THERE ARE SOME CHIPS UNDER THE COUNTER.
YOU AND ORACLE HAVE MOST OF MY LIFE DOCUMENTED HERE...
...MY PARENTS, MY RELATIVES, YOU'VE GOT PICTURES OF EVERYONE HERE...
I'M VAGUELY ALARMED.
MOST OF THE PHOTOS ARE COURTESY OF THE F.B.I. --THEY DID A LOT OF SURVEILLANCE ON THE GOTHAM MOB.
WHOEVER IS AFTER YOU KNOWS YOUR LIFE STORY, SO ORACLE FIGURED WE OUGHT TO KNOW IT, TOO.
YOU MIGHT BE... SURPRISED BY A COUPLE OF THEM, ACTUALLY.
CHIPS
MORE THAN I AM NOW?
WE MANAGED TO TRACK YOU THROUGH YOUR TIME IN SICILY. RIGHT UP TO WHEN THE ASAROS WERE CONVICTED.
THEY TRAINED YOU, RIGHT?
CHIPS
SAL DID, YEAH.
THEY'RE NOT AFTER ME, THOUGH.
THEY DIED IN PRISON.

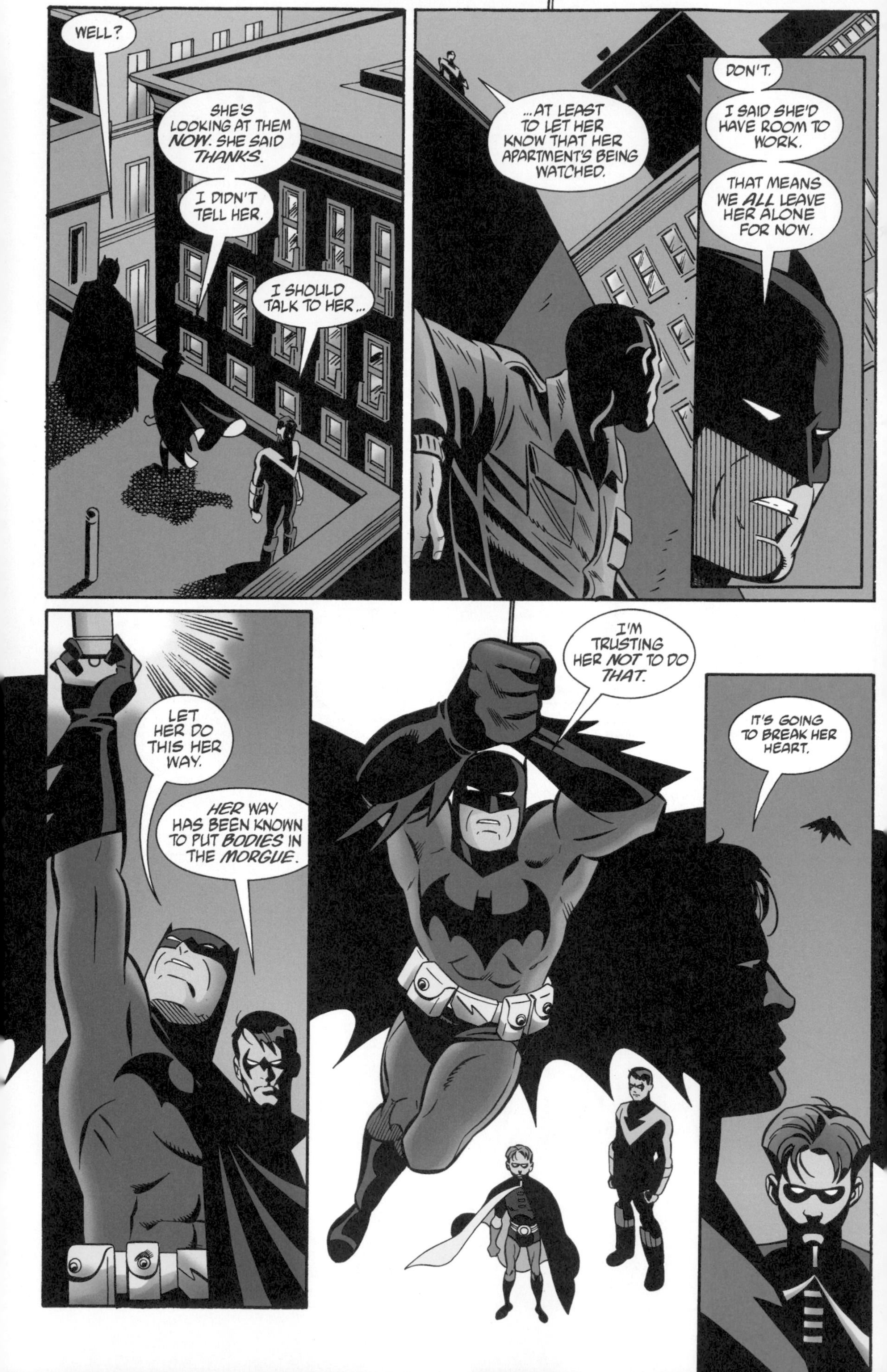
WELL?
SHE'S LOOKING AT THEM NOW. SHE SAID THANKS.
I DIDN'T TELL HER.
I SHOULD TALK TO HER...
...AT LEAST TO LET HER KNOW THAT HER APARTMENT'S BEING WATCHED.
DON'T.
I SAID SHE'D HAVE ROOM TO WORK.
THAT MEANS WE ALL LEAVE HER ALONE FOR NOW.
LET HER DO THIS HER WAY.
HER WAY HAS BEEN KNOWN TO PUT BODIES IN THE MORGUE.
I'M TRUSTING HER NOT TO DO THAT.
IT'S GOING TO BREAK HER HEART.

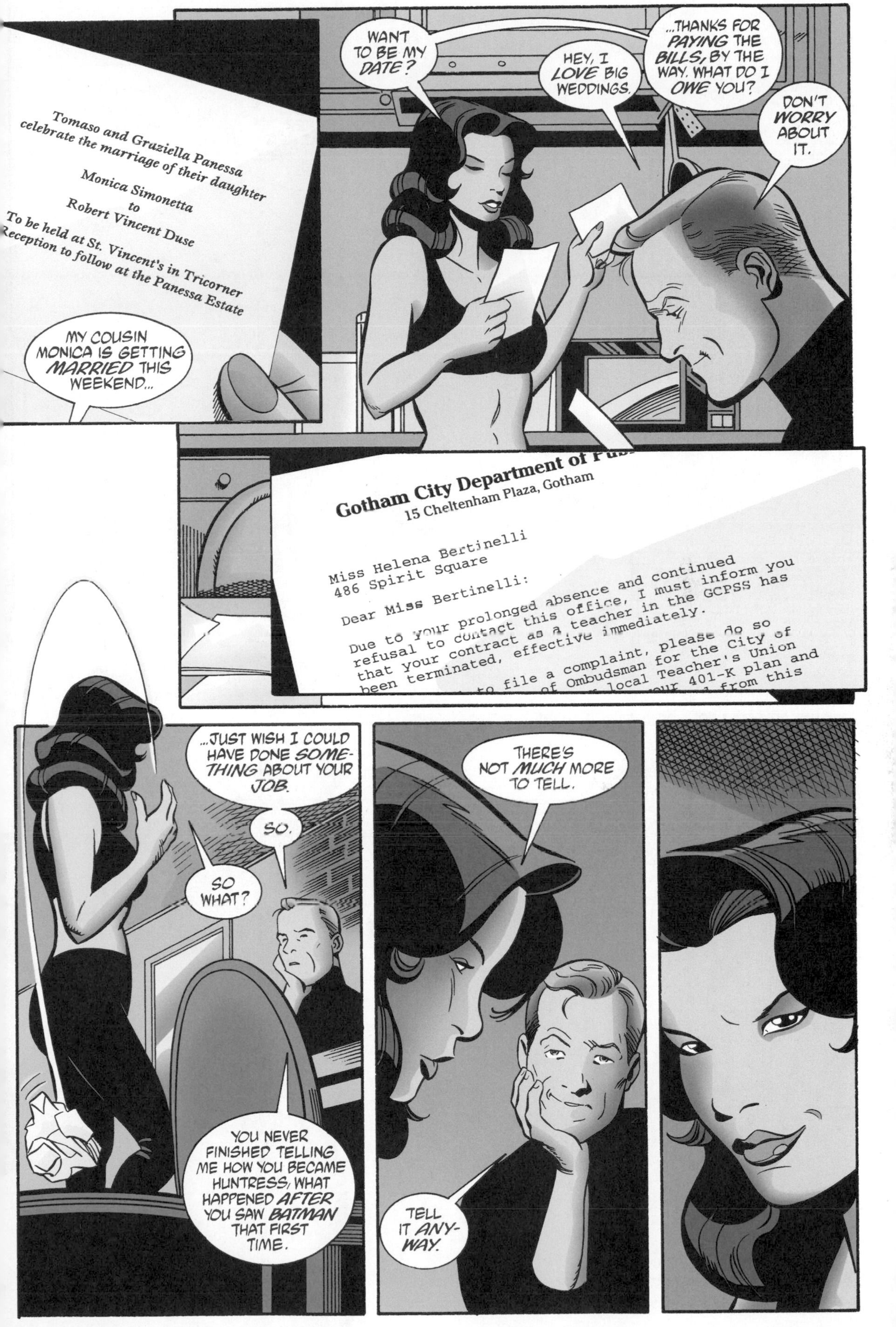
Tomaso and Graziella Panessa
celebrate the marriage of their daughter
Monica Simonetta
to
Robert Vincent Duse
To be held at St. Vincent's in Tricorner
Reception to follow at the Panessa Estate
MY COUSIN MONICA IS GETTING MARRIED THIS WEEKEND...
WANT TO BE MY DATE?
HEY, I LOVE BIG WEDDINGS.
...THANKS FOR PAYING THE BILLS, BY THE WAY. WHAT DO I OWE YOU?
DON'T WORRY ABOUT IT.
Gotham City Department of Pu
15 Cheltenham Plaza, Gotham
Miss Helena Bertinelli
486 Spirit Square
Dear Miss Bertinelli:
Due to your prolonged absence and continued
refusal to contact this office, I must inform you
that your contract as a teacher in the GCPSS has
been terminated, effective immediately.
to file a complaint, please do so
of Ombudsman for the City of
local Teacher's Union
your 401-K plan and
from this
...JUST WISH I COULD HAVE DONE SOMETHING ABOUT YOUR JOB.
SO.
SO WHAT?
YOU NEVER FINISHED TELLING ME HOW YOU BECAME HUNTRESS, WHAT HAPPENED AFTER YOU SAW BATMAN THAT FIRST TIME.
THERE'S NOT MUCH MORE TO TELL.
TELL IT ANYWAY.

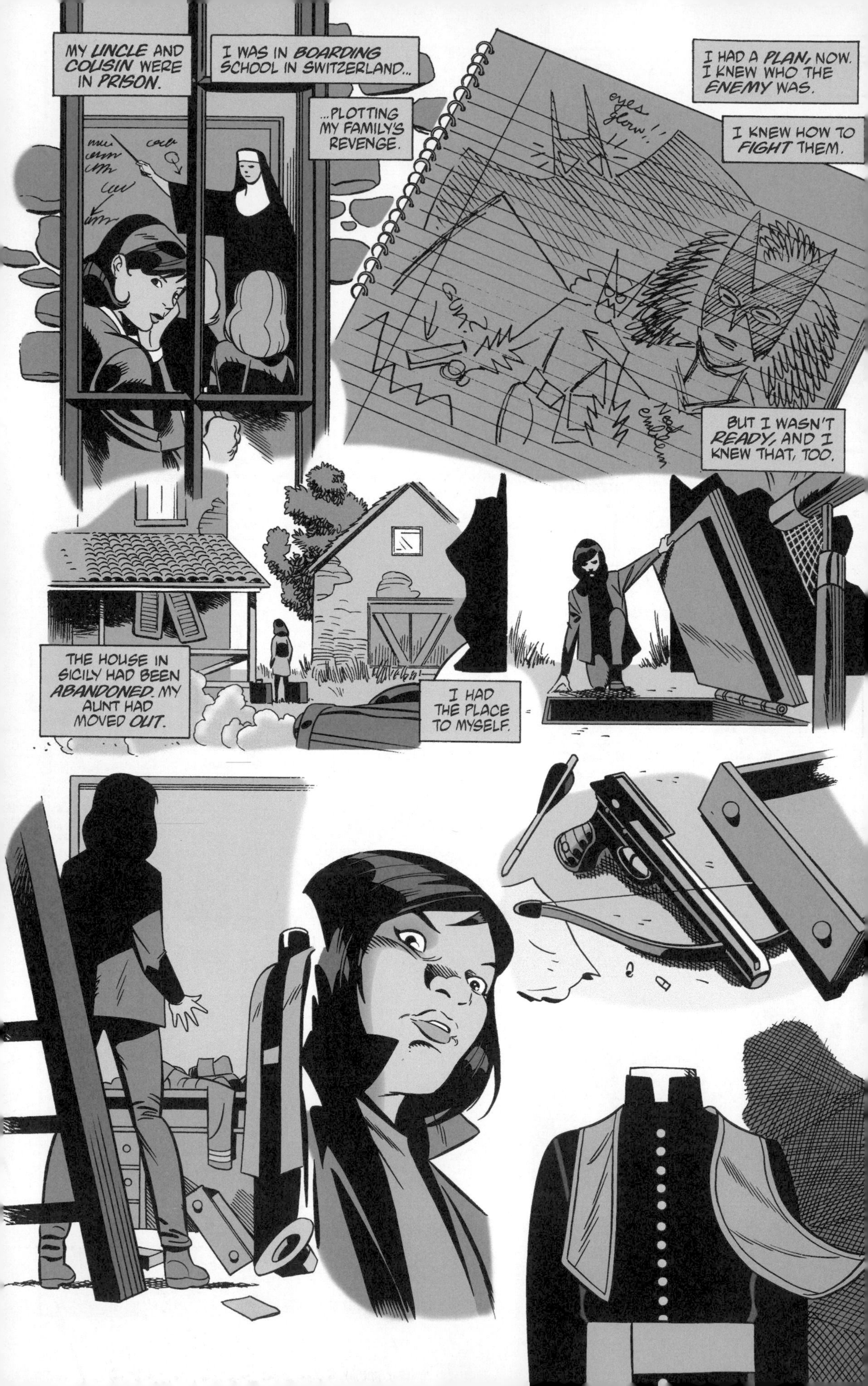
MY UNCLE AND COUSIN WERE IN PRISON.
I WAS IN BOARDING SCHOOL IN SWITZERLAND...
...PLOTTING MY FAMILY'S REVENGE.
I HAD A PLAN, NOW. I KNEW WHO THE ENEMY WAS.
eyes glow!!
I KNEW HOW TO FIGHT THEM.
BUT I WASN'T READY, AND I KNEW THAT, TOO.
THE HOUSE IN SICILY HAD BEEN ABANDONED. MY AUNT HAD MOVED OUT.
I HAD THE PLACE TO MYSELF.

I ENROLLED AT THE *UNIVERSITY* AT PALERMO.

Mandragora Organization

MANDRAGORA
Capo di tutti capi

AMERICAN
Galante (d. Bertinelli)
Boss

SICILY
Mandragora
Boss

Beretti
(Adviser)

Cassamento
Underboss
(Heroin)

Mandragora Organization

MANDRAGORA
Capo di tutti capi

AMERICAN
Galante (d. Bertinelli)
Boss

Beretti
(Adviser)

Cassamento
Underboss
(Heroin)

Panessa
Underboss
(Sicilian Connection)

Inzerillo
Underboss
(Rackets)

Soldiers | Soldiers

Soldiers | Soldiers

THEY HAD A WHOLE *DEPARTMENT* DEVOTED TO *MAFIA STUDIES.*

BUT I HAD MY *OWN* LESSON PLAN.

ENTACLES:
The Worldwide
Reach of the
Sicilian Mafia
Jason Devaulx

CAPO:
The Truth
About
Cosa
Nostra

WISEGUY
BY
VANCE
FARROW

Economic
Impact of
Organized
Crime
Euro

Gotham Gazette

Terrify them

BATMAN:
MAN OR
MYTH?

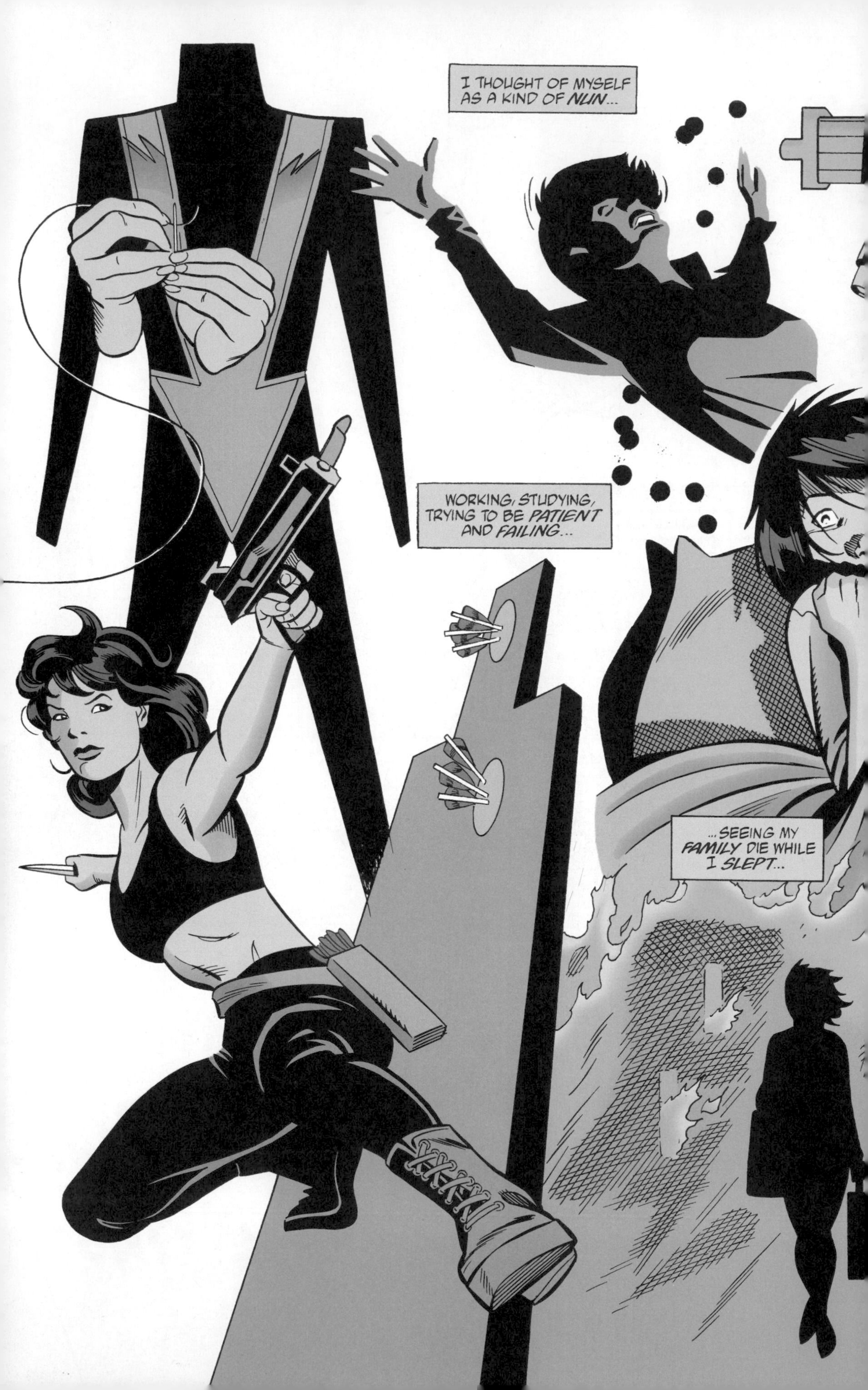
I THOUGHT OF MYSELF AS A KIND OF *NUN*...
WORKING, STUDYING, TRYING TO BE *PATIENT* AND *FAILING*...
...SEEING MY *FAMILY* DIE WHILE I *SLEPT*...

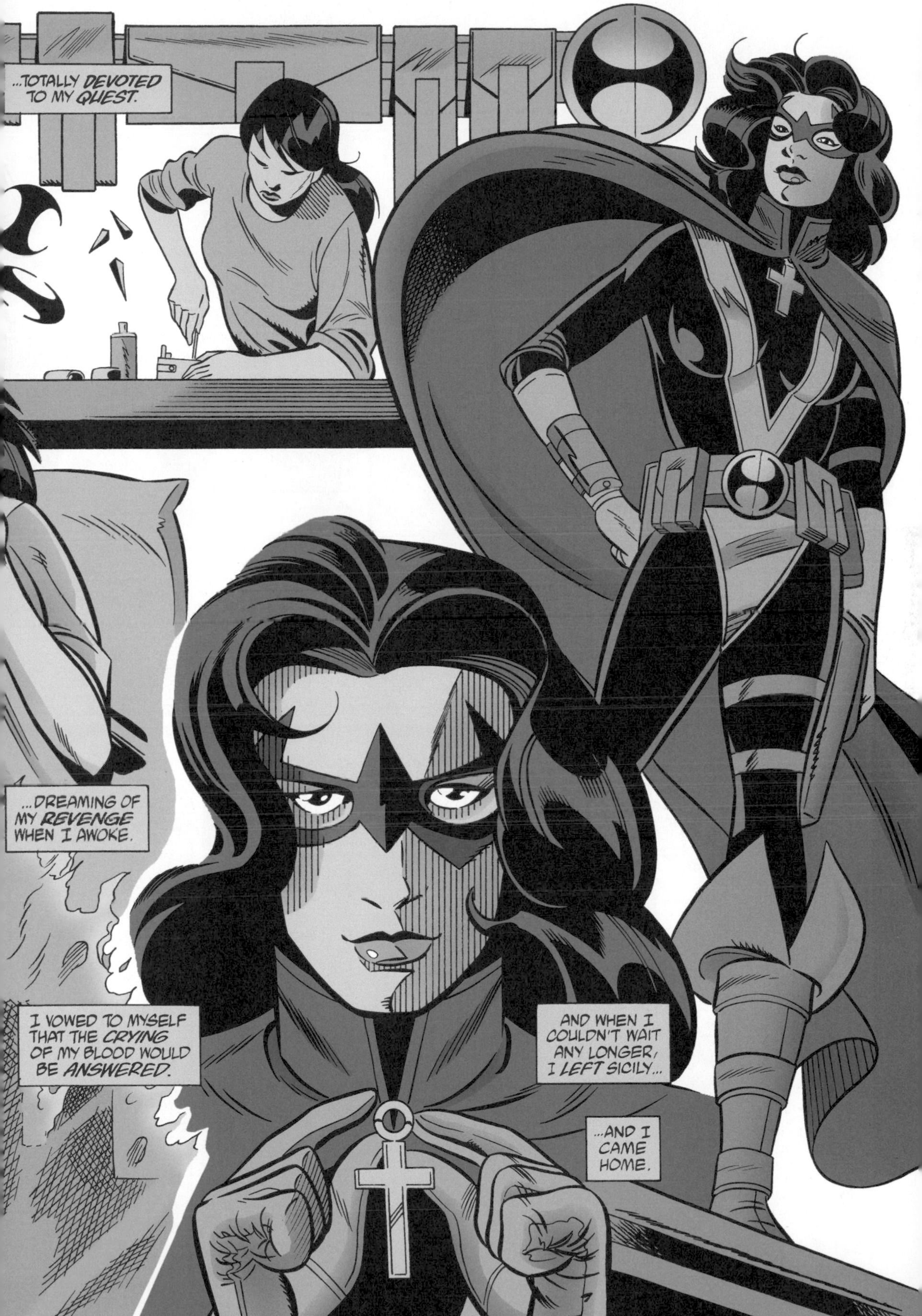
...TOTALLY DEVOTED TO MY QUEST.
...DREAMING OF MY REVENGE WHEN I AWOKE.
I VOWED TO MYSELF THAT THE CRYING OF MY BLOOD WOULD BE ANSWERED.
AND WHEN I COULDN'T WAIT ANY LONGER, I LEFT SICILY...
...AND I CAME HOME.

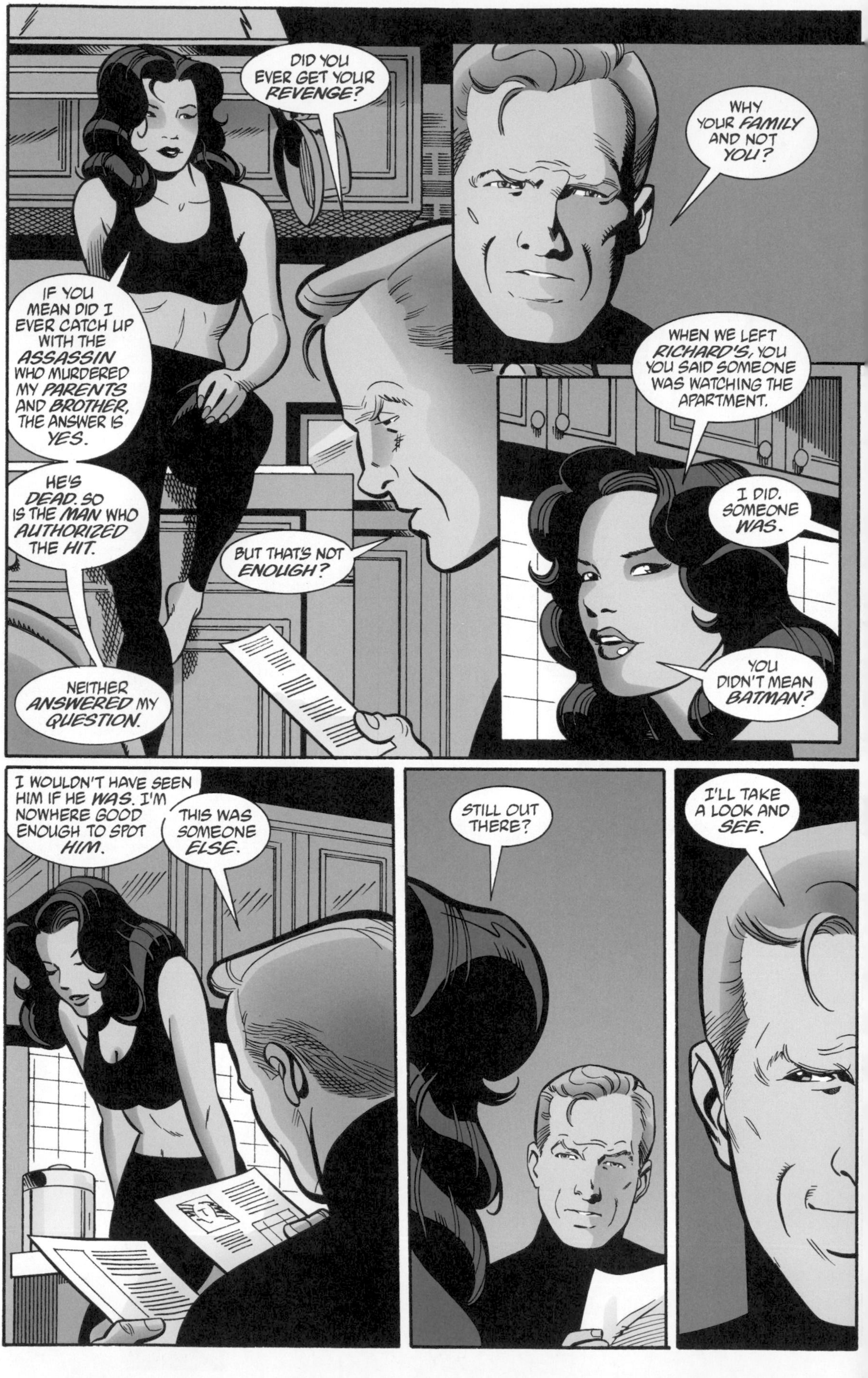
DID YOU EVER GET YOUR REVENGE?
WHY YOUR FAMILY AND NOT YOU?
IF YOU MEAN DID I EVER CATCH UP WITH THE ASSASSIN WHO MURDERED MY PARENTS AND BROTHER, THE ANSWER IS YES.
HE'S DEAD. SO IS THE MAN WHO AUTHORIZED THE HIT.
BUT THAT'S NOT ENOUGH?
NEITHER ANSWERED MY QUESTION.
WHEN WE LEFT RICHARD'S, YOU YOU SAID SOMEONE WAS WATCHING THE APARTMENT.
I DID. SOMEONE WAS.
YOU DIDN'T MEAN BATMAN?
I WOULDN'T HAVE SEEN HIM IF HE WAS. I'M NOWHERE GOOD ENOUGH TO SPOT HIM.
THIS WAS SOMEONE ELSE.
STILL OUT THERE?
I'LL TAKE A LOOK AND SEE.

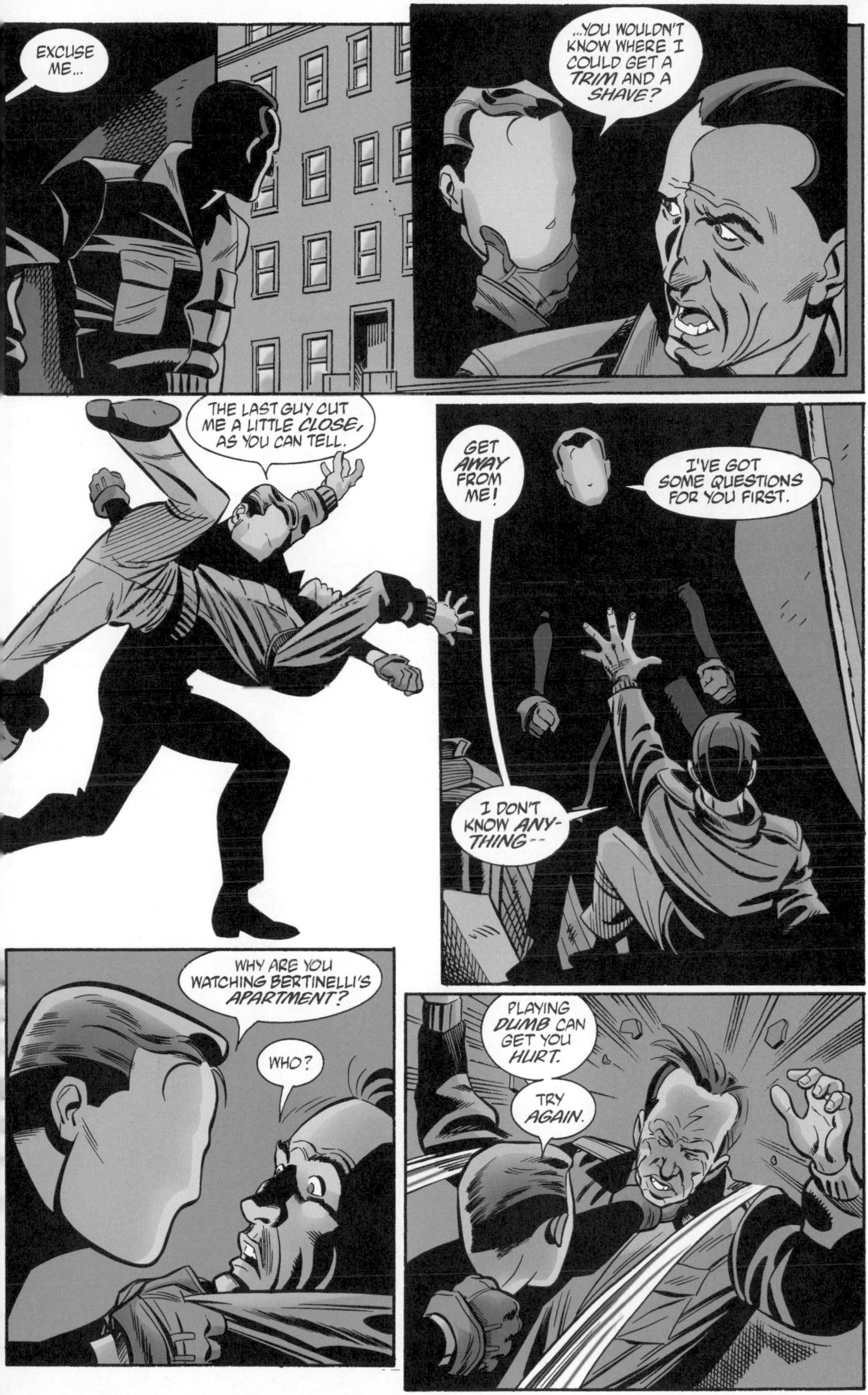
EXCUSE ME...
...YOU WOULDN'T KNOW WHERE I COULD GET A TRIM AND A SHAVE?
THE LAST GUY CUT ME A LITTLE CLOSE, AS YOU CAN TELL.
GET AWAY FROM ME!
I'VE GOT SOME QUESTIONS FOR YOU FIRST.
I DON'T KNOW ANYTHING--
WHY ARE YOU WATCHING BERTINELLI'S APARTMENT?
WHO?
PLAYING DUMB CAN GET YOU HURT.
TRY AGAIN.

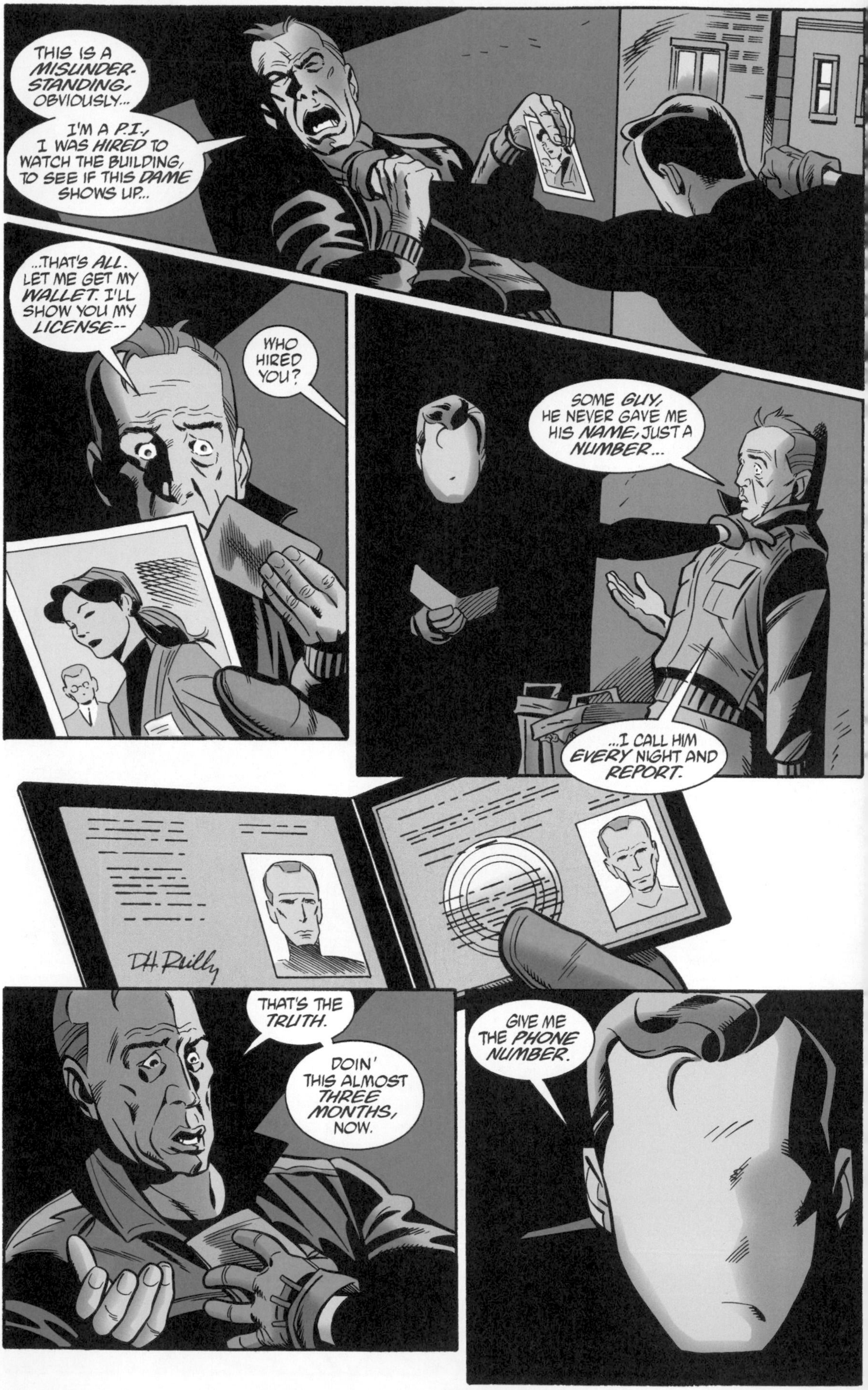
THIS IS A MISUNDER-STANDING, OBVIOUSLY...
I'M A P.I., I WAS HIRED TO WATCH THE BUILDING, TO SEE IF THIS DAME SHOWS UP...
...THAT'S ALL. LET ME GET MY WALLET. I'LL SHOW YOU MY LICENSE--
WHO HIRED YOU?
SOME GUY, HE NEVER GAVE ME HIS NAME, JUST A NUMBER...
...I CALL HIM EVERY NIGHT AND REPORT.
DH Reilly
THAT'S THE TRUTH.
DOIN' THIS ALMOST THREE MONTHS, NOW.
GIVE ME THE PHONE NUMBER.

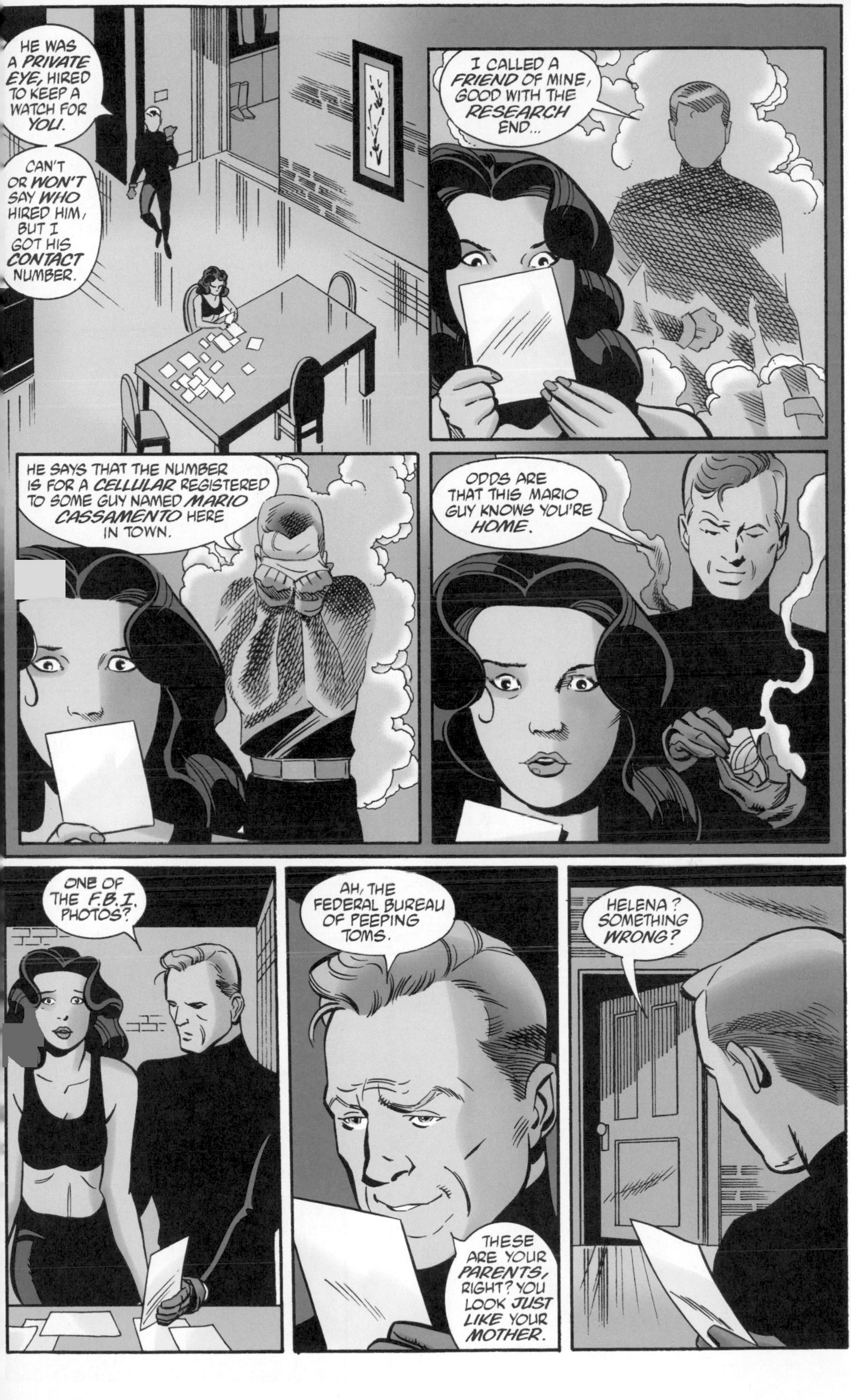
HE WAS A PRIVATE EYE, HIRED TO KEEP A WATCH FOR YOU.
CAN'T OR WON'T SAY WHO HIRED HIM, BUT I GOT HIS CONTACT NUMBER.
I CALLED A FRIEND OF MINE, GOOD WITH THE RESEARCH END...
HE SAYS THAT THE NUMBER IS FOR A CELLULAR REGISTERED TO SOME GUY NAMED MARIO CASSAMENTO HERE IN TOWN.
ODDS ARE THAT THIS MARIO GUY KNOWS YOU'RE HOME.
ONE OF THE F.B.I. PHOTOS?
AH, THE FEDERAL BUREAU OF PEEPING TOMS.
THESE ARE YOUR PARENTS, RIGHT? YOU LOOK JUST LIKE YOUR MOTHER.
HELENA? SOMETHING WRONG?

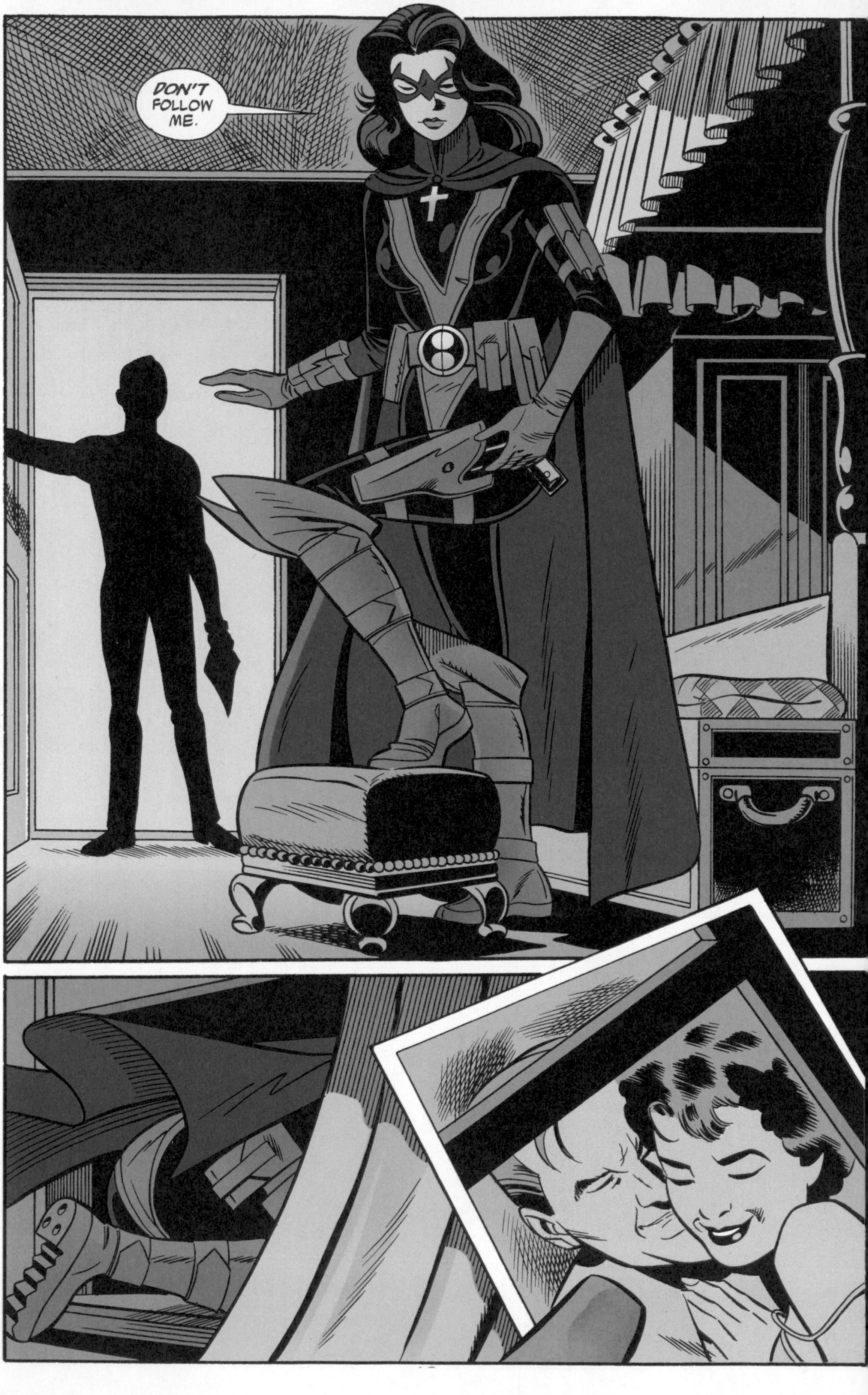
DON'T FOLLOW ME.

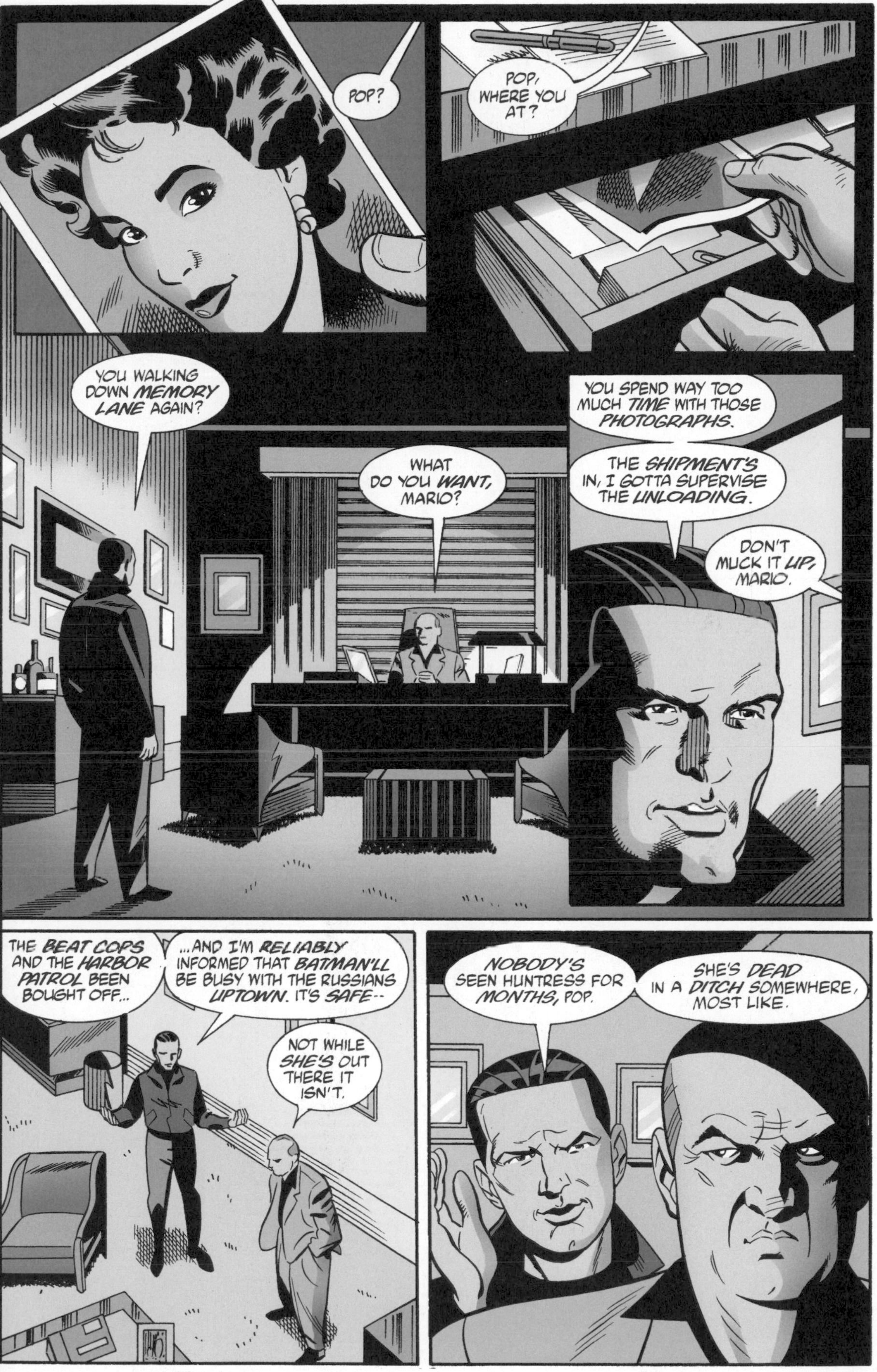
POP?
POP, WHERE YOU AT?
YOU WALKING DOWN MEMORY LANE AGAIN?
WHAT DO YOU WANT, MARIO?
YOU SPEND WAY TOO MUCH TIME WITH THOSE PHOTOGRAPHS.
THE SHIPMENT'S IN, I GOTTA SUPERVISE THE UNLOADING.
DON'T MUCK IT UP, MARIO.
THE BEAT COPS AND THE HARBOR PATROL BEEN BOUGHT OFF...
...AND I'M RELIABLY INFORMED THAT BATMAN'LL BE BUSY WITH THE RUSSIANS UPTOWN. IT'S SAFE--
NOT WHILE SHE'S OUT THERE IT ISN'T.
NOBODY'S SEEN HUNTRESS FOR MONTHS, POP.
SHE'S DEAD IN A DITCH SOMEWHERE, MOST LIKE.

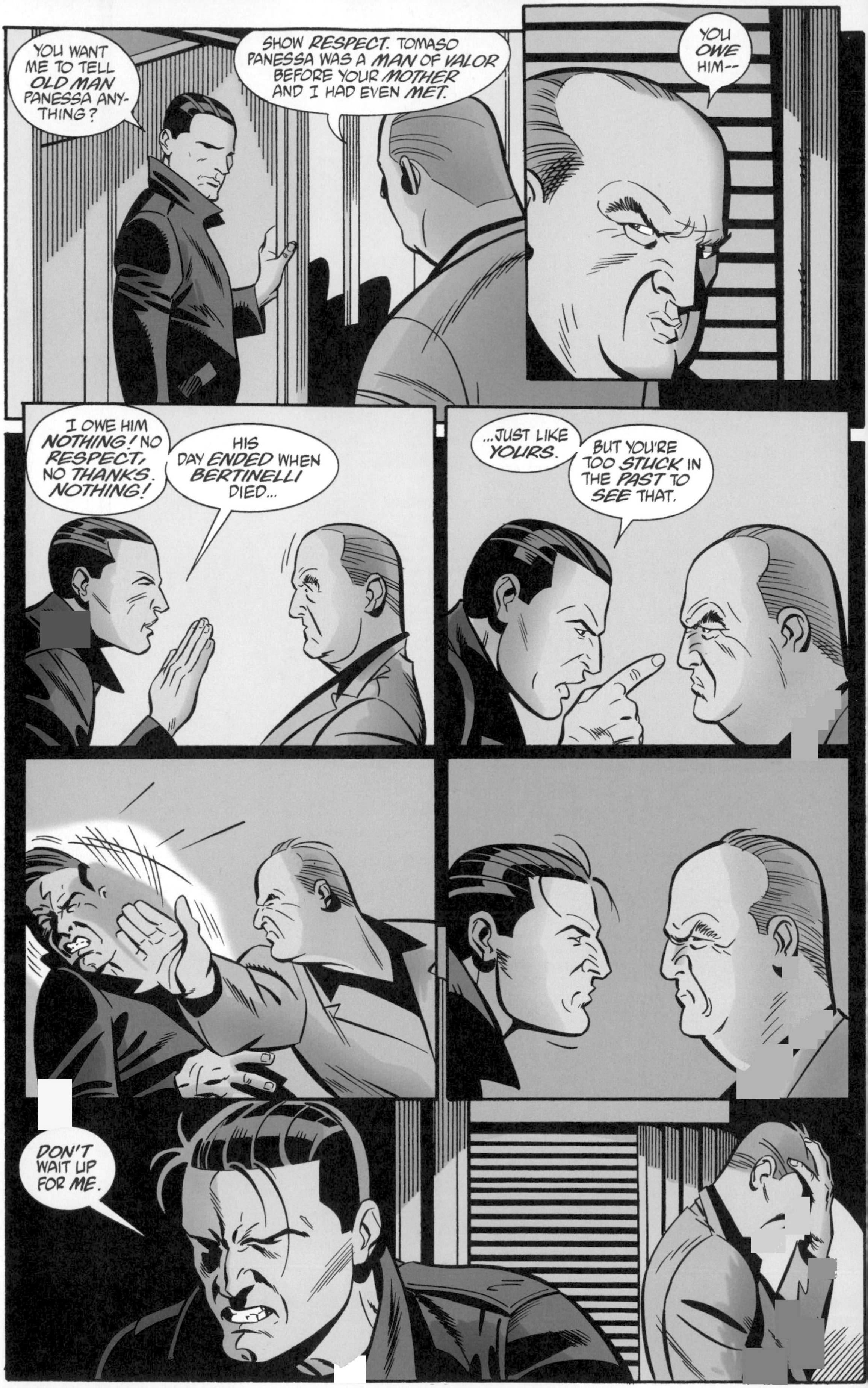
YOU WANT ME TO TELL OLD MAN PANESSA ANYTHING?
SHOW RESPECT. TOMASO PANESSA WAS A MAN OF VALOR BEFORE YOUR MOTHER AND I HAD EVEN MET.
YOU OWE HIM--
I OWE HIM NOTHING! NO RESPECT, NO THANKS. NOTHING!
HIS DAY ENDED WHEN BERTINELLI DIED...
...JUST LIKE YOURS.
BUT YOU'RE TOO STUCK IN THE PAST TO SEE THAT.
DON'T WAIT UP FOR ME.

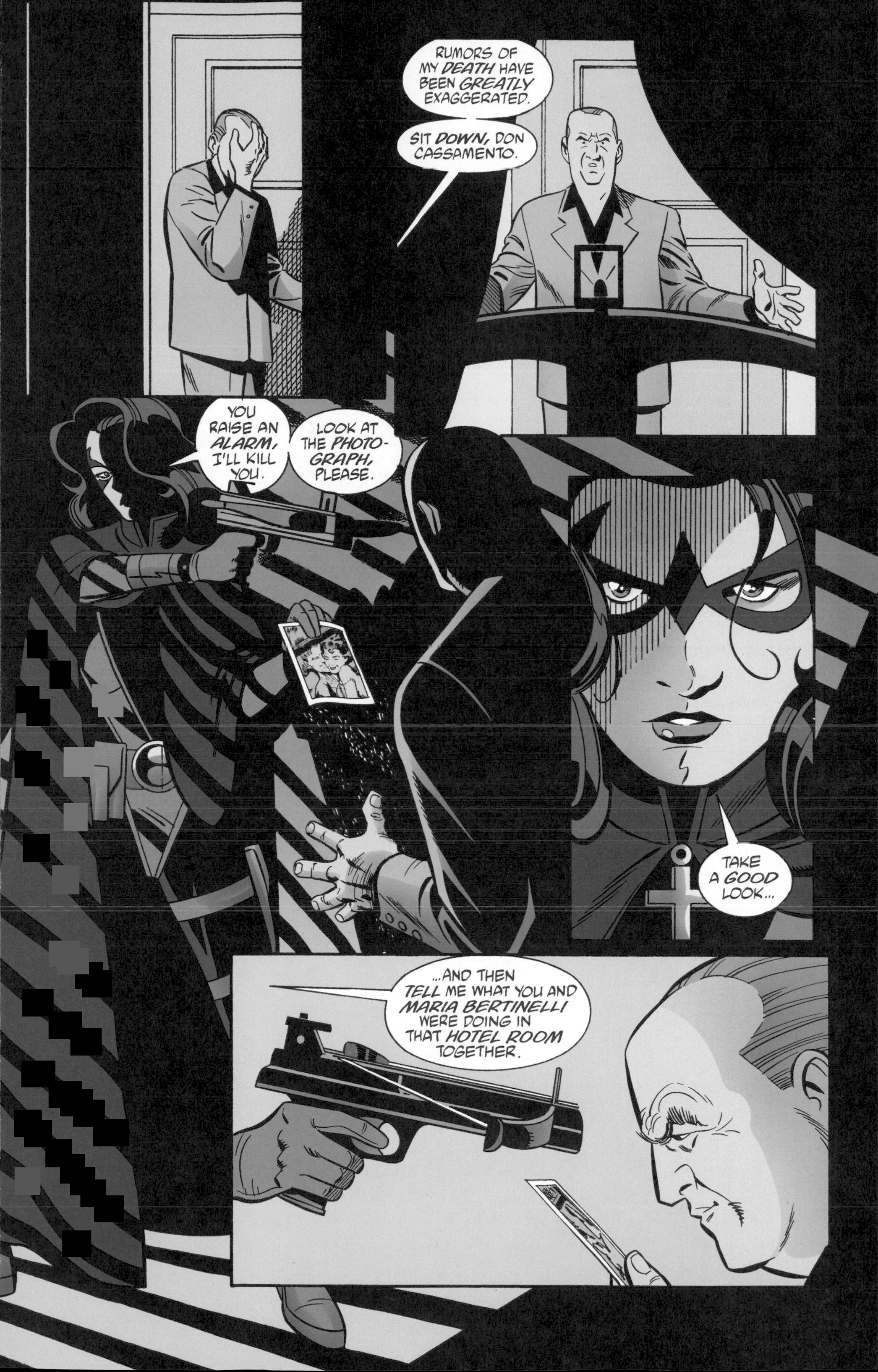
RUMORS OF MY DEATH HAVE BEEN GREATLY EXAGGERATED.
SIT DOWN, DON CASSAMENTO.
YOU RAISE AN ALARM, I'LL KILL YOU.
LOOK AT THE PHOTOGRAPH, PLEASE.
TAKE A GOOD LOOK...
...AND THEN TELL ME WHAT YOU AND MARIA BERTINELLI WERE DOING IN THAT HOTEL ROOM TOGETHER.

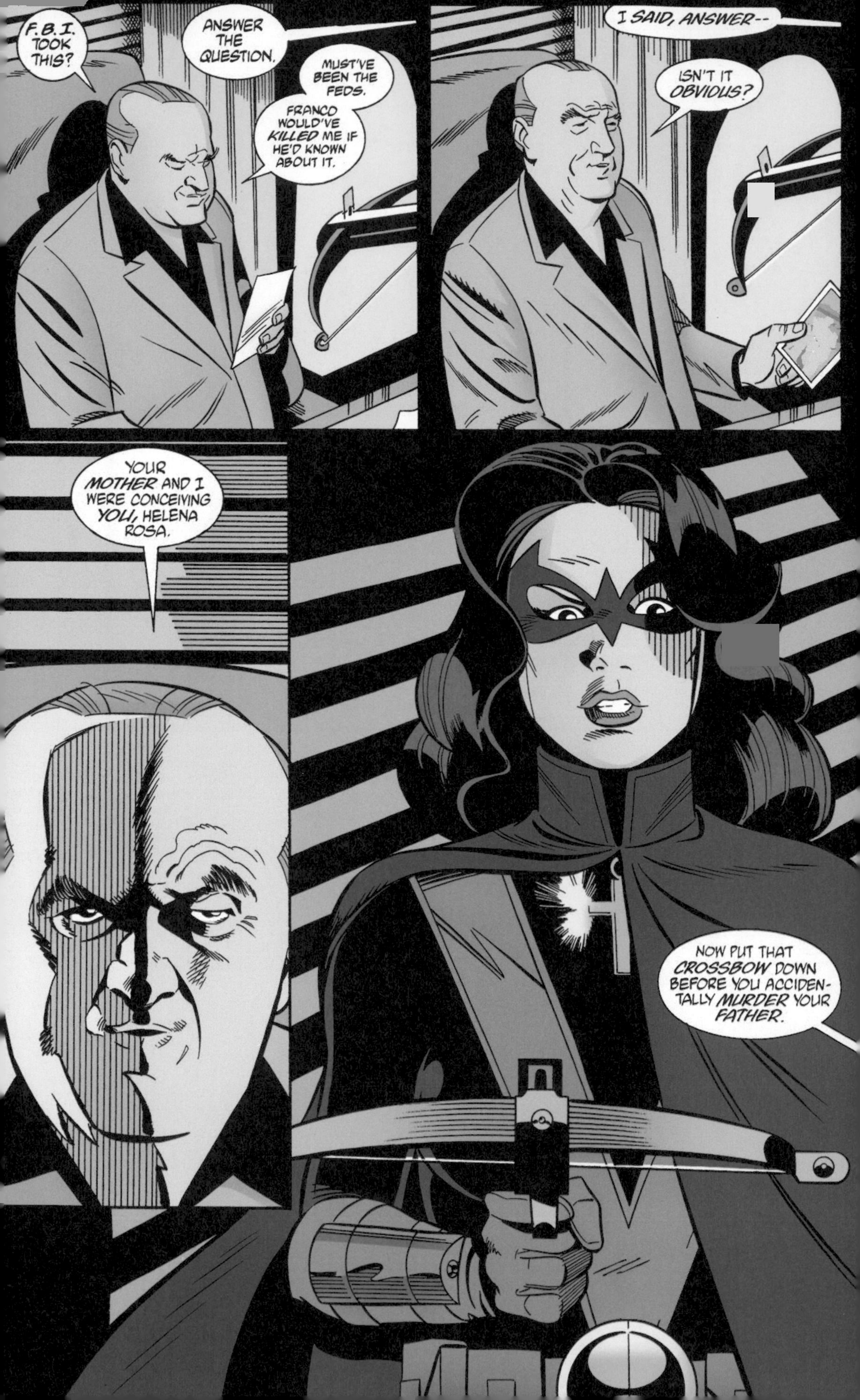
F.B.I. TOOK THIS?
ANSWER THE QUESTION.
MUST'VE BEEN THE FEDS.
FRANCO WOULD'VE *KILLED* ME IF HE'D KNOWN ABOUT IT.
I SAID, ANSWER--
ISN'T IT *OBVIOUS?*
YOUR *MOTHER* AND I WERE CONCEIVING *YOU,* HELENA ROSA.
NOW PUT THAT *CROSSBOW* DOWN BEFORE YOU ACCIDENTALLY *MURDER* YOUR *FATHER*.

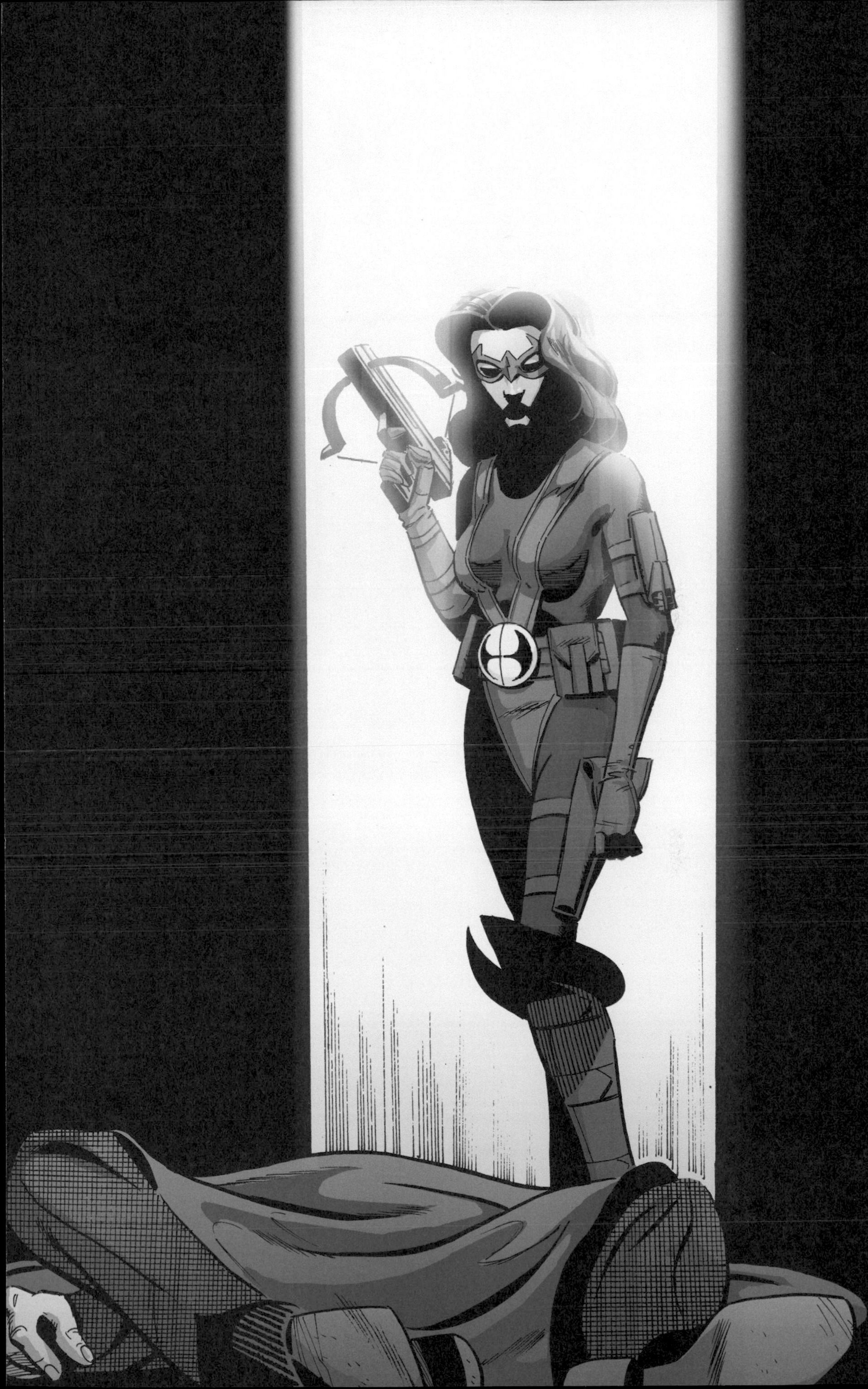

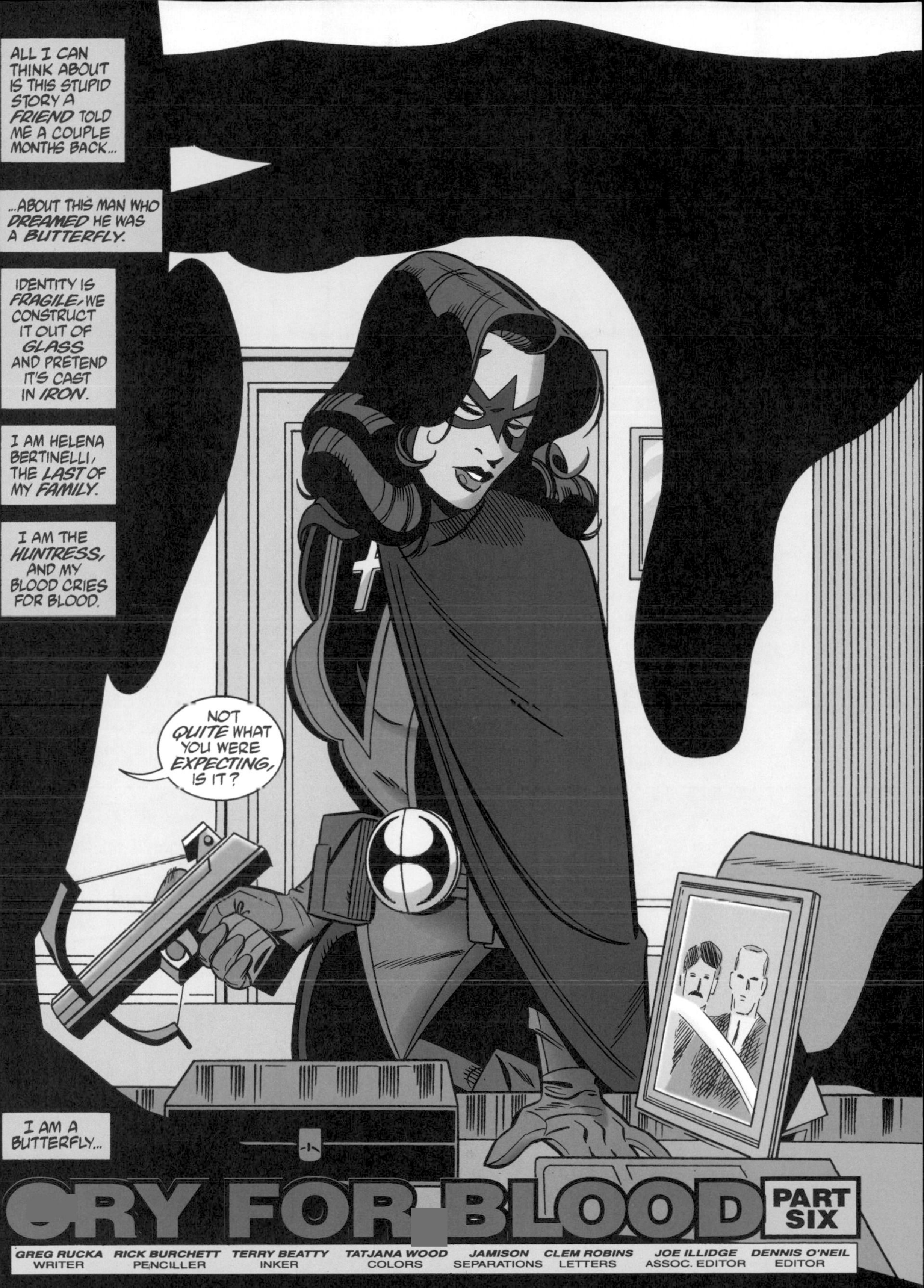
ALL I CAN THINK ABOUT IS THIS STUPID STORY A FRIEND TOLD ME A COUPLE MONTHS BACK...
...ABOUT THIS MAN WHO DREAMED HE WAS A BUTTERFLY.
IDENTITY IS FRAGILE; WE CONSTRUCT IT OUT OF GLASS AND PRETEND IT'S CAST IN IRON.
I AM HELENA BERTINELLI, THE LAST OF MY FAMILY.
I AM THE HUNTRESS, AND MY BLOOD CRIES FOR BLOOD.
NOT QUITE WHAT YOU WERE EXPECTING, IS IT?
I AM A BUTTERFLY...
[redacted]RY FOR [redacted] BLOOD
PART SIX
GREG RUCKA WRITER
RICK BURCHETT PENCILLER
TERRY BEATTY INKER
TATJANA WOOD COLORS
JAMISON SEPARATIONS
CLEM ROBINS LETTERS
JOE ILLIDGE ASSOC. EDITOR
DENNIS O'NEIL EDITOR

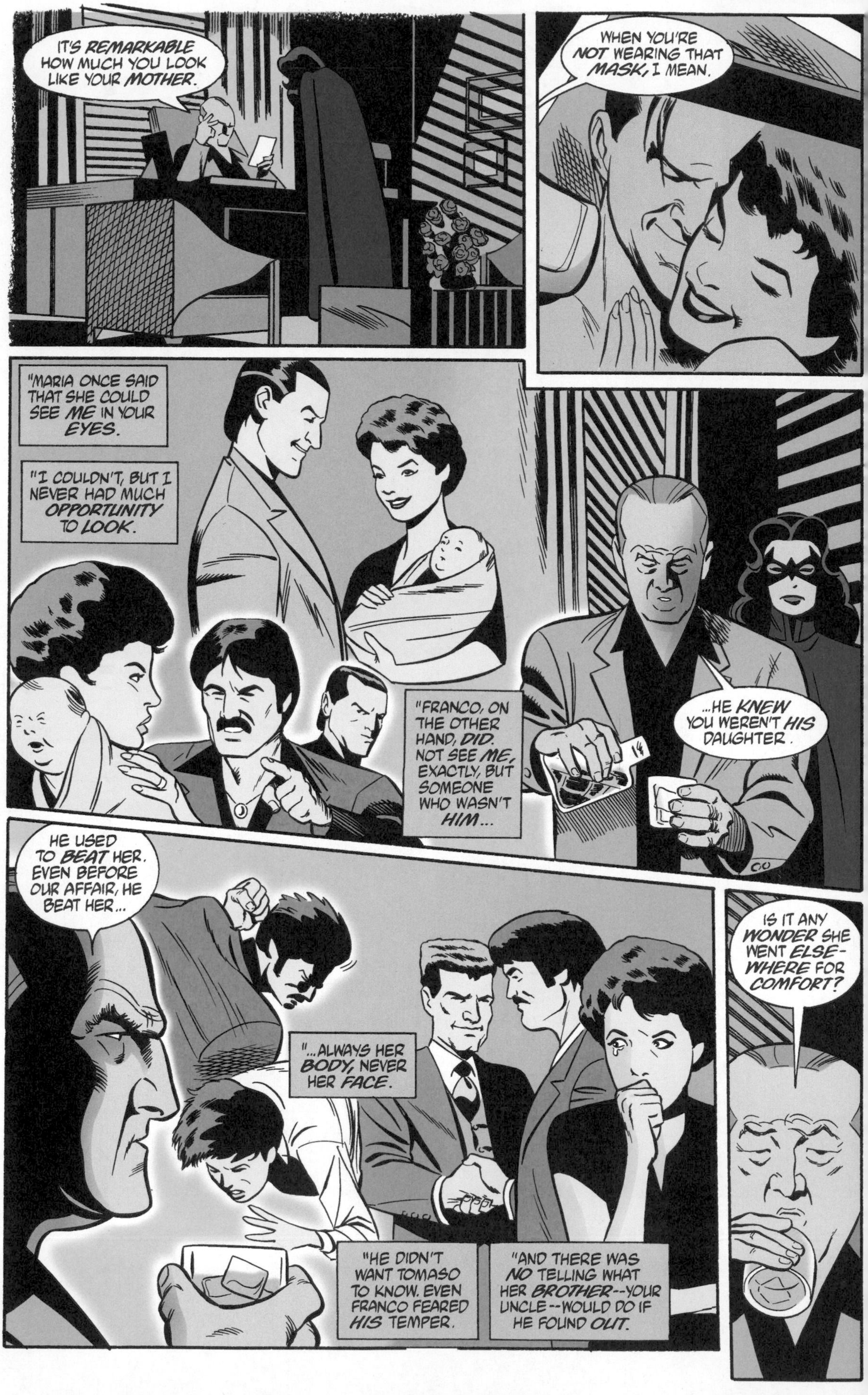
IT'S REMARKABLE HOW MUCH YOU LOOK LIKE YOUR MOTHER.
WHEN YOU'RE NOT WEARING THAT MASK, I MEAN.
"MARIA ONCE SAID THAT SHE COULD SEE ME IN YOUR EYES.
"I COULDN'T, BUT I NEVER HAD MUCH OPPORTUNITY TO LOOK.
"FRANCO, ON THE OTHER HAND, DID. NOT SEE ME, EXACTLY, BUT SOMEONE WHO WASN'T HIM...
...HE KNEW YOU WEREN'T HIS DAUGHTER.
HE USED TO BEAT HER. EVEN BEFORE OUR AFFAIR, HE BEAT HER...
"...ALWAYS HER BODY, NEVER HER FACE.
"HE DIDN'T WANT TOMASO TO KNOW. EVEN FRANCO FEARED HIS TEMPER.
"AND THERE WAS NO TELLING WHAT HER BROTHER--YOUR UNCLE--WOULD DO IF HE FOUND OUT.
IS IT ANY WONDER SHE WENT ELSEWHERE FOR COMFORT?

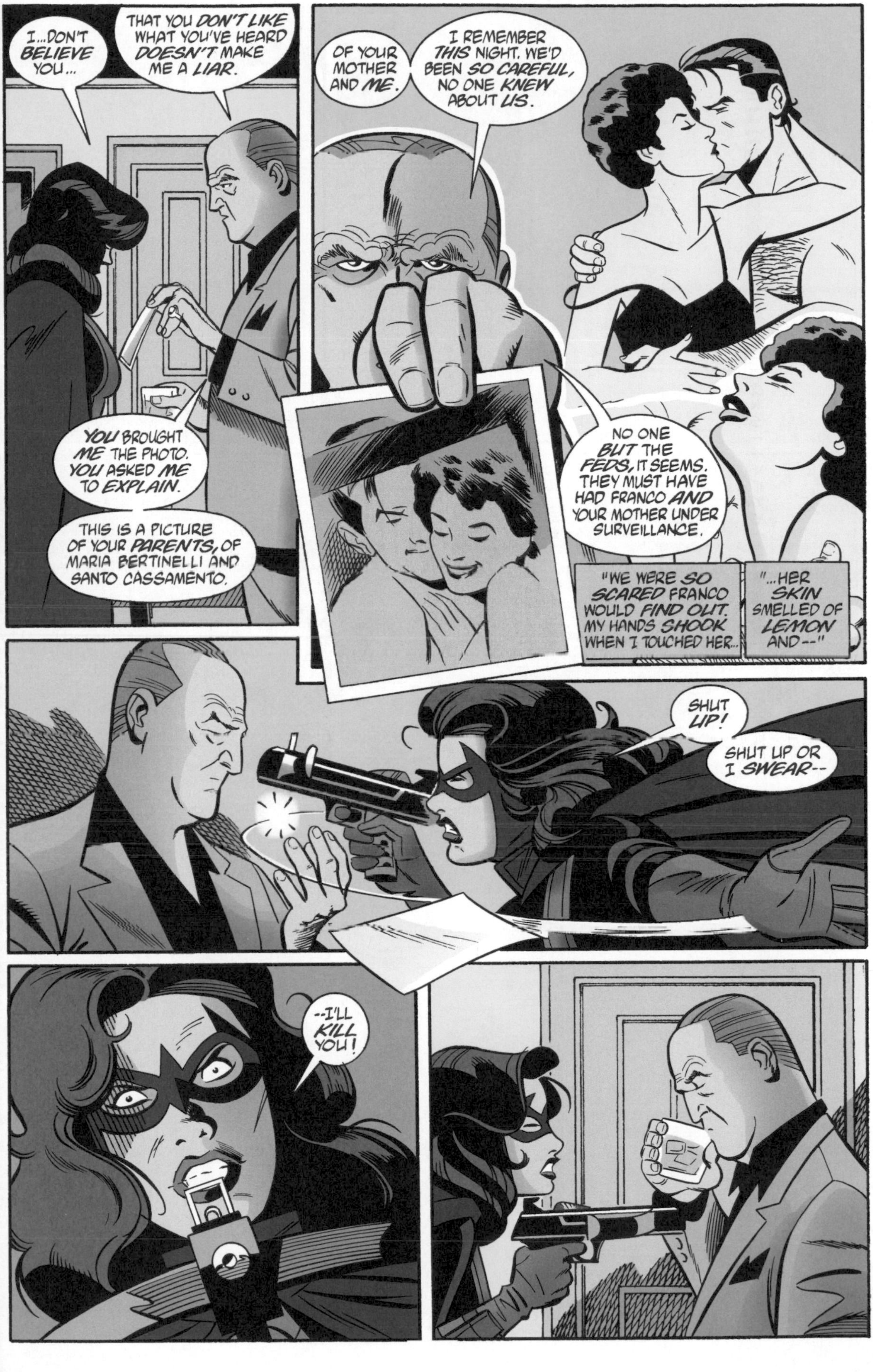
I...DON'T BELIEVE YOU...
THAT YOU DON'T LIKE WHAT YOU'VE HEARD DOESN'T MAKE ME A LIAR.
YOU BROUGHT ME THE PHOTO. YOU ASKED ME TO EXPLAIN.
THIS IS A PICTURE OF YOUR PARENTS, OF MARIA BERTINELLI AND SANTO CASSAMENTO.
OF YOUR MOTHER AND ME.
I REMEMBER THIS NIGHT. WE'D BEEN SO CAREFUL, NO ONE KNEW ABOUT US.
NO ONE BUT THE FEDS, IT SEEMS. THEY MUST HAVE HAD FRANCO AND YOUR MOTHER UNDER SURVEILLANCE.
"WE WERE SO SCARED FRANCO WOULD FIND OUT. MY HANDS SHOOK WHEN I TOUCHED HER...
"...HER SKIN SMELLED OF LEMON AND--"
SHUT UP!
SHUT UP OR I SWEAR--
--I'LL KILL YOU!

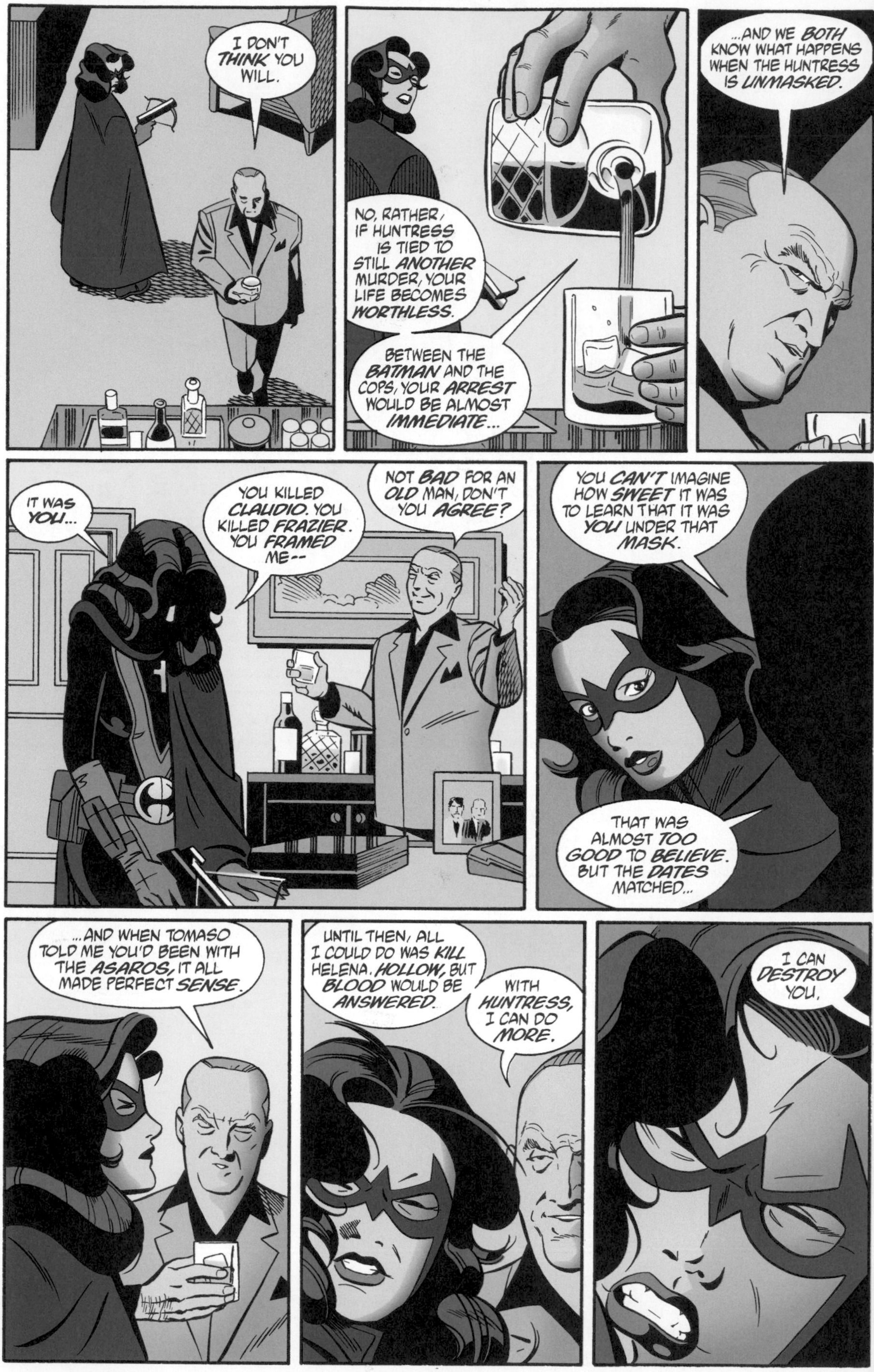
I DON'T THINK YOU WILL.
NO, RATHER, IF HUNTRESS IS TIED TO STILL ANOTHER MURDER, YOUR LIFE BECOMES WORTHLESS.
BETWEEN THE BATMAN AND THE COPS, YOUR ARREST WOULD BE ALMOST IMMEDIATE...
...AND WE BOTH KNOW WHAT HAPPENS WHEN THE HUNTRESS IS UNMASKED.
IT WAS YOU...
YOU KILLED CLAUDIO. YOU KILLED FRAZIER. YOU FRAMED ME--
NOT BAD FOR AN OLD MAN, DON'T YOU AGREE?
YOU CAN'T IMAGINE HOW SWEET IT WAS TO LEARN THAT IT WAS YOU UNDER THAT MASK.
THAT WAS ALMOST TOO GOOD TO BELIEVE. BUT THE DATES MATCHED...
...AND WHEN TOMASO TOLD ME YOU'D BEEN WITH THE ASAROS, IT ALL MADE PERFECT SENSE.
UNTIL THEN, ALL I COULD DO WAS KILL HELENA. HOLLOW, BUT BLOOD WOULD BE ANSWERED.
WITH HUNTRESS, I CAN DO MORE.
I CAN DESTROY YOU.

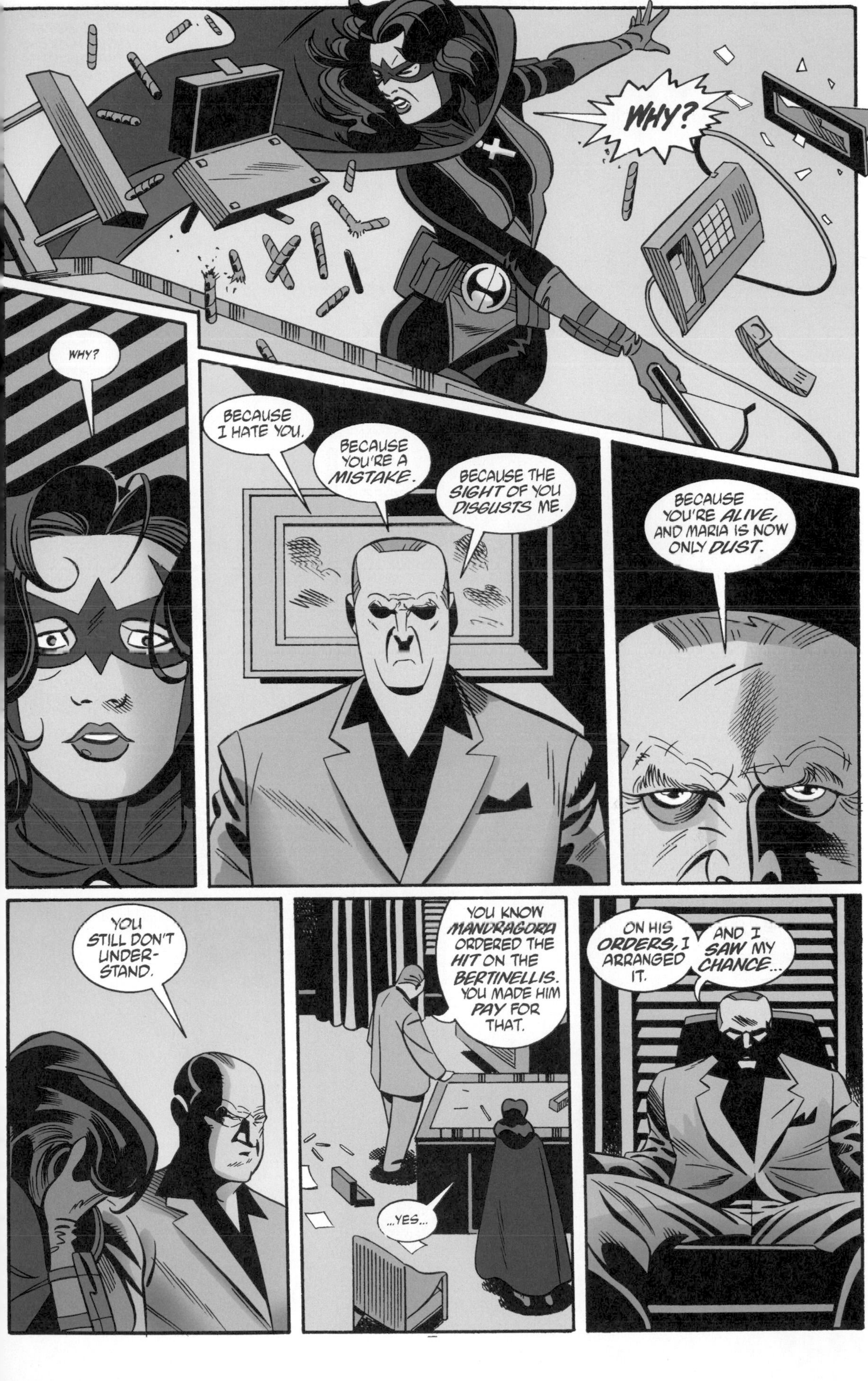

WHY?
WHY?
BECAUSE I HATE YOU.
BECAUSE YOU'RE A MISTAKE.
BECAUSE THE SIGHT OF YOU DISGUSTS ME.
BECAUSE YOU'RE ALIVE, AND MARIA IS NOW ONLY DUST.
YOU STILL DON'T UNDER-STAND.
YOU KNOW MANDRAGORA ORDERED THE HIT ON THE BERTINELLIS. YOU MADE HIM PAY FOR THAT.
...YES...
ON HIS ORDERS, I ARRANGED IT.
AND I SAW MY CHANCE...

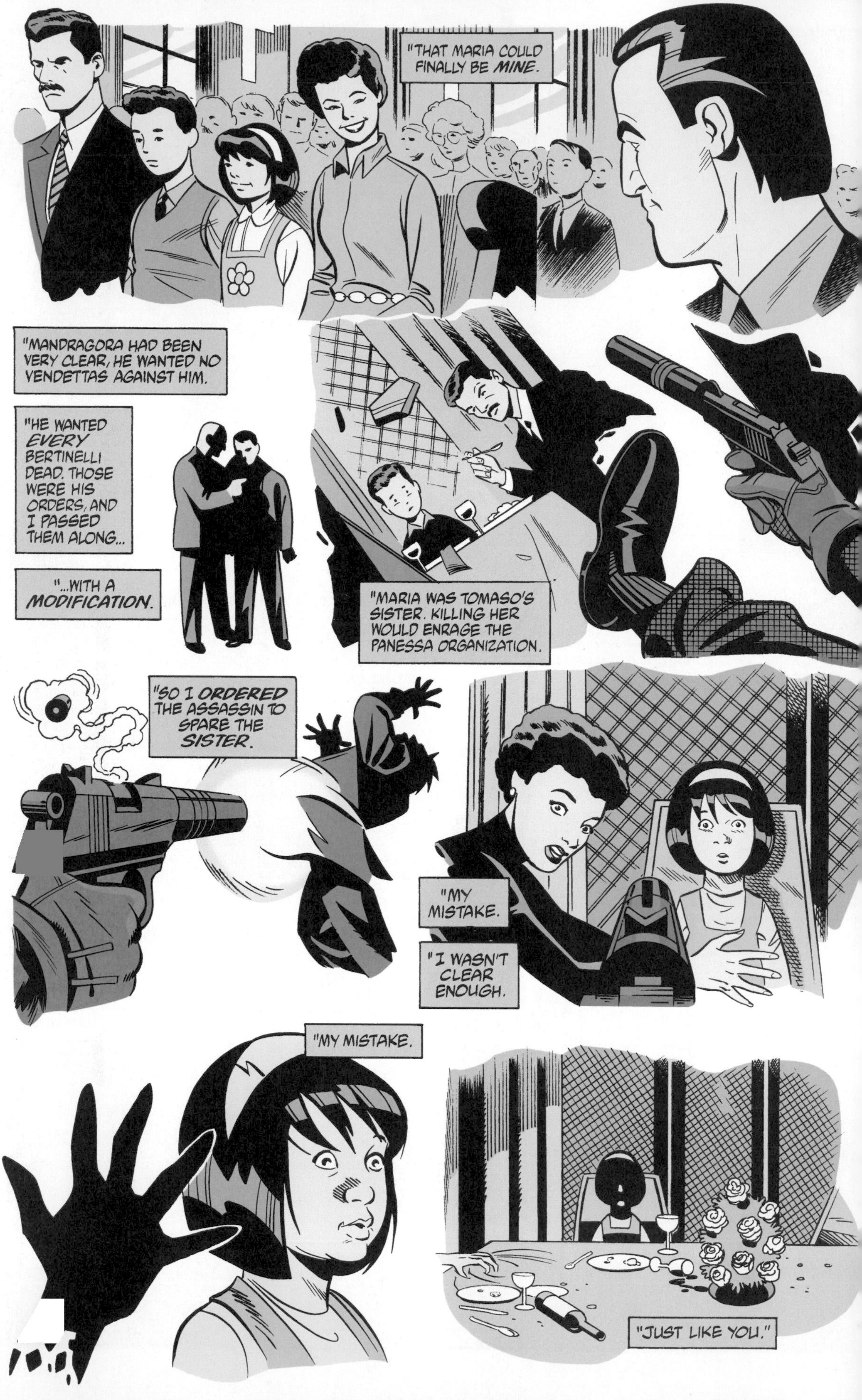
"THAT MARIA COULD FINALLY BE *MINE*.
"MANDRAGORA HAD BEEN VERY CLEAR, HE WANTED NO VENDETTAS AGAINST HIM.
"HE WANTED *EVERY* BERTINELLI DEAD. THOSE WERE HIS ORDERS, AND I PASSED THEM ALONG...
"...WITH A *MODIFICATION*.
"MARIA WAS TOMASO'S SISTER. KILLING HER WOULD ENRAGE THE PANESSA ORGANIZATION.
"SO I *ORDERED* THE ASSASSIN TO SPARE THE *SISTER*.
"MY MISTAKE.
"I WASN'T CLEAR ENOUGH.
"MY MISTAKE.
"JUST LIKE YOU."

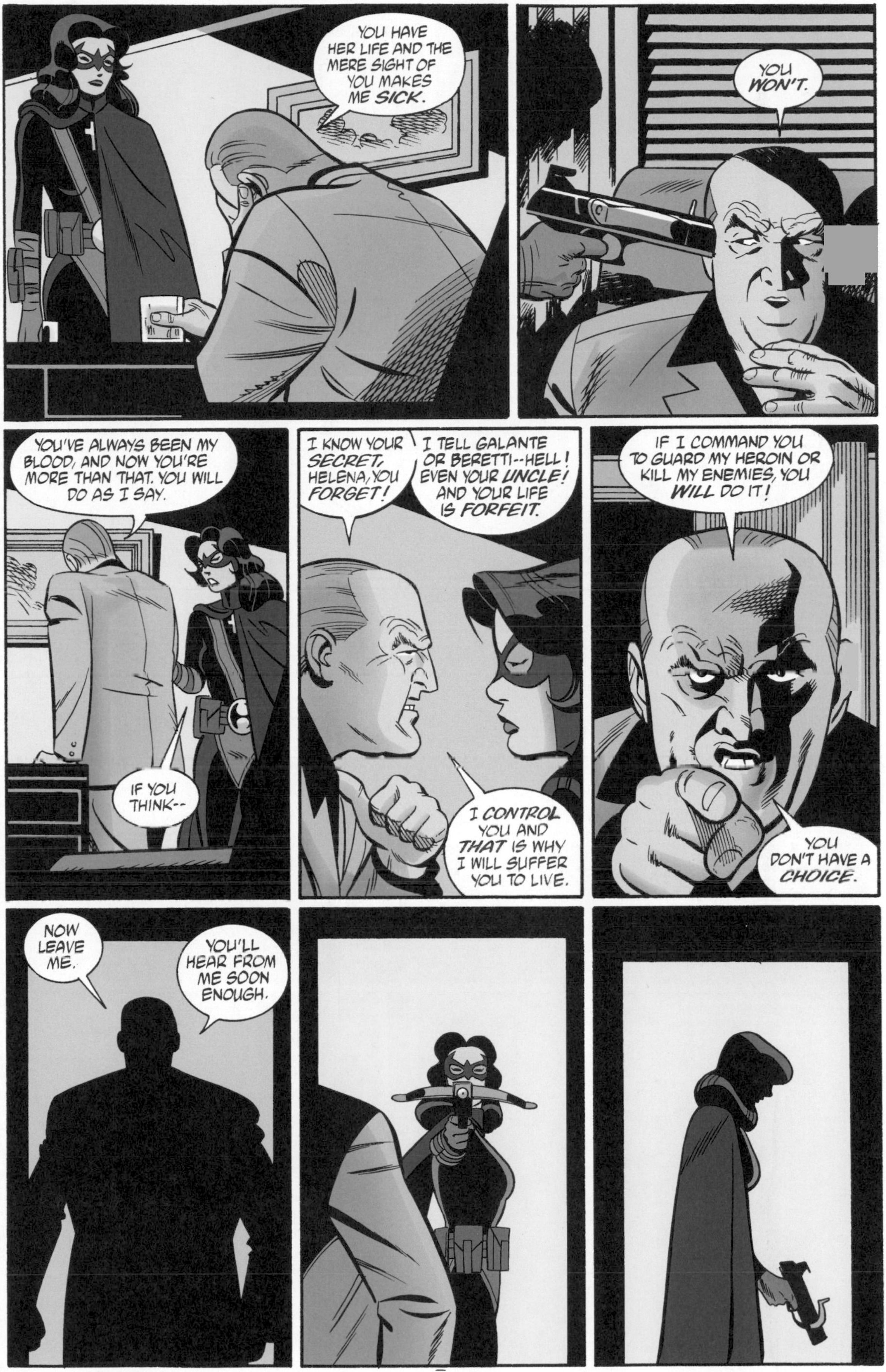
YOU HAVE HER LIFE AND THE MERE SIGHT OF YOU MAKES ME SICK.
YOU WON'T.
YOU'VE ALWAYS BEEN MY BLOOD, AND NOW YOU'RE MORE THAN THAT. YOU WILL DO AS I SAY.
IF YOU THINK--
I KNOW YOUR SECRET, HELENA, YOU FORGET!
I TELL GALANTE OR BERETTI--HELL! EVEN YOUR UNCLE! AND YOUR LIFE IS FORFEIT.
I CONTROL YOU AND THAT IS WHY I WILL SUFFER YOU TO LIVE.
IF I COMMAND YOU TO GUARD MY HEROIN OR KILL MY ENEMIES, YOU WILL DO IT!
YOU DON'T HAVE A CHOICE.
NOW LEAVE ME.
YOU'LL HEAR FROM ME SOON ENOUGH.

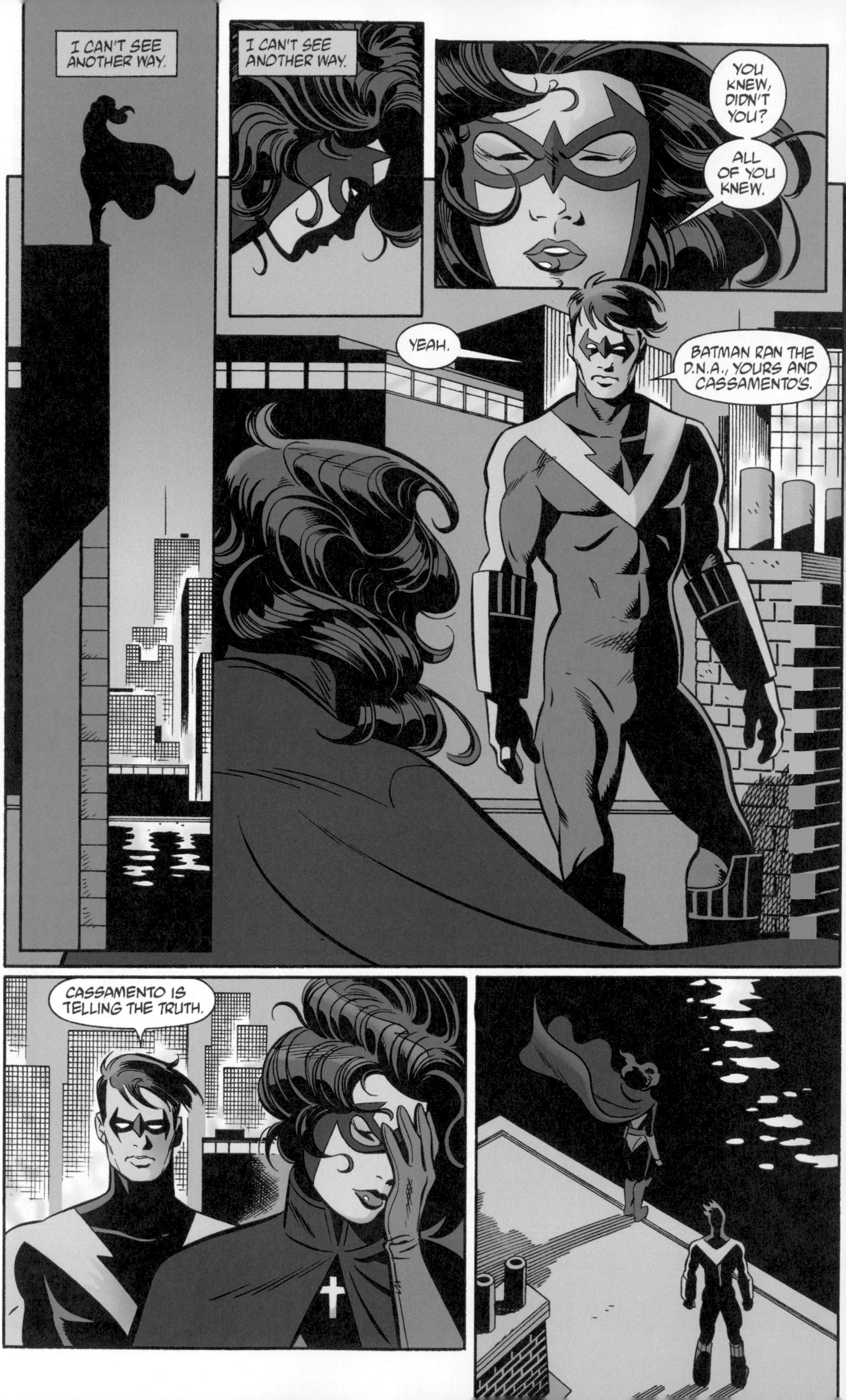
I CAN'T SEE ANOTHER WAY.
I CAN'T SEE ANOTHER WAY.
YOU KNEW, DIDN'T YOU?
ALL OF YOU KNEW.
YEAH.
BATMAN RAN THE D.N.A., YOURS AND CASSAMENTO'S.
CASSAMENTO IS TELLING THE TRUTH.

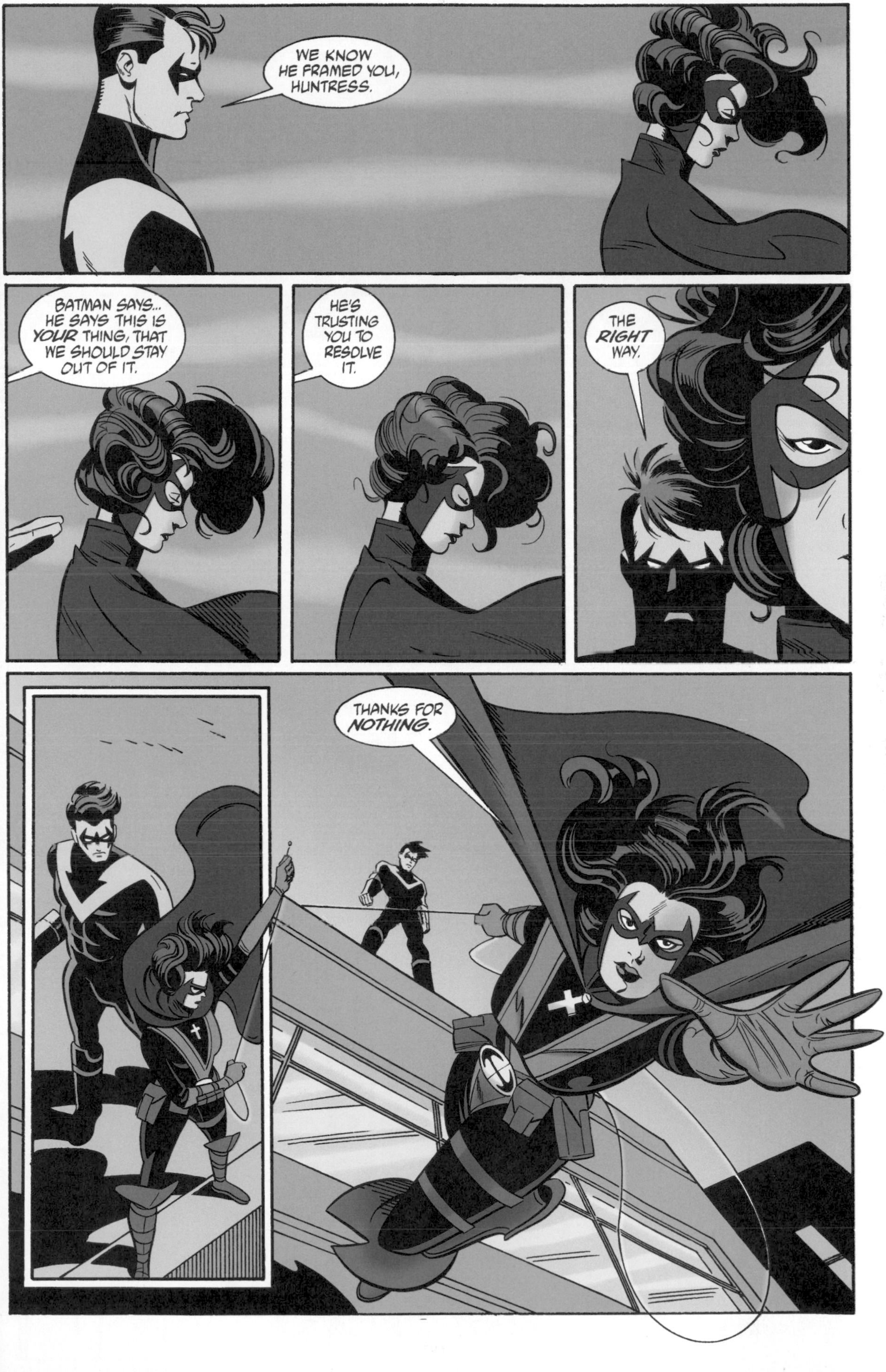
WE KNOW HE FRAMED YOU, HUNTRESS.
BATMAN SAYS... HE SAYS THIS IS YOUR THING, THAT WE SHOULD STAY OUT OF IT.
HE'S TRUSTING YOU TO RESOLVE IT.
THE RIGHT WAY.
THANKS FOR NOTHING.

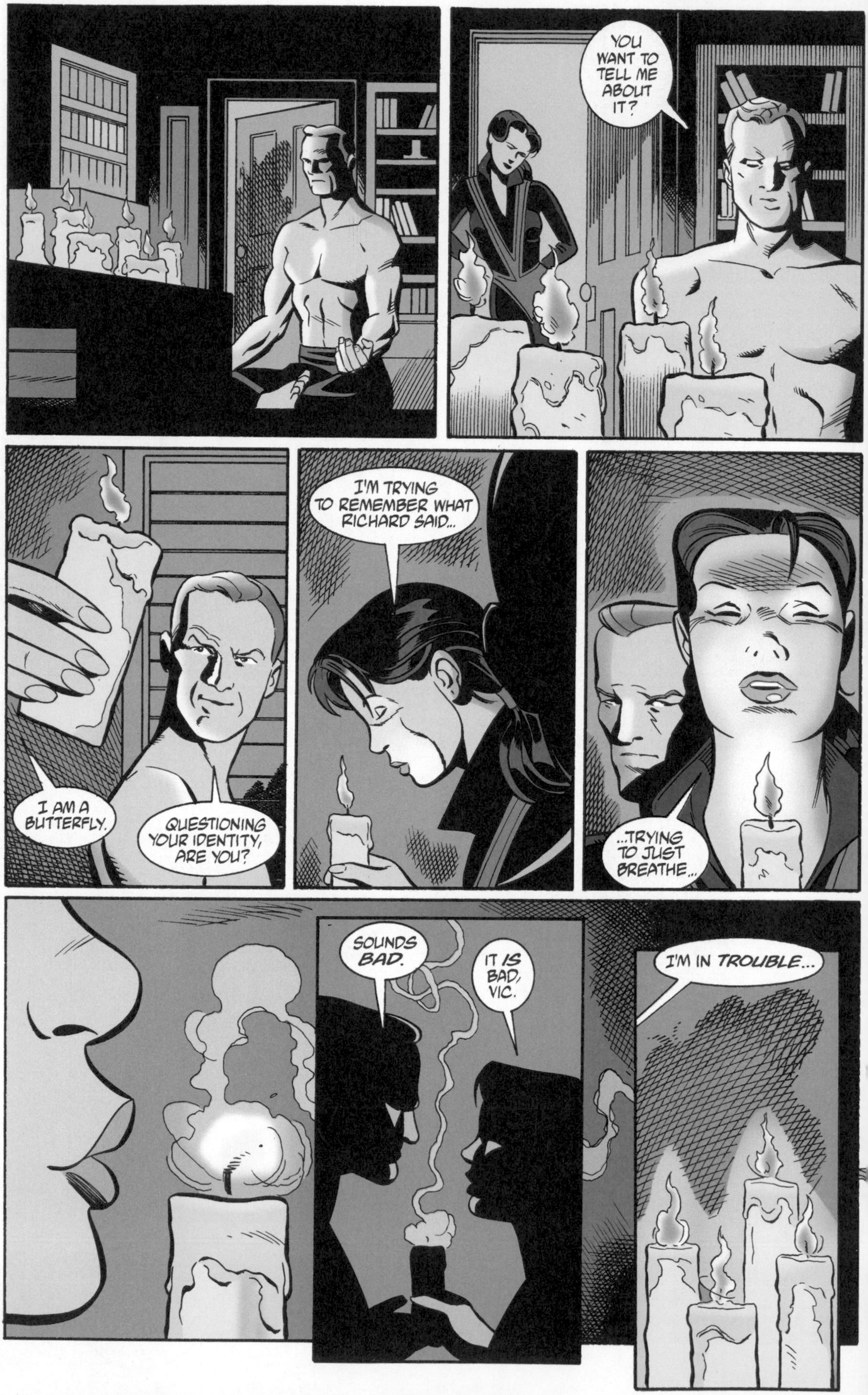
YOU WANT TO TELL ME ABOUT IT?
I AM A BUTTERFLY.
QUESTIONING YOUR IDENTITY, ARE YOU?
I'M TRYING TO REMEMBER WHAT RICHARD SAID...
...TRYING TO JUST BREATHE...
SOUNDS BAD.
IT IS BAD, VIC.
I'M IN TROUBLE...

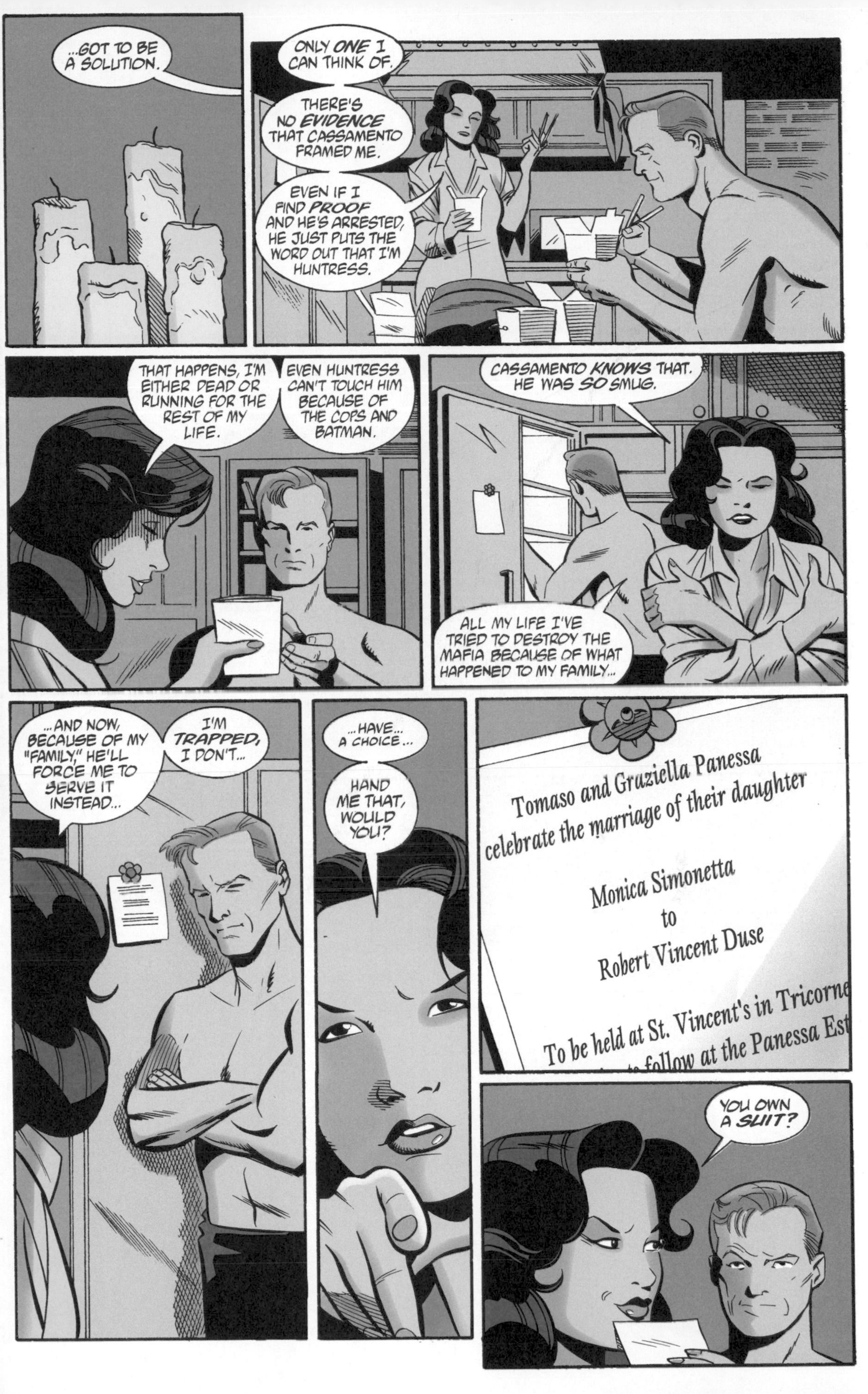
...GOT TO BE A SOLUTION.
ONLY ONE I CAN THINK OF.
THERE'S NO EVIDENCE THAT CASSAMENTO FRAMED ME.
EVEN IF I FIND PROOF AND HE'S ARRESTED, HE JUST PUTS THE WORD OUT THAT I'M HUNTRESS.
THAT HAPPENS, I'M EITHER DEAD OR RUNNING FOR THE REST OF MY LIFE.
EVEN HUNTRESS CAN'T TOUCH HIM BECAUSE OF THE COPS AND BATMAN.
CASSAMENTO KNOWS THAT. HE WAS SO SMUG.
ALL MY LIFE I'VE TRIED TO DESTROY THE MAFIA BECAUSE OF WHAT HAPPENED TO MY FAMILY...
...AND NOW, BECAUSE OF MY "FAMILY," HE'LL FORCE ME TO SERVE IT INSTEAD...
I'M TRAPPED, I DON'T...
...HAVE... A CHOICE...
HAND ME THAT, WOULD YOU?
Tomaso and Graziella Panessa
celebrate the marriage of their daughter
Monica Simonetta
to
Robert Vincent Duse
To be held at St. Vincent's in Tricorne
follow at the Panessa Est
YOU OWN A SUIT?

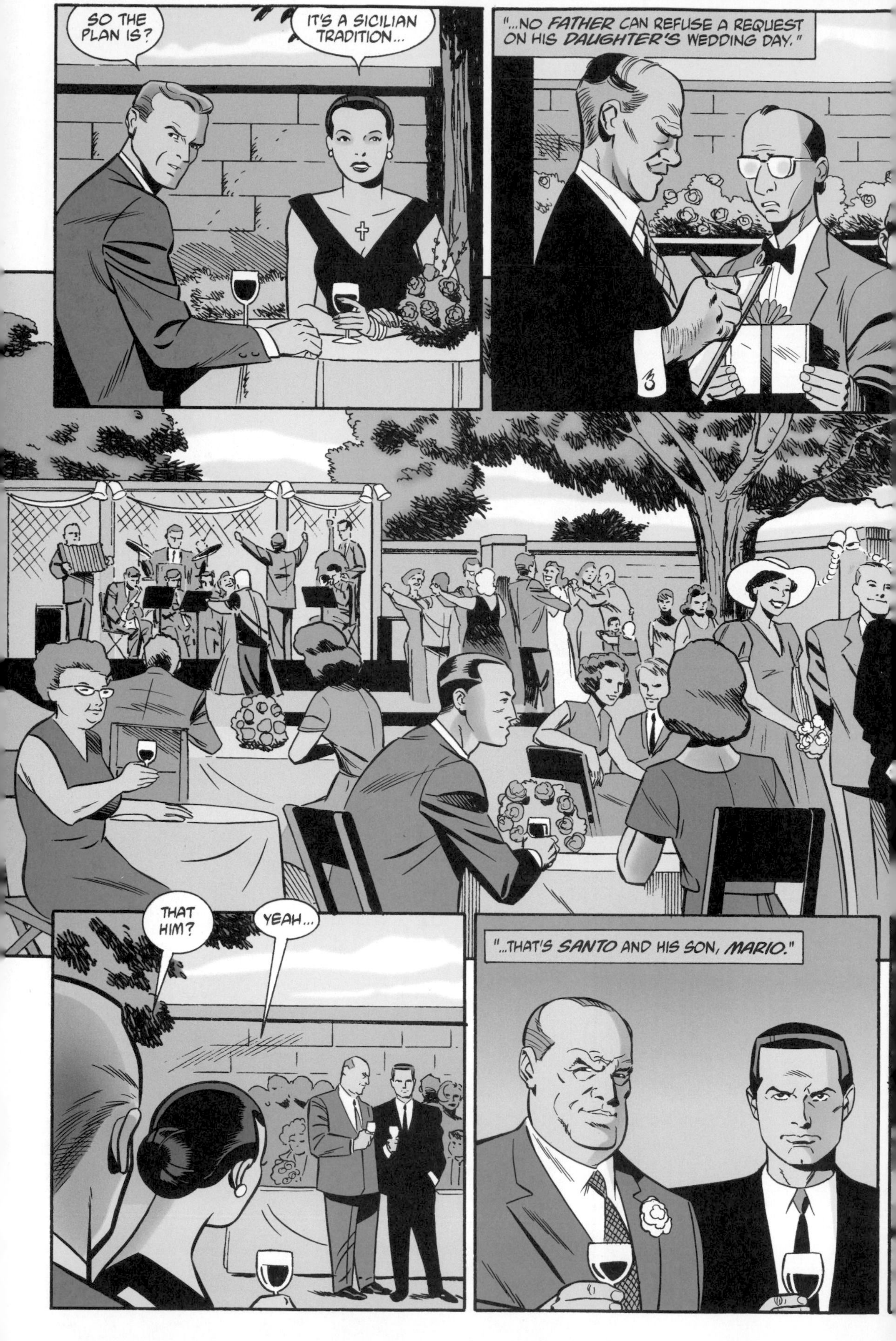
SO THE PLAN IS?
IT'S A SICILIAN TRADITION...
"...NO FATHER CAN REFUSE A REQUEST ON HIS DAUGHTER'S WEDDING DAY."
THAT HIM?
YEAH...
"...THAT'S SANTO AND HIS SON, MARIO."

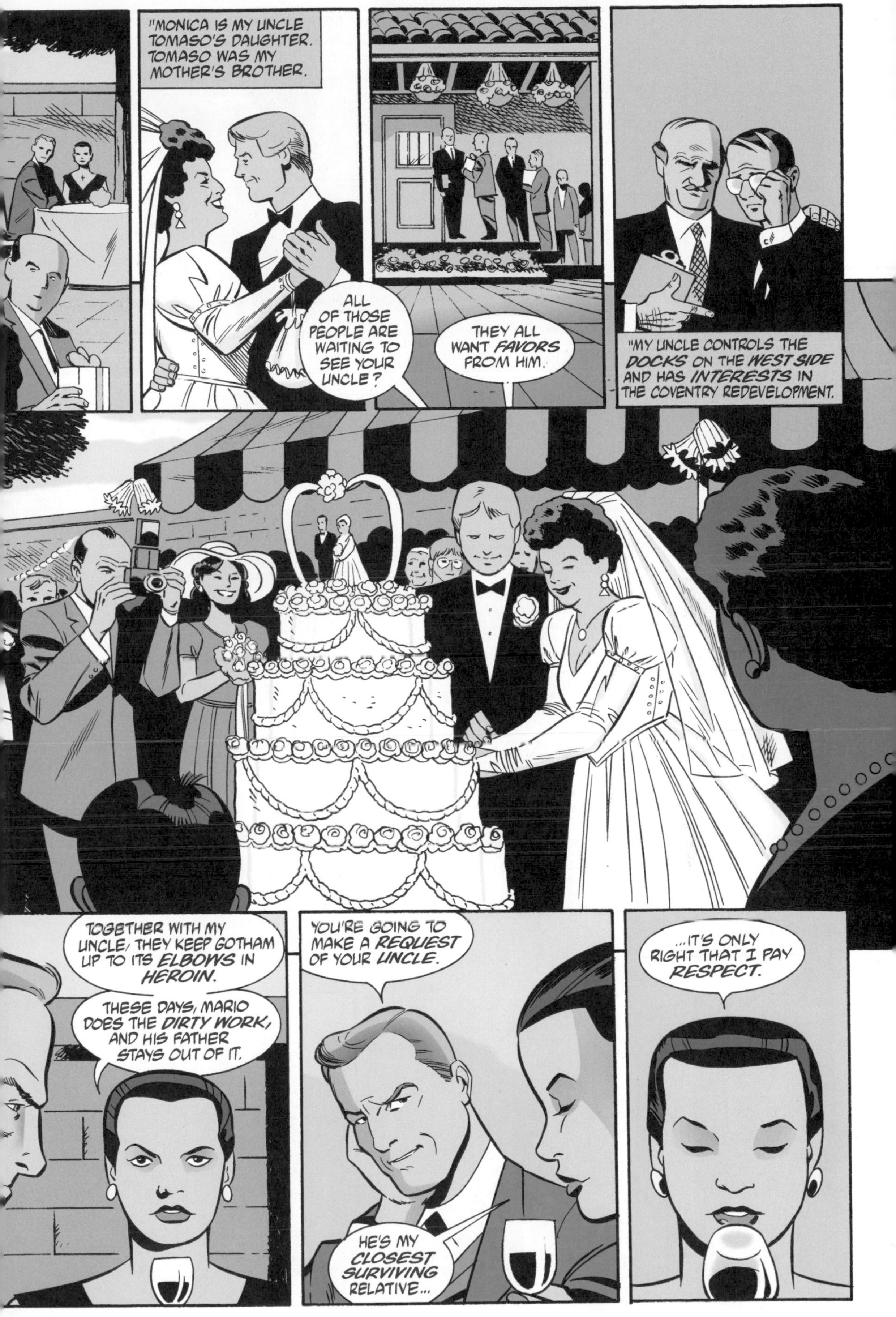
"MONICA IS MY UNCLE TOMASO'S DAUGHTER. TOMASO WAS MY MOTHER'S BROTHER.
ALL OF THOSE PEOPLE ARE WAITING TO SEE YOUR UNCLE?
THEY ALL WANT FAVORS FROM HIM.
"MY UNCLE CONTROLS THE DOCKS ON THE WEST SIDE AND HAS INTERESTS IN THE COVENTRY REDEVELOPMENT.
TOGETHER WITH MY UNCLE, THEY KEEP GOTHAM UP TO ITS ELBOWS IN HEROIN.
THESE DAYS, MARIO DOES THE DIRTY WORK, AND HIS FATHER STAYS OUT OF IT.
YOU'RE GOING TO MAKE A REQUEST OF YOUR UNCLE.
HE'S MY CLOSEST SURVIVING RELATIVE...
...IT'S ONLY RIGHT THAT I PAY RESPECT.

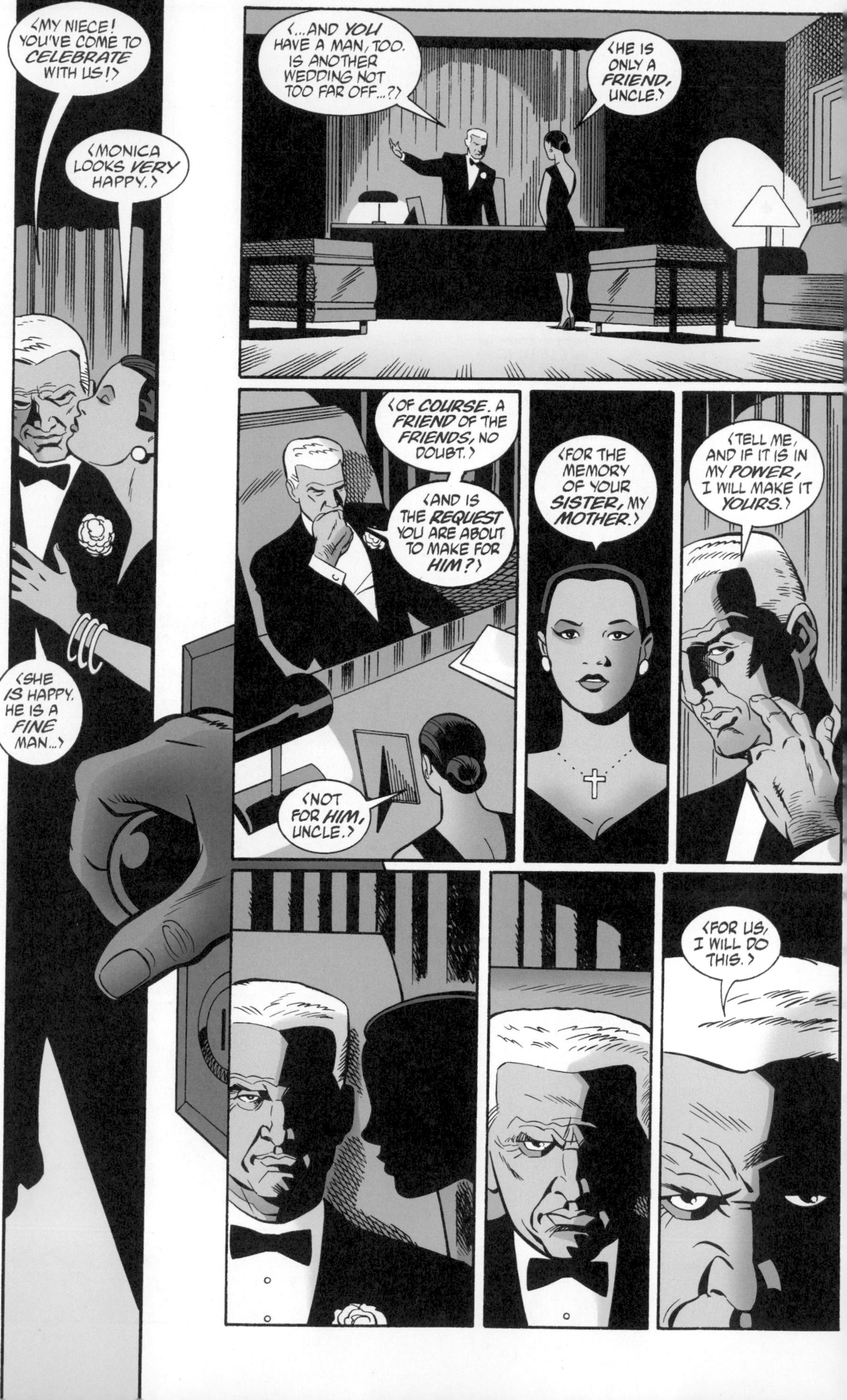

<MY NIECE! YOU'VE COME TO CELEBRATE WITH US!>
<MONICA LOOKS VERY HAPPY.>
<SHE IS HAPPY. HE IS A FINE MAN...>
<...AND YOU HAVE A MAN, TOO. IS ANOTHER WEDDING NOT TOO FAR OFF...?>
<HE IS ONLY A FRIEND, UNCLE.>
<OF COURSE. A FRIEND OF THE FRIENDS, NO DOUBT.>
<AND IS THE REQUEST YOU ARE ABOUT TO MAKE FOR HIM?>
<NOT FOR HIM, UNCLE.>
<FOR THE MEMORY OF YOUR SISTER, MY MOTHER.>
<TELL ME, AND IF IT IS IN MY POWER, I WILL MAKE IT YOURS.>
<FOR US, I WILL DO THIS.>

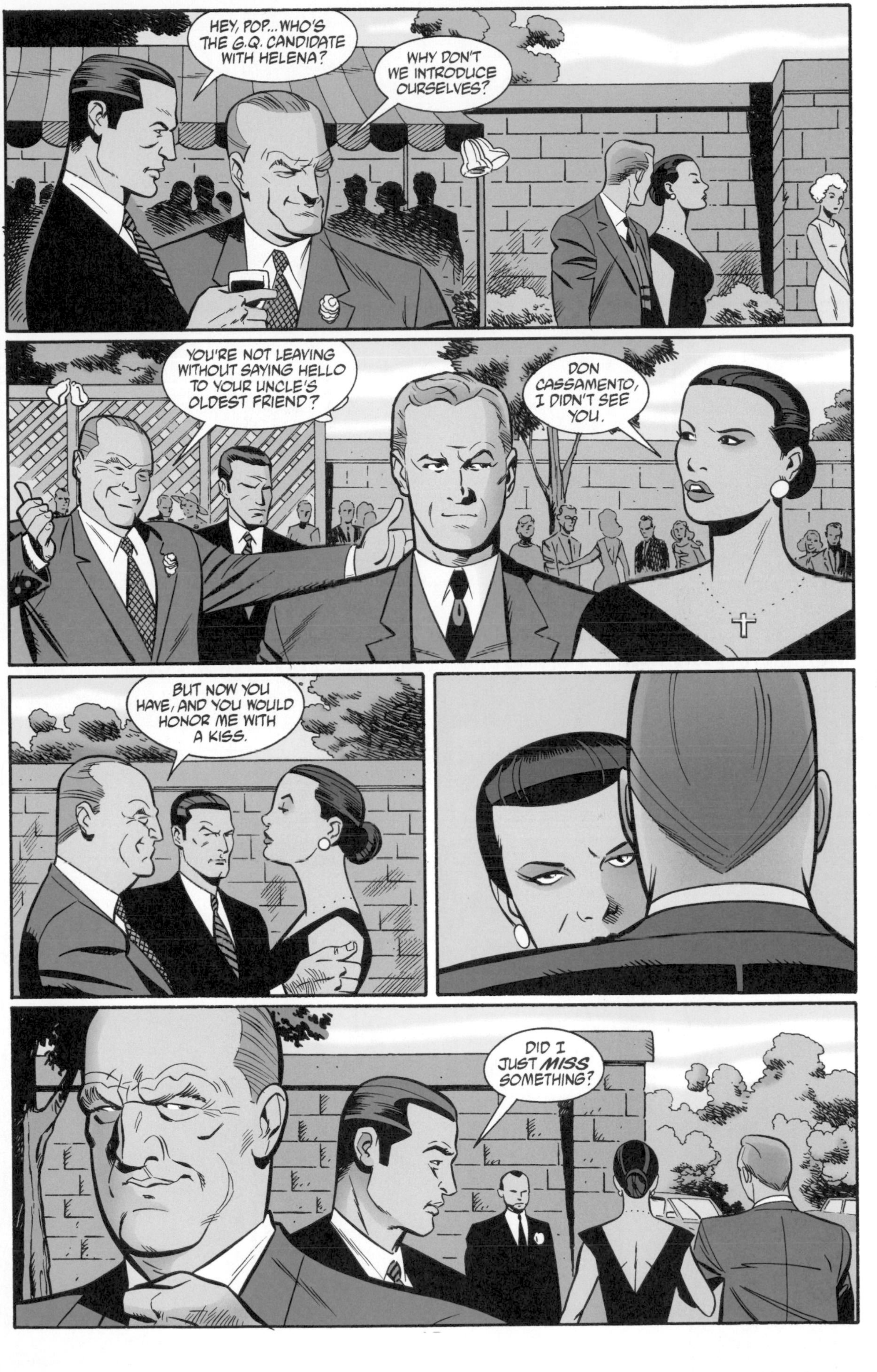
HEY, POP... WHO'S THE G.Q. CANDIDATE WITH HELENA?
WHY DON'T WE INTRODUCE OURSELVES?
YOU'RE NOT LEAVING WITHOUT SAYING HELLO TO YOUR UNCLE'S OLDEST FRIEND?
DON CASSAMENTO, I DIDN'T SEE YOU.
BUT NOW YOU HAVE, AND YOU WOULD HONOR ME WITH A KISS.
DID I JUST MISS SOMETHING?

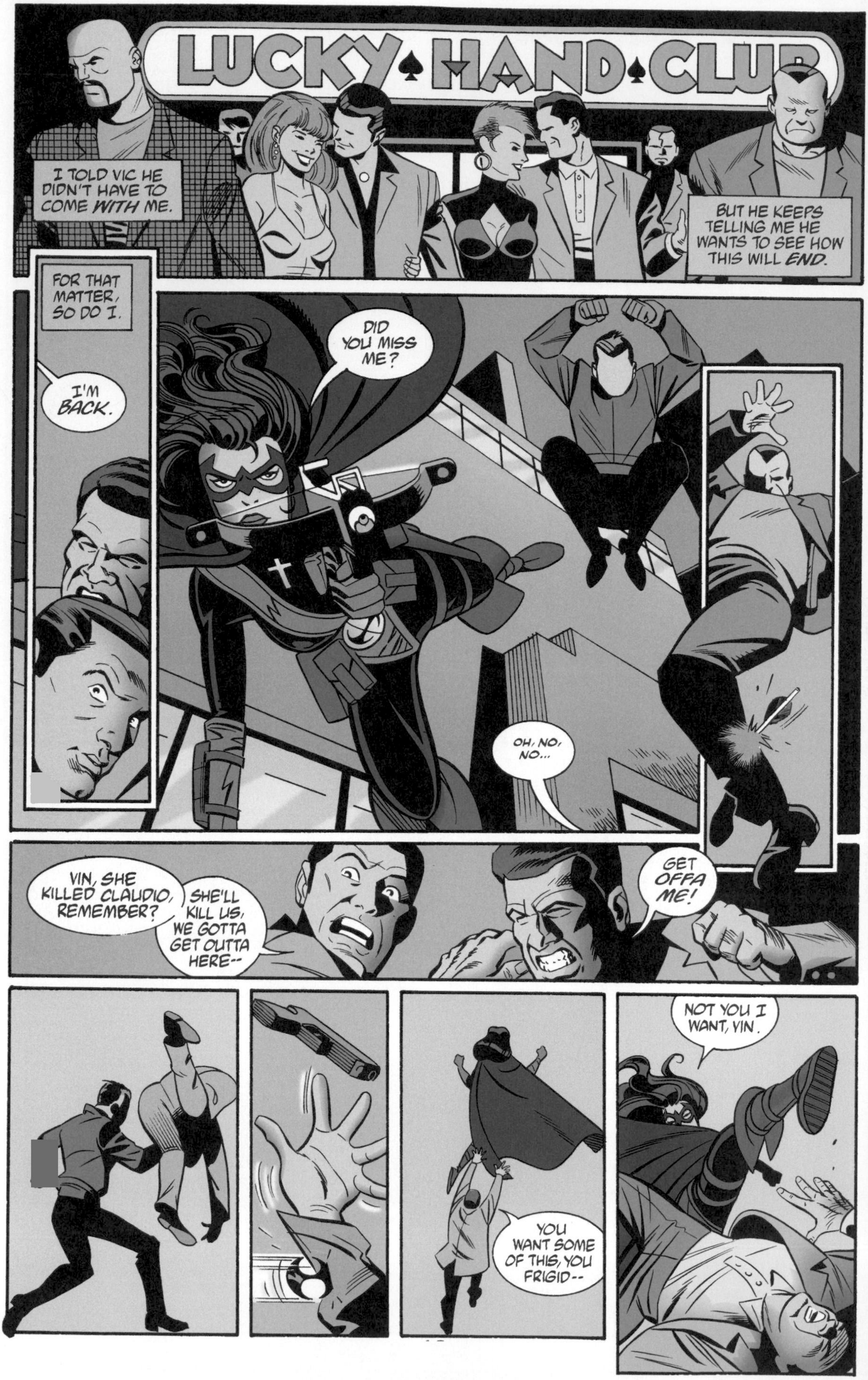
LUCKY HAND CLUB
I TOLD VIC HE DIDN'T HAVE TO COME WITH ME.
BUT HE KEEPS TELLING ME HE WANTS TO SEE HOW THIS WILL END.
FOR THAT MATTER, SO DO I.
I'M BACK.
DID YOU MISS ME?
OH, NO, NO...
VIN, SHE KILLED CLAUDIO, REMEMBER?
SHE'LL KILL US, WE GOTTA GET OUTTA HERE--
GET OFFA ME!
YOU WANT SOME OF THIS, YOU FRIGID--
NOT YOU I WANT, VIN.

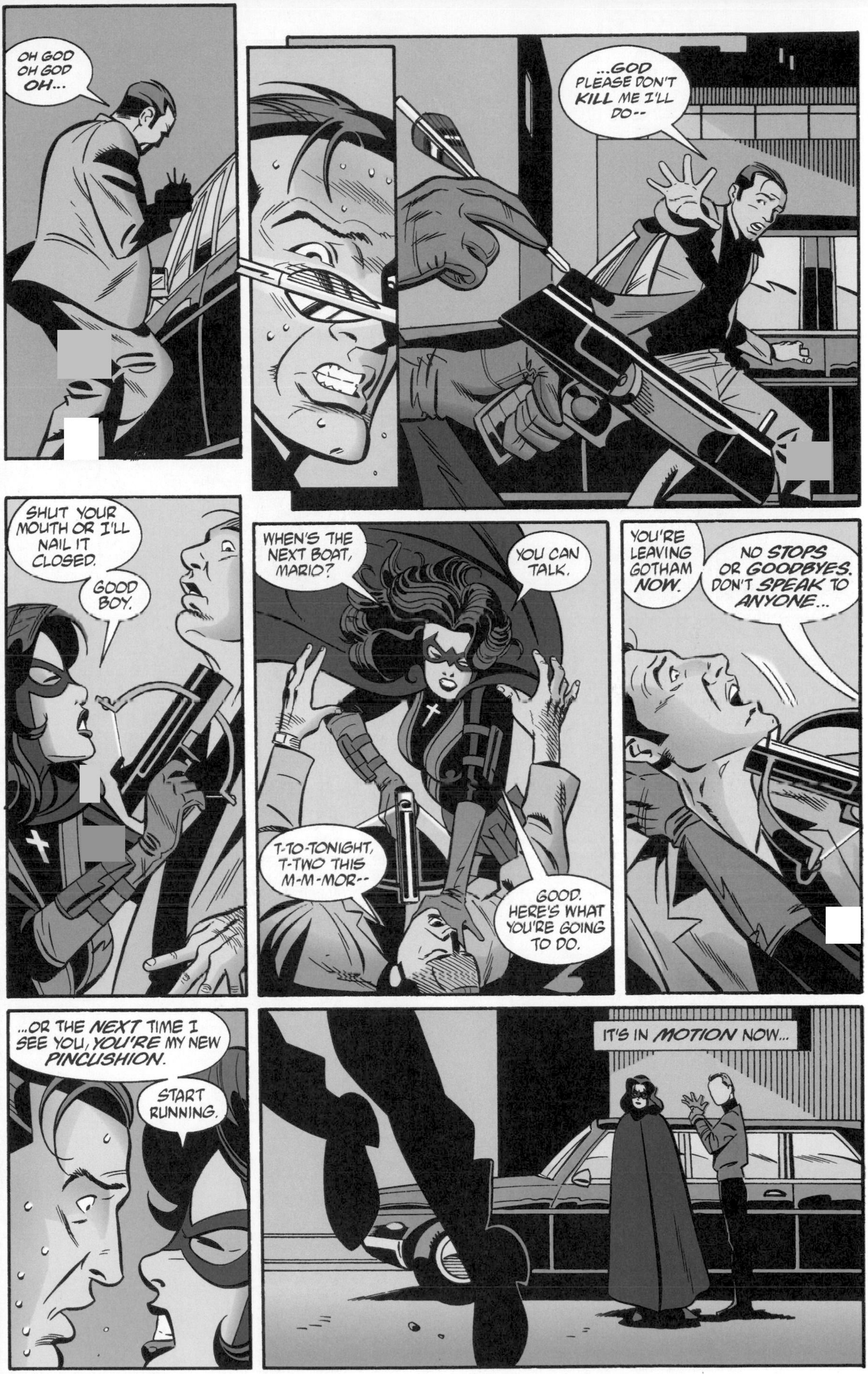
OH GOD OH GOD OH...
...GOD PLEASE DON'T KILL ME I'LL DO--
SHUT YOUR MOUTH OR I'LL NAIL IT CLOSED.
GOOD BOY.
WHEN'S THE NEXT BOAT, MARIO?
YOU CAN TALK.
T-TO-TONIGHT, T-TWO THIS M-M-MOR--
GOOD. HERE'S WHAT YOU'RE GOING TO DO.
YOU'RE LEAVING GOTHAM NOW.
NO STOPS OR GOODBYES. DON'T SPEAK TO ANYONE...
...OR THE NEXT TIME I SEE YOU, YOU'RE MY NEW PINCUSHION.
START RUNNING.
IT'S IN MOTION NOW...

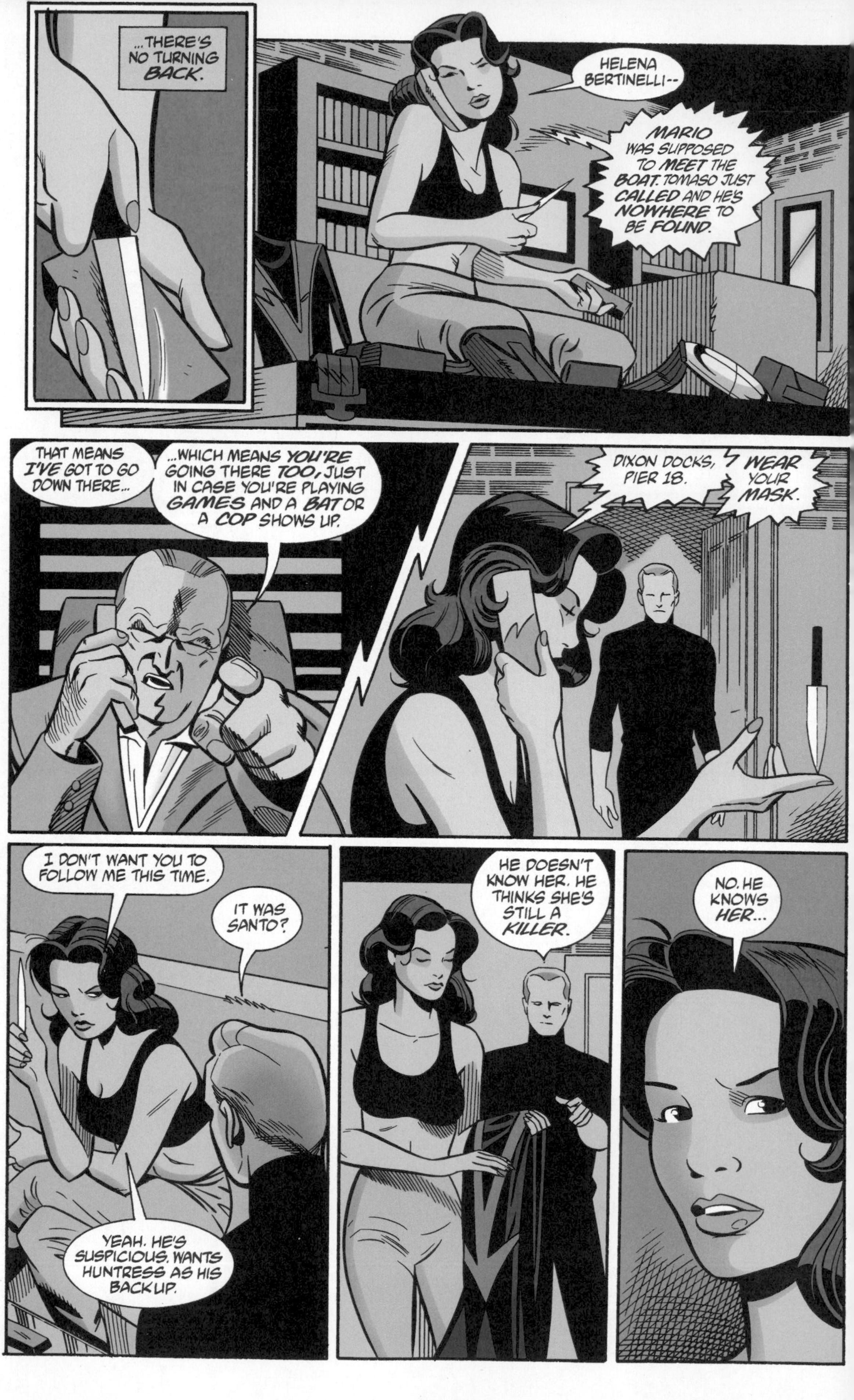
...THERE'S NO TURNING BACK.
HELENA BERTINELLI--
MARIO WAS SUPPOSED TO MEET THE BOAT. TOMASO JUST CALLED AND HE'S NOWHERE TO BE FOUND.
THAT MEANS I'VE GOT TO GO DOWN THERE...
...WHICH MEANS YOU'RE GOING THERE TOO, JUST IN CASE YOU'RE PLAYING GAMES AND A BAT OR A COP SHOWS UP.
DIXON DOCKS, PIER 18.
WEAR YOUR MASK.
I DON'T WANT YOU TO FOLLOW ME THIS TIME.
IT WAS SANTO?
YEAH. HE'S SUSPICIOUS. WANTS HUNTRESS AS HIS BACKUP.
HE DOESN'T KNOW HER. HE THINKS SHE'S STILL A KILLER.
NO. HE KNOWS HER...

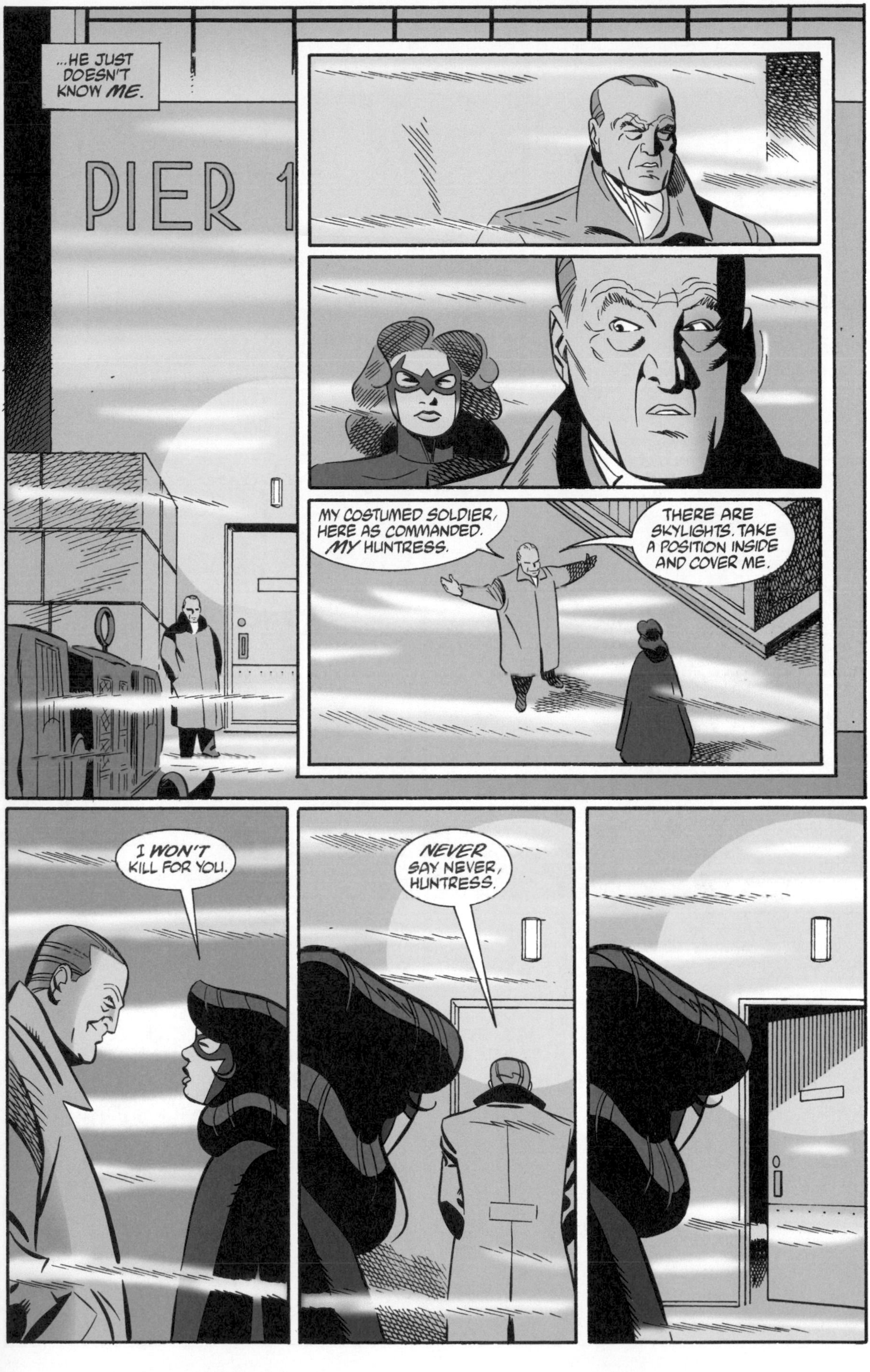
...HE JUST DOESN'T KNOW *ME*.
PIER 1
MY COSTUMED SOLDIER, HERE AS COMMANDED. *MY* HUNTRESS.
THERE ARE SKYLIGHTS. TAKE A POSITION INSIDE AND COVER ME.
I *WON'T* KILL FOR YOU.
NEVER SAY NEVER, HUNTRESS.

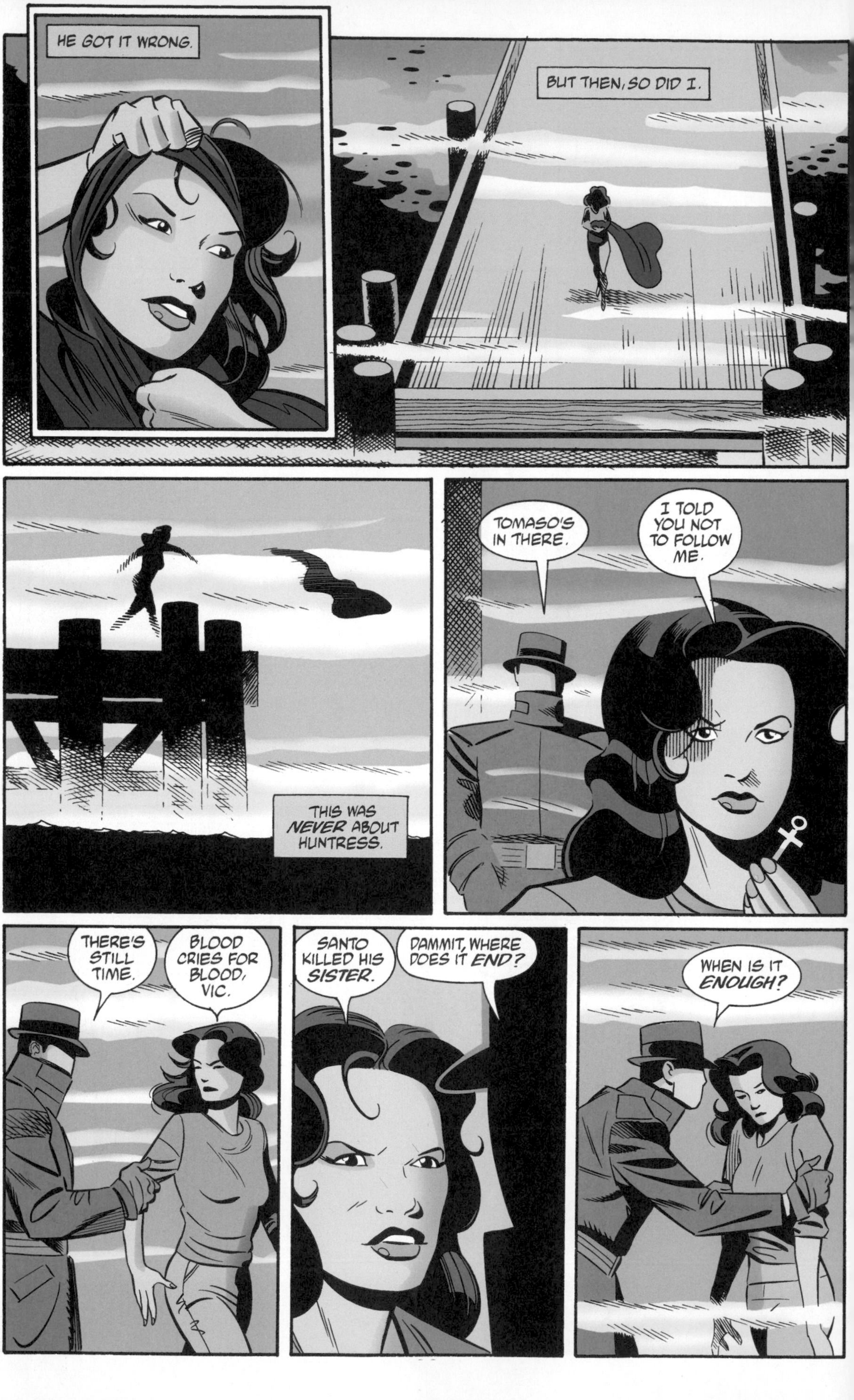

HE GOT IT WRONG.
BUT THEN, SO DID I.
THIS WAS *NEVER* ABOUT HUNTRESS.
TOMASO'S IN THERE.
I TOLD YOU NOT TO FOLLOW ME.
THERE'S STILL TIME.
BLOOD CRIES FOR BLOOD, VIC.
SANTO KILLED HIS *SISTER*.
DAMMIT, WHERE DOES IT *END*?
WHEN IS IT *ENOUGH*?

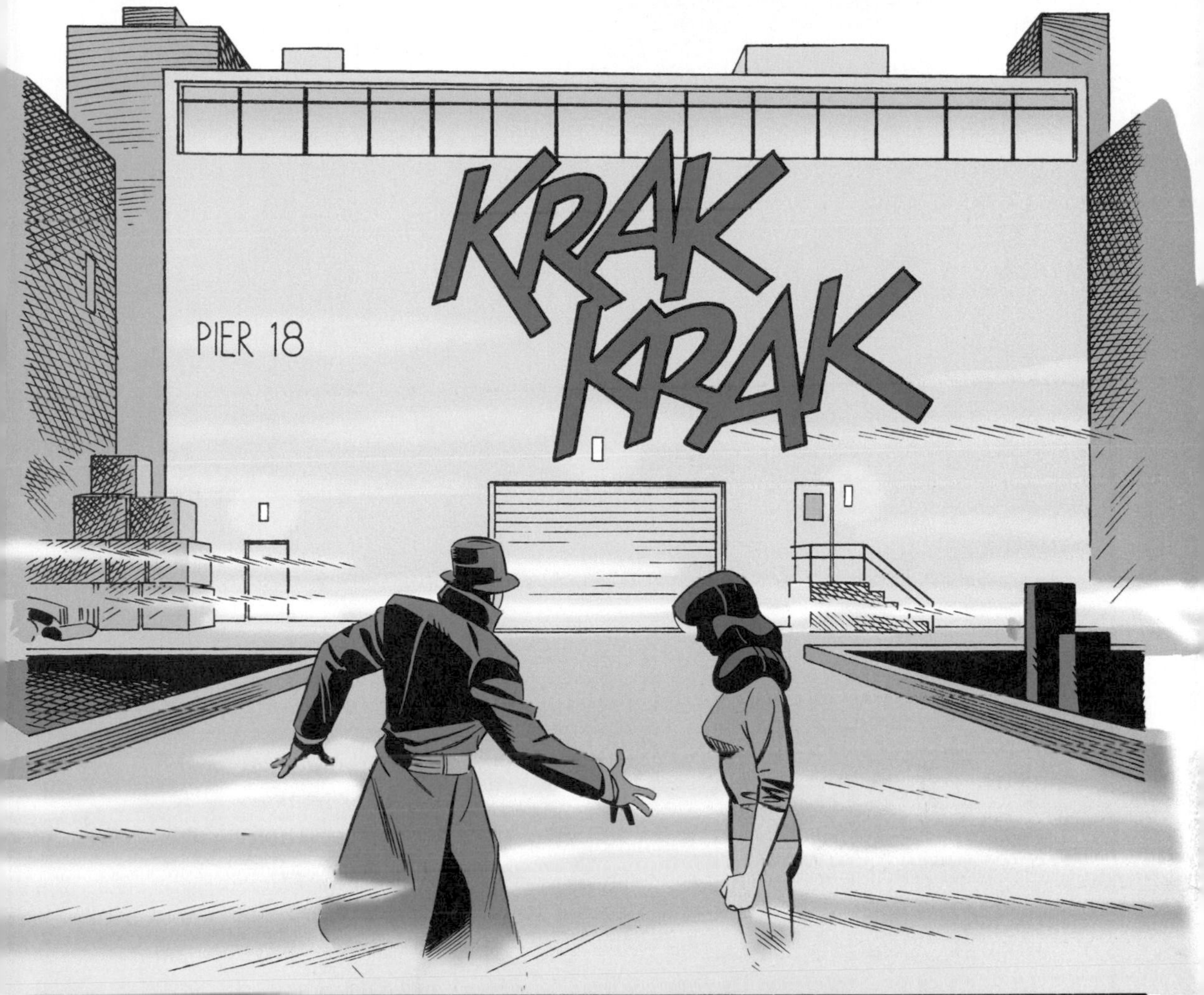
KRAK
KRAK
PIER 18

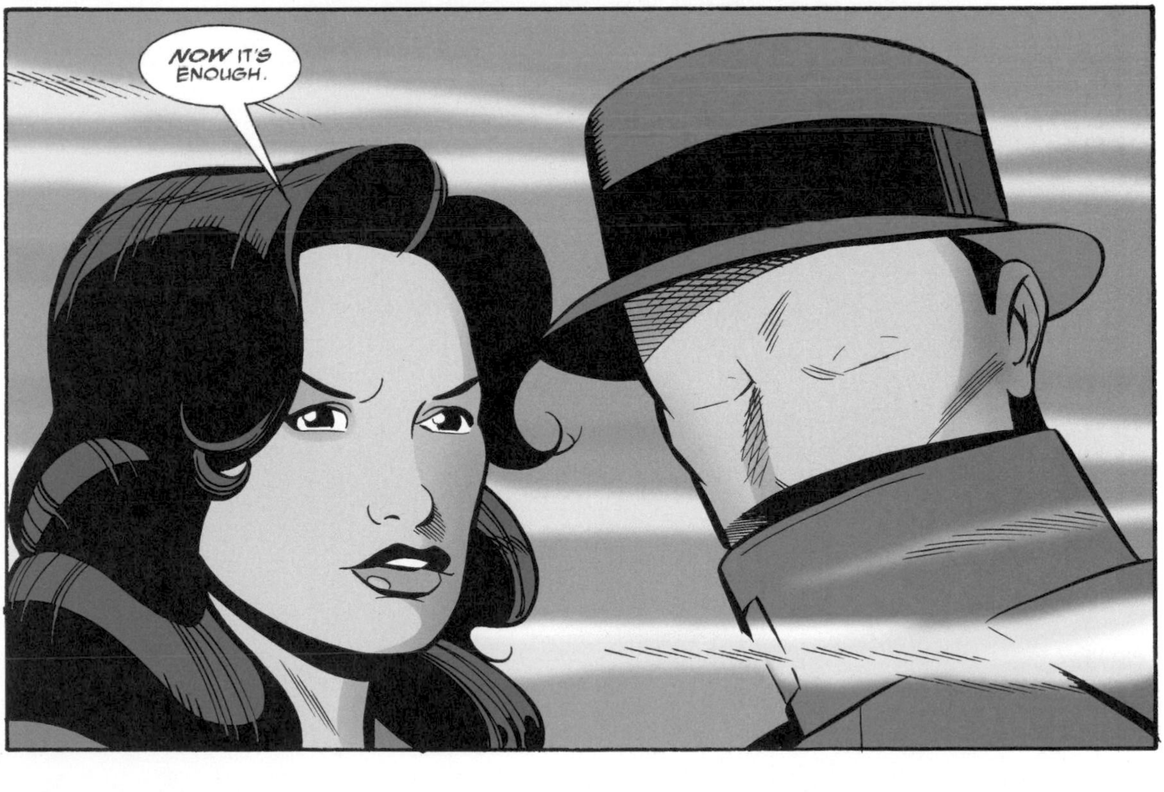
NOW IT'S ENOUGH.

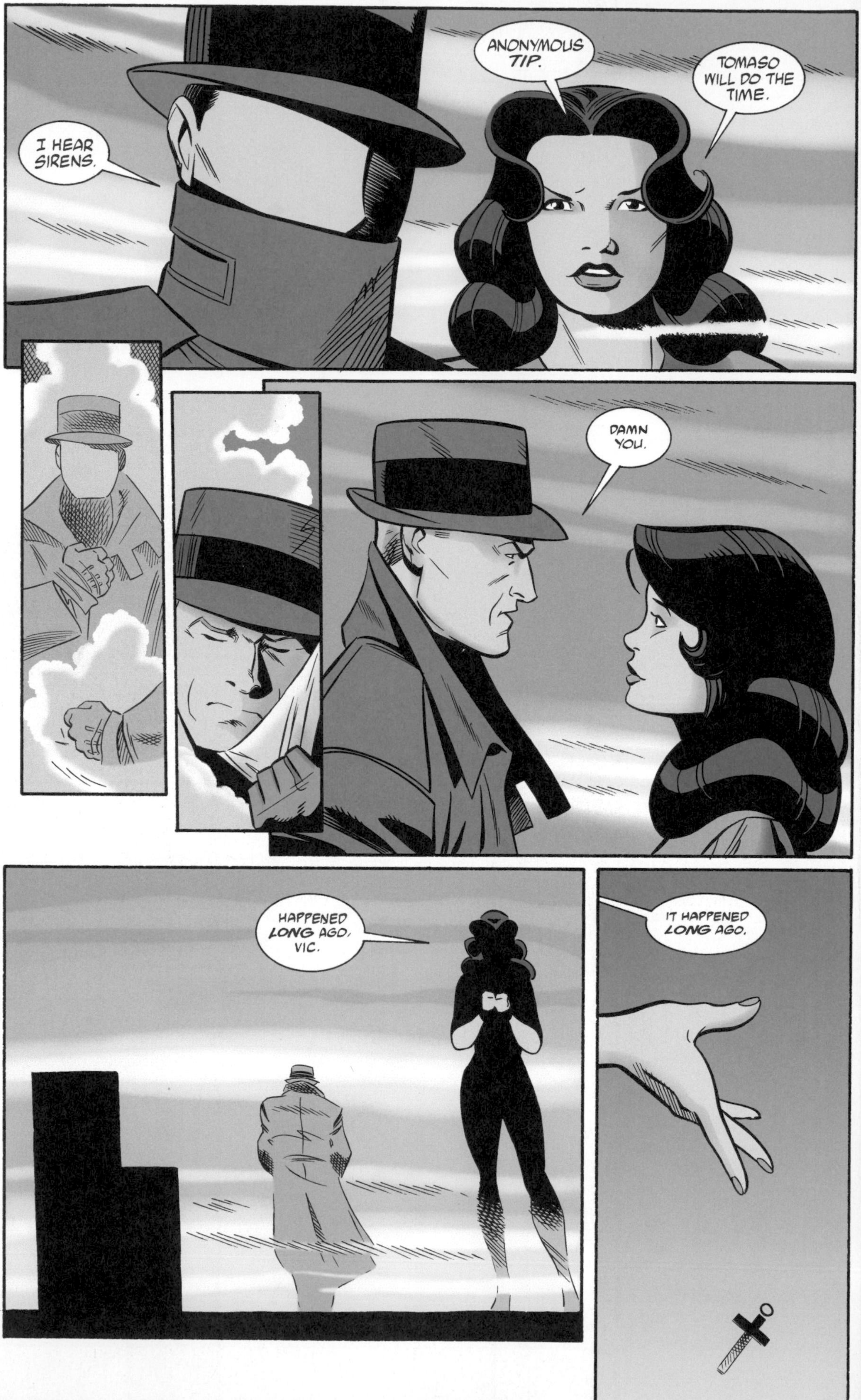
I HEAR SIRENS.
ANONYMOUS TIP.
TOMASO WILL DO THE TIME.
DAMN YOU.
HAPPENED LONG AGO, VIC.
IT HAPPENED LONG AGO.

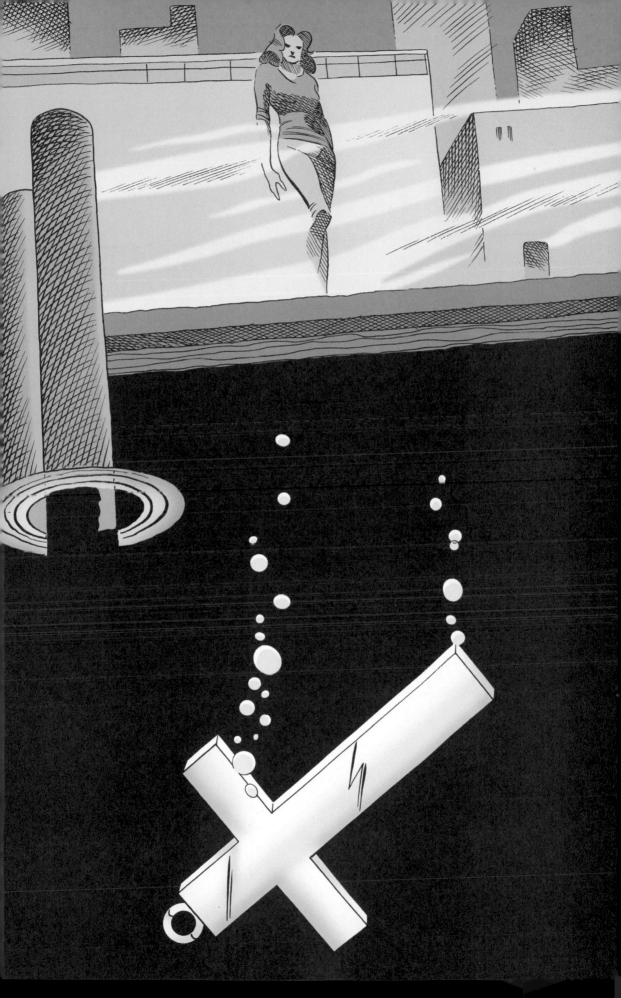

BATMAN/HUNTRESS: CRY FOR BLOOD
2002 COLLECTION COVER
ART BY RICK BURCHETT

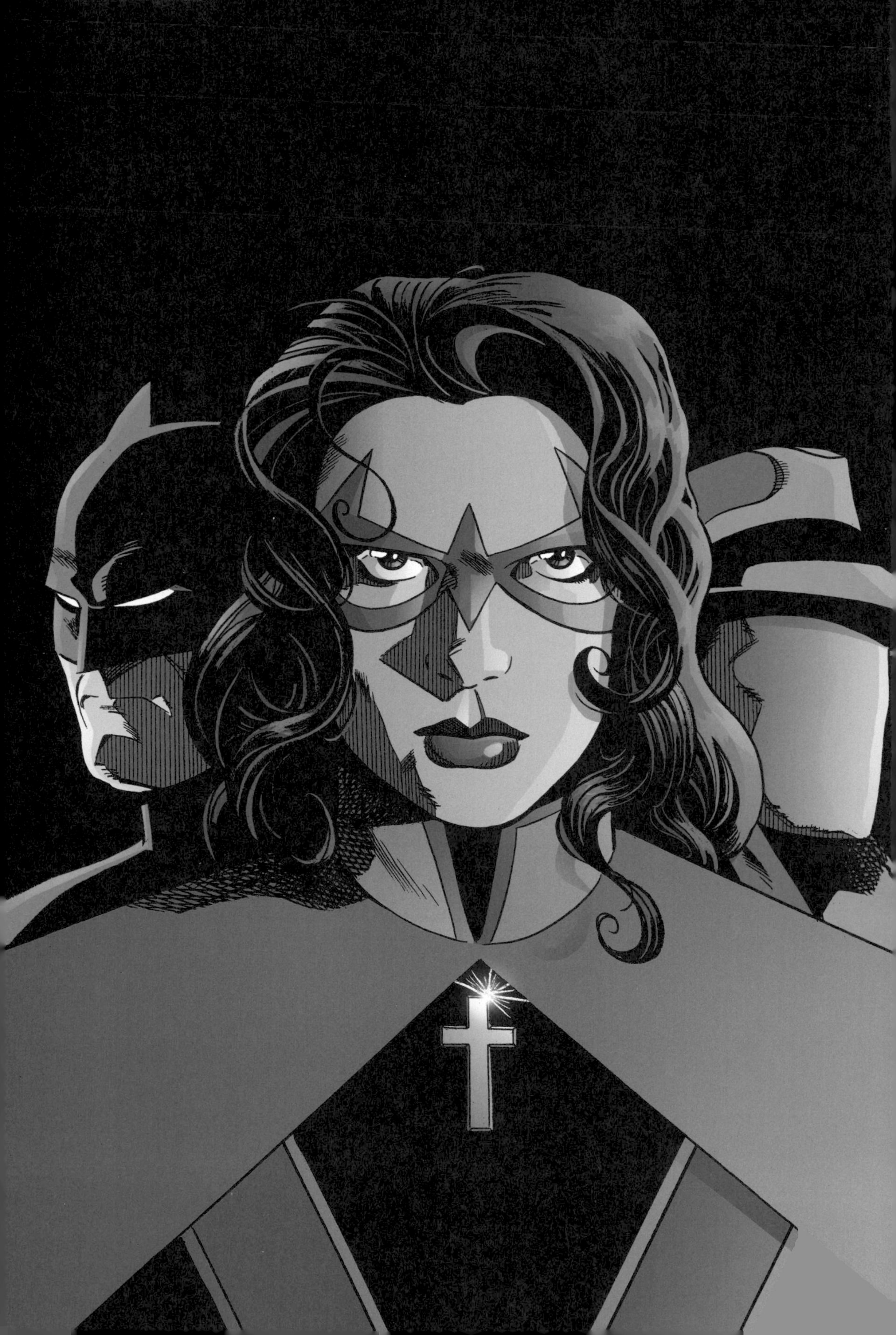

BIRDS OF PREY: HUNTRESS
COLLECTION COVER
ART BY **TULA LOTAY**

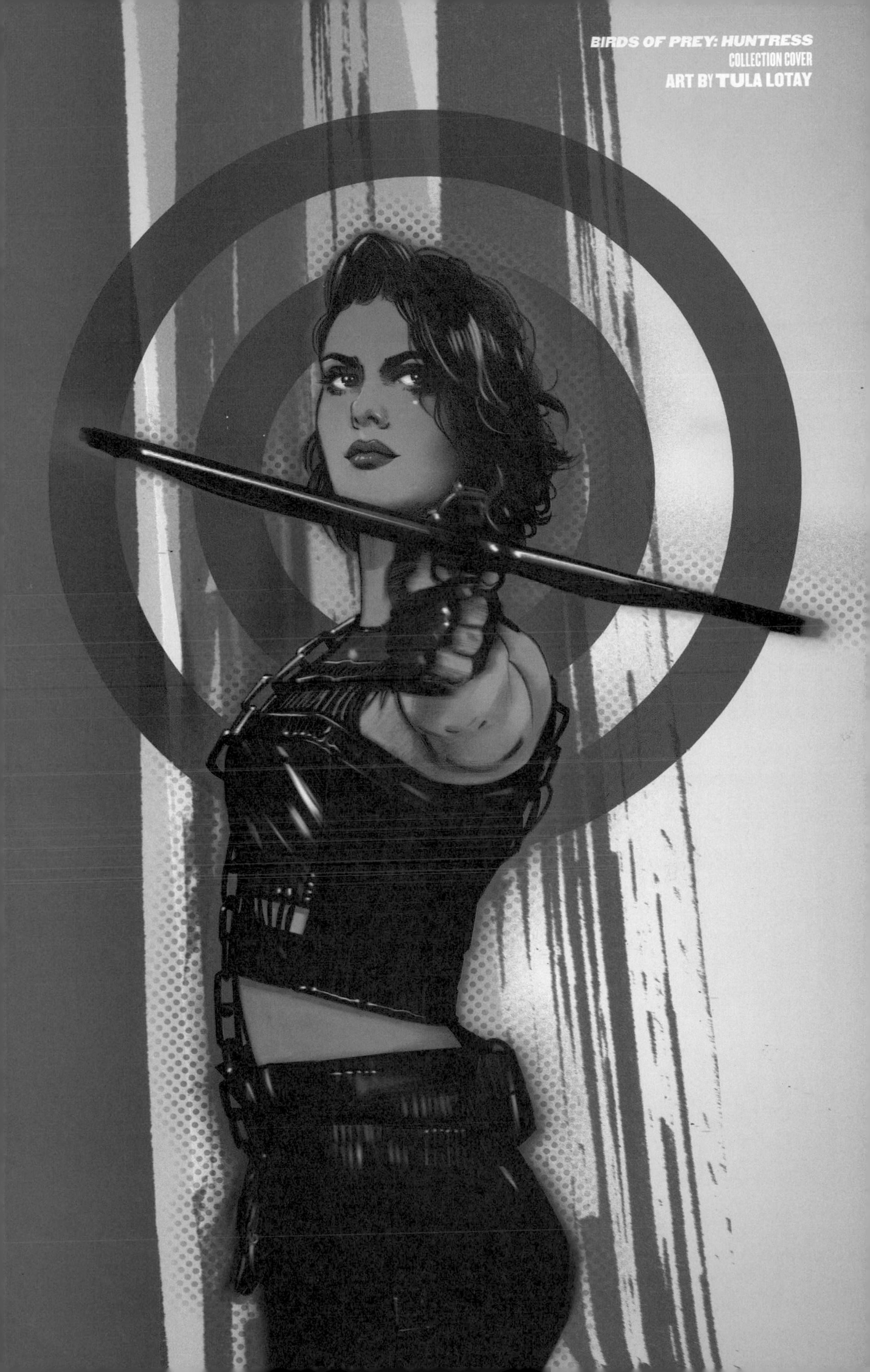

> "A smart concept, snappy one-liners and a great twist to match a tag-team of talented artists."
> **—NEWSARAMA**

> "Every bit as chaotic and unabashedly fun as one would expect."
> **—IGN**

HARLEY QUINN

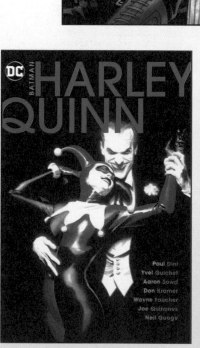

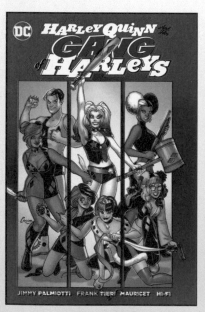

HARLEY QUINN AND HER GANG OF HARLEYS

BATMAN HARLEY QUINN

HARLEY QUINN: PRELUDES AND KNOCK-KNOCK JOKES

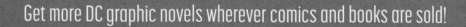